2000 YEARS OF
Amazing Grace

2000 YEARS OF

Amazing Grace

THE STORY AND MEANING OF THE CHRISTIAN FAITH

The Christianity Primer

PAUL F.M. ZAHL

ROWMAN & LITTLEFIELD PUBLISHERS, INC.
Lanham • Boulder • New York • Toronto • Plymouth, UK

ROWMAN & LITTLEFIELD PUBLISHERS, INC.

Published in the United States of America
by Rowman & Littlefield Publishers, Inc.
A wholly owned subsidiary of The Rowman & Littlefield Publishing
Group, Inc.
4501 Forbes Boulevard, Suite 200, Lanham, Maryland 20706
www.rowmanlittlefield.com

Estover Road
Plymouth PL6 7PY
United Kingdom

Distributed by National Book Network

Grateful acknowledgment is made for permission to reprint the excerpt
that appears on page 312, here entitled "A Text Concerning St. August
and Pelagius" from *Augustine of Hippo—A Biography* by Peter Brown
copyright 1967 by Peter Brown.

British Library Cataloguing in Publication Information Available

Library of Congress Catalog Number: 2006936334
ISBN-13: 978-0-7425-5276-4 (cloth : alk. paper)
ISBN-10: 0-7425-5276-0 (cloth : alk. paper)

Printed in the United States of America

♾™ The paper used in this publication meets the minimum requirement
of American National Standard for Information Sciences—Permanence
Paper for Printed Library Materials, ANSI/NISO Z39.48-1992.

CONTENTS

INTRODUCTION

T he world's most widely practiced religion can use a primer, a basic, simple digest of its beliefs and how it has come to be what it is. Christianity is a huge and complex subject, very old and many layered. But it is still possible to say what the essence of it is. It should not be hard to get the basic facts about a thing. Those facts may not describe the thing exhaustively. Yet they can capture its essence.

The purpose of *The Christianity Primer* is to state clearly and simply the main facts about Christianity: how it started; how it developed over the years and centuries; how it split, like an amoeba, into several different forms of itself; and how it survives and even thrives today.

The main facts about Christianity

Who were and are its main thinkers? Who are its main activists? Who are its saints? Who are its statesmen? Who are its villains? Who are its unsung heroes?

What is Christianity's influence on the world stage today? How does Christianity relate to other religions, especially to high-profile religions such as Islam, and also Judaism and Buddhism? What are Christianity's strengths? What are its weaknesses? What questions about life does it claim to answer? What questions does it leave unanswered? How does Christianity, in its vastness of numbers and many expressions, relate to its founder, Jesus of Nazareth? What would *he* think of worldwide Christianity today? What do *you* think of it?

The Christianity Primer offers straight facts, in chronological order, with some interpretation for the lay reader. It surveys the big ideas and history of the Christian faith, right from its first-century beginning. It offers short biographies of the important personalities, from then to now. It also includes a few of the main, primary sources — the original documents themselves — that have been the charter texts for the religion.

To avoid the use of footnotes and make for easier reading, descriptions of key subjects, events, and writings mentioned in the text are given in alphabetical order in a glossary at the back of the book, commencing at page 371. Similarly, biographical sketches of significant persons mentioned in the text are also listed in alphabetical order in a separate section at the back of the book, commencing at 433.

Aside from the most important event of Christianity, the coming of Christ, there are two other watershed events that I would like you to keep in mind as you read the *Primer*. One is the splitting or Great Schism of the Christian church into two parts, the Roman Catholic Church and the Eastern Orthodox (or simply "Orthodox") Church, in 1054. The other is the Protestant Reformation, which began in Germany in 1517 under the leadership of Martin Luther. The Reformation further divided the Roman Catholic Church, result-

Two watershed events you should keep in mind

ing in the establishment of Protestantism. Since that time, the Christian church has consequently consisted of three branches: Roman Catholic, Eastern Orthodox, and Protestant.

As the author of the *Primer,* I hope you have before you a clear and easy digest of almost everything you need to know about Christianity to comprehend it, critique it, embrace it, or even reject it — in short, to understand it as it really is.

A clear and easy digest

I myself am a convinced Christian. I am also made uncomfortable by the contradictions and hypocrisies of many people and groups who call themselves Christian. I am trying to follow the founder, and what he taught. Yet sometimes, when I look around me at the Christian churches, it makes me want to drop out. I shall try to give you a sympathetic view, but not one that hides the scar tissue and the fault lines.

†

I

WHAT IS CHRISTIANITY?

A RELIGION OF SALVATION BY GRACE

WHAT IS CHRISTIANITY?

Christianity is a religion based on the moral teachings and the life's work of a single person, Jesus the carpenter-prophet who came from Nazareth. It is a religion based on both moral concepts and a single life. It is not just a list of dos and don'ts, like the sayings of Confucius. Nor is it just the worship of a divine figure, the emissary from God; or, as most Christians believe, God in a human body. Christianity is a religion of morality *and* a religion of worship.

To understand Christianity, you have to get your mind around both parts of it: what it commands us to do, and how, through this one man, we are said to be able to do those things. Some forms of Christianity focus on the things he told us to do, such as love our neighbors as ourselves, turn the other cheek, and be compassionate to sufferers. Other forms of Christianity focus on the religious side of it: worshipping God in the figure of Christ, adoring him through praise, contacting

A religion based upon moral concepts and a single life

him through prayer and reading the Bible, walking and talking with him.

In fact, there is an unbreakable link between the teachings of Jesus and the actual person. It is proper to say that what he said and who he was are uniquely yoked together. You have to understand both parts of that to understand Christianity.

I have always admired many of the things Christ said. Even as a child, I was impressed by his compassion and his love for troubled, wounded people. But I could not make the link between the impressive things he said and did and the idea that he was God's Son. That seemed beyond belief. To go from inspired wisdom to "God in Christ" was an awesome leap.

Later, in college and then after becoming a husband and a father, I felt as though I needed him. Or rather, I needed his compassion. In the middle of my own struggles and losses, even impasses, it was not enough to be like him — and my life experience showed that my being like him was impossible. What I craved was his sympathy, his outstretched hand.

That hand I experienced. Who he was — the "friend of sinners," to use the old words — trumped the very excellent things he taught. The quality of him as savior — the truly religious side of the Christian religion — overwhelmed in importance the quality of him as teacher. In terms of personal impact, it almost submerged it. Both factors are important, the teaching and the saving. But the

What Jesus said and who he was are uniquely yoked together

saving part became more important for me than the teaching part.

Yet there was more to it than even the simple, emotional superiority of personal saving over moral teaching. My doing of the good deeds he taught actually *hinged* on the person of Christ saving me, I who had found myself paralyzed and blocked from doing those deeds. When I felt myself loved in my chains, in my paralyses, that feeling of being loved seemed to trigger the very motivation and strength that had failed me before. Being treated forgivingly in my faults and fears freed me up. The faults themselves lost some of their binding strength. The confining fears ceased to restrict so tightly. There was an empowering connection between his saving me (who he was for me) and the fuel to do what he said I should do (what he taught).

I take this connection between saving and the response to being "saved" that results in morally good actions to be the heart of Christianity. It is the relation of being loved to loving. Being loved creates an environment inside a person by which the works of love begin to take place naturally. Loving is born from being loved. This actually happens. We shall see it again and again in the unfolding story of Christianity.

The heart of Christianity is the relation of being loved to loving

Belovedness is closely allied to a concept called Grace. Grace is unconditional love toward a person who does not deserve it. The result of Grace is that the undeserving person is made more deserving. "Love to the loveless shown, that they might lovelier be" is a seventeenth-century way of saying it. This is Grace, and Grace summarizes all that is essential for Christianity to operate in a human being's life.

Grace summarizes all that is essential for Christianity to operate

This *Primer* on Christianity is based on a full-field or comprehensive theory about Jesus of Nazareth's importance in history. He embodied and exemplified Grace in action: "love to the loveless." This Grace-core of his ministry had enormous, long-term impact. It made the religion that bears his name a religion of mercy par excellence. It made articulate preachers out of fishermen. It made prime witnesses out of women, who in ancient times were considered in no way reliable or credible. It made cosmopolites and world traders out of insular ethnic people. The experience of Grace turned the early Christians' lives upside down.

A RELIGION OF GRACE IN TENSION WITH LAW

Grace also put Christianity on an unintended collision course with the religion that had birthed it. It put Christians on a collision course with the Jewish Law. This is because Grace does not depend on personal performance or adherence to a code or on any kind or degree of personal achievement. Grace is love without conditions attached. Grace pole-vaults over merit. It makes no distinction between people. It loves for its own reasons. This is an important concept, critical to an understanding of Christianity, and therefore worth spending a little more time on.

Martin Luther taught that the Bible cannot be properly understood unless the reader knows the difference between the part of the Bible that comes under the category of Law and the part of the Bible that comes under the category of Grace.

I believe Luther was exactly right. But what did he mean? Luther meant that God's Word has two parts. The first part of God's Word is condemnation and Law. It is the Word of God's perfection or righteousness, which no human being can imitate. The Law drives us to our knees. This is what St. Paul meant when he wrote that the Law is a schoolmaster (Galatians 3:24). *God's Word has two parts*

The Grace of God, on the other hand, is God's saying, "Even though you are an impossible and paralyzed mess, I will save you anyway. You cannot save yourself, but I shall save you *from yourself.*" Grace is what is meant by the verse "While we were yet helpless, Christ died for the ungodly" (Romans 5:6).

Thus, Law berates and convicts, Grace forgives and restores. It is that simple and that profound.

Thus, approaches to life that are based on deserving or earning anything are left in the dust. *Christianity,* to the extent that it has been true to its founding message of Grace, *has always existed in tension with legal or exhorting approaches to human endeavor*. Christianity undercuts moralism.

This means that the core of Christianity is typically in conflict with its versions that stress being good or doing this or that thing because it is expected. Sadly, the Christian church has regularly reverted to moralism throughout its long history. The *Primer* narrates, in case after case after case, the sorry and amazing history of tension between Christianity's core, Grace, and Christianity's tendency to revert to dos and don'ts, which is the Law.

A RELIGION OF GRACE IN TENSION WITH THE CHURCH

Grace has found itself in strenuous and perpetual conflict with the church. The extravagant love of God as Christianity asserts it comes into conflict with the institutional expression or embodiment of that love, the church. This is an unending wonder! Whenever the Grace taught and demonstrated by Jesus of Nazareth comes alive in Christian people's life experiences, it acts like dynamite. It is so powerful in reconstructing and transforming human lives that it demolishes the structures of the past.

Grace acts like dynamite

You see an old building, the visible church, in which is buried or held unknowingly a very combustible substance — the message of the Grace of God. When that substance is unwrapped and held up to the light, it ignites and burns.

Core Christianity exists not only in opposition to religions that stress demand and Law-keeping, such as Islam and to some extent Judaism, but also in opposition to the church. We shall see this tension frequently in the life of the early church and in the various "revival" movements of the later Middle Ages, such as those of the Franciscans and the Hussites. We shall also see that the tension turns to spontaneous combustion at the time of the Protestant Reformation. The tension occurs again in the eighteenth century with the Great Awakening, or evangelical movement, which so imprinted the history of the United States. It bursts out in East Africa during the twentieth century, then flames out over South America and, in recent years, in China. Can the old wineskins that Jesus talked about (Matthew 9:17; Mark 2:22; Luke 5:37) hold the new wine? Can the church hold within itself the chemistry of Grace? History says no, or at best, very, very rarely.

This problem — the gulf between the kernel of Christianity, which is Grace, and its husk, the church — is expressed powerfully in a three-hundred-year-old woodcut displayed in my study. The left half shows an ancient church building being demolished by construction workers. On the top of the collapsing building is the word

The kernal of Christianity is Grace; the husk is the church

superstition. There are ornate statues on the building's front elevation, all of which are being pulled down. On the right half of the woodcut, a minister or bishop is holding the Holy Bible and pointing to a picture of workers constructing a new building. It is a new church, simple and with clear lines. The foundations are deep, and a worker is shoveling down in them, to show us how truly deep they are. Overhead is the title of the woodcut: "The History of the Reformation." Clearly the "new" or reformed church has been founded on the Scriptures. But the erection of the new one has also meant the demolition of the old.

Some Christians shrink from such a picture. It implies negativity. It looks antichurch, or anti–*old* church. It places the Bible, the founding charter of Christianity, in opposition to the church. And yes, it does that.

To understand the history and development of Christianity, you have to see that it is a yes but it is also a no. It is a yes to Grace and forgiveness, compassion and love, both human and divine, which exist without conditions. But it is also a no — a no to the Law as an end in itself and a no to the institutional church as the possessor or decider of divine truth. The old woodcut in my study displays a church exploded by the Grace of God in the Bible; a new, alternative church, footed on fresh foundations.

I have experienced this. I grew up alongside and within a denomination, the Episcopal Church,

Christianity is a yes, but it is also a no

that has been in an uneasy relationship with religious revival right from the start of its almost 450-year history. Revival broke out with the Protestant Reformation, and it took at least 150 years for the church (in those days, the Church of England) to catch up with the religion of Grace that so exploded in its belly when Martin Luther's teachings reached England and people began to read the Bible again. The same church was uncomfortable with John Wesley later. It has been uncomfortable with evangelicals and Pentecostals in our own time. In fact, most of these kinds of Christians have departed from the Episcopal Church. The "new wine" Christ talked about could not be held within the old wineskins.

"New wine" could not be held within the old wineskins

When I experienced a religious conversion to Grace and a living Christ thirty years ago, I became like one with leprosy to the church I knew so well. I came to feel like the big bad wolf trying to get inside the well-constructed house of the third little pig: "Let me in, let me in." I was never let in.

Or was it the other way around? Who was the wolf, and who was the little pig? Where was the problem? Was it with the fiery young "newborn" Christian or the old structure with its orderly forms and processes? We probably threatened each other, like the deformed man who looks in the mirror and cries out against himself.

I have never, or very seldom ever, felt comfortable with the old church. With me, it is always a case of ardor and freshness versus control and order. And that collision, which is the precise case of my own life and ministry, is repeated again and again in the history of Christianity. Of course, the dynamic works both ways. There are many sincere Christians, in all times and places, who regard themselves as comfortable with the old church.

A RELIGION OF WEAKNESS IN TENSION WITH STRENGTH

If Christianity is a religion of Grace in tension with Law and the Gospel in tension with the church, it is also a religion of weakness in tension with strength. This is the third prism through which our *Primer* sees the religion.

Jesus was raised in glory, but he lived and died in weakness

Jesus lived in weakness and died in weakness. To be sure, Christians affirm that he was raised in strength from the dead. He was raised in glory. But "the man for others" was shamed before he was ever exalted. He spent his working life with fishermen and sick people, with tax collectors and tavern keepers, and, strange for his time, with women. He talked unendingly about the last becoming first and about those who had lost their lives — given up their own prerogatives — and been given back their lives again. Christ ended his life in bitter aloneness and ironic rejection, in forsakenness lived to the maximum. This is simply how things turned out.

St. Paul, the great interpreter of Christianity (who will be discussed in chapter 3), dwelt on these facts. He actually lived them. These facts stamped Christianity forever. Paul wrote: "God chose what is foolish in the world to shame the wise, God chose what is weak in the world to shame the strong, God chose what is low and despised in the world, even things that are not, to bring to nothing things that are" (I Corinthians 1:27–28). Paul later added, in an enduring and decisive point of theological interpretation, that God's "power is made perfect in weakness. . . . For when I am weak, then I am strong" (II Corinthians 12:9–10).

"For when I am weak, then I am strong"

Christianity has from its beginning placed enormous value on the strength of weakness and the weakness of strength. Christianity's conviction is that true power consists in powerlessness. This has been "proven," so to speak, again and again in history, in events such as the triumph of nonviolence — in the American civil rights movement, in the unstoppable moral power emanating from such figures as Mother Teresa, in the sheer appeal of children, and in the child in us all — in getting adults to change their minds. It is the underdog factor in life, by which human sympathy almost always turns from the victors to the defeated.

For Christianity as I understand it, the third spoke in the wheel is the power of weakness. Martin Luther called this a "theology of the Cross," in distinction to a theology of glory. He saw the power of weakness as central, absolutely essential, to the Christian view of life.

Christianity is a religion of salvation for people

who are failures. In saving such people, Christianity makes them into something like successes. This is the dynamite. Christianity creates a confrontation with religions of rigor and demand. It also negates all attempts to get visible things to represent invisible things. These negations, as well as the positive essence of them, which is God's Grace, have made the history of Christianity what it is.

If you understand that, the last two thousand years of Christian history make sense. They add up. *The Christianity Primer* presents the basic facts and invites the reader on a passionate journey from Grace to Law and back, from first love to church and back, from weakness to strength and back, always in a repeating cycle and in dynamic ways that have created the world in which we live.

A passionate journey from Grace to Law and back

†

II

JESUS OF NAZARETH

THE BIRTH OF JESUS

Jesus, the founder of Christianity, is thought to have been born just before the year zero, the year that B.C. ("before Christ") turned to A.D. (*anno Domini,* "in the year of the Lord").

The precise date of Jesus' birth is not certain. The best evidence we have, based on the report of a famous census that occurred in Israel under the Roman emperor Augustus, was that Jesus was born as early as 6 B.C. or possibly 4 B.C., or as late as 2 B.C. The calendar we use today is based on Christ's appearance in world history as it was calculated and finalized in the Middle Ages (when astronomy and time measuring were not exact sciences). The day of his birth was first celebrated on December 25 during the fourth century.

The mother of Jesus, Mary, came from a very religious family who lived near the city of Jerusalem. She was married to Joseph, who was a carpenter from Nazareth, a small town in the northern section of Israel, called Galilee. According to the belief of most Christians, Mary was a virgin when she conceived Jesus, and God was his Father through the divine intervention of his Holy

Spirit. Thus Joseph is regarded as Jesus' nominal or adoptive father.

Jesus was born, it is believed, during a Roman census, by the rules of which Mary and Joseph were required to leave their home in Nazareth and travel to the town of Bethlehem, outside Jerusalem, to be registered in the town from which Joseph's tribe had originated. Bethlehem was then (as it is today) a singularly unprepossessing place, and of course, all the world is familiar with the humble circumstances of Jesus' birth there in a lowly manger.

As time went by, so impressive were Jesus' life and words, and later so awesome were the manner of his death and his witnessed resurrection from the dead, that the first Christians came to believe and treasure stories they heard (originally as told by his mother Mary) about his birth. They called it Christmas or the Nativity. It is a beautiful festival surrounding the historical fact of a famous man being born in such massively humble circumstances; and it has become the basis for one of the world's most appealing stories. This is Christianity's "magnitude of meekness," as the English poet Christopher Smart put it 250 years ago.

THE HISTORICAL SETTING

Into what kind of world did Christ come?

Into what kind of world did Christ come? What sort of family, what sort of culture, what sort of thought world, what kind of customs, what sort of hopes surrounded him? What were the givens of his life as he actually lived it? Jesus was born into the period of piety, or religious practice, that is known to religious scholars as Second Temple Judaism. The First Temple was built in Jerusalem by King Solomon roughly between 960 and 926 B.C. It was destroyed by the Babylonians in 587 B.C. The Temple at Jerusalem (the Second Temple) was rebuilt after 520 B.C. and then improved and enlarged much later by King Herod the Great, who was king over Jerusalem when Jesus was born. *Second Temple* refers as much to an ethos or cultural world as to a building. Second Temple Judaism was a thriving and somewhat diverse religious structure in the framework of which Jews lived their entire lives.

This religious structure consisted of a number of factions. There were conservative but not fanatical doers of the Law, known as Pharisees. There were theologically liberal scholars, known as Sadducees, who loved the Law but did not believe in life after death. There were "whole hog" monastic-style extremists, known as Essenes, who lived in the desert or wilderness and copied manuscripts, prayed, denied themselves pleasures, and waited for the Messiah to come who would end the world as we know it. There were left-wing activists, called Zealots, who plotted to overthrow the Roman occupiers of Israel by the use of force. And there were tens of thousands of average Jewish people who observed the religious festivals seriously, listened to their rabbis in the synagogues week after week, and sought to frame their whole lives, private as well as public, according to the Law of Moses, or what Christians call the first five books of the Old Testament.

It is fair to say that the people who lived according to Second Temple Judaism were overwhelmingly serious religious people. Of course, Judaism allowed for human nature and its layers. It was a humane religion. You could go wrong in your life and still be forgiven and restored. There were many allowances for human beings, and all sorts of ways to get back on track with your life. But as a whole, the people practiced their religion. They sought to practice it from their hearts. We know this from writings by individuals such as Flavius Josephus, who gave a detailed and accurate picture of Second Temple Judaism in the period of Christ's life.

Second Temple Judaism was a humane religion

It is important to keep in mind that at this time, *Israel was an occupied country*. It had been occupied by the Romans since a war in A.D. 63. However, the Romans gave considerable freedom to the Jewish people, as well as to Herod, their approved and also very smart and powerful client-king. But the Romans ruled Israel, absolutely and unequivocally. They could intervene at any time in any aspect of the life of the Jews if they did not like something that was going on.

A few religious scholars want to add another factor to this picture of Second Temple Judaism:

the influence of Greek civilization — of high and refined Greek or Hellenistic art, science, and literature — upon the world into which Jesus was born. They point to a beautiful city in Galilee, known as Sepphoris, which was recently excavated and found to be filled with fewer Jewish and more Hellenistic cultural influences. Thus, it is reasonable to conclude that the world into which Jesus was born existed side by side with non-Jewish and therefore more cosmopolitan cultures.

. Yet apparently, these other cultural influences had little effect upon Christ himself. The New Testament Gospels, which tell the story of Jesus' life, refer very, very little to such influences. The thought world that breathes through the Gospels, almost every bit of it, is Second Temple Judaism. We can find Greek or Hellenistic influences in some of the writings of St. Paul, and also of St. John, but the Gospels of Matthew, Mark, and Luke reflect an overwhelmingly Jewish culture.

The thought world that breathes through the Gospels

Thus, although Jesus would later become the first Christian in history, he grew up initially, and more or less solidly, Jewish. There is no question about this. His teachings are all engagements with Jewish ideas concerning God and religion. His teaching illustrations all relate to daily life in a primarily agricultural, Jewish Law–regulated society. Except at the very end of his life, when he came up against Roman justice and Pontius Pilate, he engaged with Jews and Jewish ideas in one hundred percent of his personal interactions. He did not think philosophically, in the sense of Greek or Roman philosophy. Not a bit.

An important fact of Second Temple Judaism — although this was by no means restricted to Jewish people in ancient times — was the absolute requirement of loyalty to one's family of origin, one's blood relatives. As in agricultural societies everywhere, in Second Temple Judaism it was the ironclad obligation and understanding of everyone that a child owed his first loyalty to his nuclear family, to his parents. Second loyalty was to extended family — brothers and sisters, and then, in turn, to one's children and more distant relatives. Everyone else was outside the circle. Everyone else was not part of a person's first and binding responsibility.

In adulthood, when Jesus decided to refer to his followers as family — as in Matthew (chapter 12) and Mark (chapter 3), as well as in Luke's Gospel — he was absolutely and radically breaking with the entrenched structures of Second Temple family life. Its absolute given of loyalty to one's nuclear family and blood relatives had never before been challenged. Jesus changed this.

Another key part of the Second Temple Jewish world into which Jesus was born and of the values that he acquired in his education was the sacrificial system of the Jerusalem temple. Jewish males were required to travel to Jerusalem once a year to make a sacrifice to God at the temple. Although this was not enforced in a police-state way, the incentive to make these sacrifices was very high.

Loyalty to one's blood relatives was an absolute requirement

Sacrifice to God, for the purpose of atoning for your sins, was *the* barter in that keenly religious world. You bought an animal and killed it or had it killed by a priest or subpriest, and then your debt to God was paid, for a period. The honor due God's name was paid. The idea of propitiation (i.e., appeasing God by means of personally sacrificing the gift of something precious to you) was pervasive in Second Temple Judaism.

Finally, there also ran through Second Temple Judaism the political hope of a reversal of fortune. Everyone hoped for a better time. It was God who would finally intervene and make things better. Concretely, God would give Israel its political independence from the Romans and from all future occupiers and oppressors.

Everyone hoped for a better time

Second Temple Jews believed that one way God's intervention would occur was through a reform or renewal of Jewish spiritual life. At different periods of national decline and decadence, prophets had been chosen by God to come and preach the hope implicit in religious renewal and more fervent, consecrated practice of the Law. Sometimes prophets just gave comfort and consolation. They preached that there would come a better time. They reminded the Jews that God had not forgotten his people. Even now, they could look to better things coming. Second Temple Judaism was that turbulent with hope. Yet the hope took different forms. When John the Baptist inquired of Christ, "Are you he who is to come, or shall we look for another?" (Matthew

to watch and wait (Matthew 24:42; 25:13; Mark 13:35; Luke 21:36).

Jesus never taught the idea of human perfectionism

This means that Jesus never taught the idea of human perfectionism. Christians often think their religion demands perfection of them. That is why so many of them leave their churches, or, as I often say, take sabbaticals from God. To them, the bar of God looks so high that they would just as soon flee, or give up, or put on a false front.

Christ did not teach perfectionism. Of course, God is perfect. But Christ saw people as existing both in the now, as they are, and also in the then, as they shall one day be in the coming kingdom of God. The "already and not yet" philosophy of Christ sprang directly from his encounter with the massive — but disappointed — hopes of John the Baptist for a speedy finish to everything: the end of history. There were consequences in this for the birth and later development of Christian theology.

Thus, the Jesus of Nazareth whom we know as our Savior did not emerge onto the stage of world history fully grown. He grew up in the bosom of Second Temple Judaism. He was surrounded by the literal smell of sacrifice and by the temple system of animal sacrifice. He was the master of one book: the Jewish Law and Jewish Chronicles, the Psalms, and the Prophets — what Christians call the Old Testament. And as we have discussed, his nuclear family and also his extended family were extremely tight. They expected nothing less than complete loyalty and attention. There was also the matter of the Roman occupation. You couldn't miss that. Christ also had this high-profile cousin, John, who was banging the drum of apocalyptic hope, and not slowly. All these factors were to affect everything Jesus did and was.

And yet he came as something new, and something very big. His humanity, Christians would say, was touched by an inspired divinity. One thing, his human legacy and circumstances, interacted with another, a divine destiny. Thus, when Christ was baptized in the Jordan by John, such a thunderclap of future chosenness burst over him that everyone who was there heard a voice from heaven saying, "Thou art my beloved Son" (Matthew 3:17; Mark 1:11; Luke 3:22).

He came as something new, and something very big

THE TEACHINGS OF JESUS

What did Jesus teach? What words came out of his mouth? Did he teach Jewish things? Did he teach Christian things? How did the world he had grown up in interact with his personal insights, which were to make the world regard him as unique?

Jesus taught many things. Three of the things that he taught were completely new within the history of religion. We can call these Christ's *novum*s, taken from the Latin word for new thing or innovation.

The first *novum* of Christ was his assertion that his words were superior to the words of Moses. Christ said, "Moses [i.e., the old Law] said unto you such and such, but I say unto you . . ." In the fifth chapter of the Gospel according to St. Matthew, Jesus contrasted what "was said to the men of old" with what he was saying now. Thus, for example, Moses (the old Law) had condemned the *act* of adultery. But Jesus said, "If you even look at a woman with lust, you have committed adultery with her in your heart." Ouch!

By putting things this way, Christ not only placed himself on a par with Moses the lawgiver but asserted a superior wisdom. This way of representing his authority put him on a collision course with Judaism. It was a costly *novum*.

Christ's second *novum* was his attitude toward the Jewish Sabbath, or day of rest. In Mark, he declared that "the Sabbath was made for man, not man for the Sabbath" (2:27). This was to say that the Law exists for the good of mankind, not the other way around. For Christ, the human being was an end in himself. He had significance. The human being in and for himself was an object of highest interest to God.

In both of these *novum*s, Christ was setting his personal authority over that of Moses the lawgiver. This could only create tension with his context, which was Second Temple Judaism.

The third *novum* of Christ's teachings was his rejection of the purity regulations set forth by the Law. He had been criticized for failing to require his students to wash their hands before they ate. Christ shot back, "Do you not see that whatever goes into the mouth passes into the stomach, and so passes on? But what comes out of the mouth proceeds from the heart, and this defiles a man. For *out of the heart* come evil thoughts, murder, adultery, fornication, theft, false witness, slander. These are what defile a man; but to eat with unwashed hands does not defile a man" (Matthew 15:17–20; italics added).

This *novum* put the blame for, and the source of, all human wrongdoing on the inward person himself rather than on outward circumstances or other people. It was a frontal assault on the victim mentality, by which everything and everyone outside you has caused your problems. Jesus shunted the burden of guilt back onto its source: the human heart. This called into question all theories of blame and scapegoating. It committed Christ's religion to humility on the basis of admitted sin.

The practical result of these three *novum*s in Jesus' teaching was what we today might call the birth of Christian compassion. Jesus understood the purpose of the Law as being its service to the human race. The object of the divine "exercise" in giving the Law was the well-being of men and women. In other words, Jesus centered on the needs of people. His view of sin as being entirely evenly distributed and directed inward birthed the idea of equality. All people were in bondage to their inner selves. There was no "good, better, best" in the population of Israel, not to mention the world at large. Because Christ leveled the playing field, his address included everybody: beggars as well as kings, Good King Wenceslas as well as the "poor man at the gate." Jesus' under-

The birth of Christian compassion

standing of human nature, his *anthropology,* produced compassion. Self-righteousness and New Testament Christianity do not go hand in hand. Jesus' sermons could only result in self-knowledge and humility in those he addressed.

Moreover, Christ acted this out:

> And as he sat at table in the house, behold, many tax collectors and sinners came and sat down with Jesus and his disciples. And when the Pharisees saw this, they said to his disciples, "Why does your teacher eat with tax collectors and sinners?" But when he heard it, he said, "Those who are well have no need of a physician, but those who are sick. . . . For I came not to call the righteous, but sinners."   (Matthew 9:10–13)

Jesus expended his energies on *sinners*

Jesus expended his energies on *sinners.* This sounds a little heavy to our modern ears. The word *sinner* can sound heavy, even oppressive. It can come off like a put-down. Yet it is what fueled Christ's celebrated compassion. According to him, everyone in the world is trapped by his own internal drives. "For out of the heart come evil thoughts," lying, and the rest (Matthew 15:19). We are all self-deceived. We also have a lot less freedom than we think we have. Bad things, in the main, come from inside us. To be sure, there are tornadoes, diseases, and droughts. There are wars, betrayals, and bullying. But the core of our problems lies within us.

Jesus Christ had a groundbreaking compassion for inwardly trapped people. This extended to his celebrated mercy for lepers and blind people and disabled persons, not to mention for helpless infants and undefended children. He lived out the implications of what he taught.

There are two other aspects of Jesus' teaching that need to be stressed.

Jesus preached the arrival of what he called the kingdom of God. This was an agenda with him. It filters through almost everything he said. "The time is fulfilled, and the kingdom of God is at hand; repent, and believe in the gospel" (Mark 1:15). He announced this fact continually: The *kingdom of God* is just around the corner. So you have to *repent* and believe in the *Gospel*. I put those three very loaded expressions in italics because they require short and simple definitions.

Jesus preached the arrival of the kingdom of God

The *kingdom of God* is the reign or acted-out power of God, complete and ruling to the uttermost in all affairs of the world and in all corners. Jesus believed that the kingdom of God was on the way. Yet Jesus also differed somewhat from many preachers of his time, especially John the Baptist. Most preachers who were predicting the end of the world were convinced that the Messiah was just over the horizon. He was in range! They could feel it in their bones. Jesus agreed with them, and with John, that the kingdom was coming, but he also taught that its exact timing could not be known by anyone on earth. No human being could know the exact time. Only God knows that.

As we have observed, Christ was a prophet of

doom *delayed*. The end was on its way, but no one knew when. This may sound like a small distinction. After all, what is the real difference between saying something is going to happen very, very soon (i.e., what John the Baptist said) and saying that something is going to happen soon but we cannot pin down when (i.e., what Jesus said)? But this was an important difference. It had a huge effect on the development of Christianity after Jesus. This is because many of Jesus' parables, which were homespun stories to illustrate a larger point, assumed a "time being" — a period in which we can expect something to happen, but not yet. We long for a better world. Our faith in God endures with hope for a better day. We do believe that all wrongs will be righted one day and that "the earth shall be filled with the glory of the Lord" (Numbers 14:21). But we are still living in the "not yet."

Do you see how the effects of this idea could be quite awesome? You say to yourself, "I believe that God will one day 'wipe away every tear from [our] eyes' " (Revelation 21:4). But in the now, in the present, assuming he will not do that until he is ready, "I think I might try to wipe some tears away from the faces of others." Jesus' teaching has you thinking toward a glorious future but also living in the needy now and doing something about it.

It has to be said finally that Jesus considered something fantastic was taking place through his ministry. He expected that as a result of his announcement about the kingdom of God, people would *repent*. He came to believe that he was the Messiah and that the kingdom of God was, in a preliminary way, already here. How could you not sink to the ground and turn your face away in humiliation if the Messiah of God were before you in person?

Jesus called on people to repent as a consequence of the coming of the kingdom of God, its advance presence in his presence. And he called on people to believe the *Gospel*.

What was the Gospel in this context? It was the coming of God's Holy Word to unworthy humans — the "finger of God," as he said, extended in service to the broken, undeserving human race.

So in addition to the three *novum*s of Christ, there was the hurtling train of the *kingdom of God* — although it might be delayed and no man could know its estimated time of arrival. The natural response to this train would be humble *repentance* and the conviction that God's *Gospel* had introduced the touch of divinity into earthly human affairs.

Christ's teachings were accompanied by a specific manifestation of his authority, which followed him, so to speak, everywhere he went. This manifestation of his authority was the exorcism of demons or hostile spirits. From the very beginning of his work, which lasted about three years (although some scholars argue two), men and women with mental illnesses were attracted

A specific manifestation of his authority

to Christ. Wherever he went, "possessed" (psychotic) people were drawn to him. He would cure them. The word used for this cure at the time (and still used today) was *exorcism*. When Jesus came near a possessed person, the evil spirits would fly out of the one possessed. Sometimes these evil spirits spoke to Jesus, often challenging him. In every such confrontation, Christ addressed the spirits as if they were detached from and did not occupy the mind of the person they were oppressing. Today we would say that Christ distinguished between the illness and the person afflicted by the illness. He detached the sickness from the patient. This was unknown in ancient times, and it is still a rare feat. Who among us does not identify an alienating or "sick" characteristic with the person who evinces it? To depersonalize your problems is an easy thing to say, but it rarely happens. Yet Christ distinguished between the demon and the sufferer. It was a master stroke. To the people who saw this happen with their own eyes, it was pure miracle.

Christ distinguished between the demon and the sufferer

Christ's exorcisms confirmed his message. They gave it authenticity and weight. We shall get to his many other miracles next, but it is important to say here that his casting out of evil spirits was a living demonstration of his superiority to Moses. It was also right in line with his extremely impressive compassion for people with deep problems.

A concluding note on the teachings of Jesus: The best place to look for them is in the Sermon on the Mount, which is given in the fifth chapter of Matthew's Gospel. (The Sermon on the Mount is included on page 303 in the appendix to the *Primer.*) Some of the same material is also found in the sixth chapter of Luke, known as the Sermon on the Plain. The Sermon on the Mount

Christ also used a form of teaching called parables — simple stories from the natural world around us that convey a larger truth about God. Many of his parables grew names in later Christian tradition, such as the parable of the prodigal son (Luke 15:11–32), the parable of the wicked tenants (Matthew 21:33–41), and the parable of the talents (Matthew 25:14–30). The parables all served Jesus' key ideas that God grants Grace to the sinful, that the Gospel is in tension with the synagogue, that strength is hidden in weakness, and that the kingdom of God is to be hoped for but the time of its arrival is still hidden.

THE MIRACLES OF JESUS

Jesus performed many miracles of physical and psychological healing. He also stopped a thunderstorm on the Sea of Galilee. He multiplied five loaves of bread and two fish to make enough food to feed five thousand people.

In Christian theology, the time of his miracles is sometimes referred to as the Galilean ministry. The time of his suffering and death is then entitled his Judean (or Jerusalem) ministry.

It is absolutely true that as Christ traveled from one city or town of Galilee to another, he had a huge impact because of his miracles.

What are we to make of these miracles as they are reported in the four Gospels? They certainly created a climate for the whole future history of Christianity — a climate of hope in a wonder-working savior. Some Christians have deliberately rejected the notion that his miracles continue in the present day, on the idea that they were confined to his glorious thirty-three years on earth. This view of things is called dispensationalism. It asserts that God works differently in different dispensations or time periods — that was then, this is now, so forget about miracles today. Others, mainly Pentecostal Christians who believe God's Holy Spirit works in all times and places, believe that miracles of healing still take place today. Christian Scientists also have underscored the nowness of God's healing power.

Miracles proved the compassion of Jesus

One thing we can say definitely about the miracles of Jesus is that they proved his compassion. But to say they proved his wonder-working power to be absolute goes against a larger and even more visible tendency in Jesus' life, and certainly in his death: his tendency to work through weakness. For example, his final vulnerability in Jerusalem is so dazzlingly untriumphalistic. Christ actually said to his disciples near the end, on the night of his arrest, "Put your sword back into its place. . . . Do you think that I cannot appeal to my Father, and he will at once send me more than twelve legions of angels?" (Matthew 26:52–53) In other words, Christ could have called in an airstrike of miracles, but he refrained.

To focus primarily on the miracles is to focus on the power side of religion. That would not be fully characteristic of Jesus. Nevertheless, he healed and he helped and he fed and he even stilled a storm out of compassion. This is the meaning of the miracles. They were the compassion of God to people who could be aided in no other way.

Did the miracles happen? Did they actually happen? I believe they did, simply because I have seen and experienced transforming miracles in many people's lives today, my own included. But did they happen as reported? Water into wine, a virgin giving birth, a dead man raised? Well, we cannot take a camera back to those years and satisfy ourselves in a scientific way. But the titanic imprint of Christ's personality, his magnetism and appeal on every front you can name, makes it believable. Such a person must have had God with him. He certainly *could* have done what was reported.

And then there is his resurrection from the dead, Easter Day. We shall get to Easter soon. *That* miracle, the empty tomb and Christ's resurrection appearances, puts everything else to one side. And the evidence (if that is the right word) for the Resurrection is credible but also disturbing; extremely odd, also oddly plausible; out of left field, as they say, but therefore all the way home. The facts reported of Christ's resur-

Did the miracles happen?

rection, linked as they inevitably are to the many lesser miracles from his time in Galilee, and confirmed by the answers to prayer I have witnessed on several occasions — these have made a believer out of me.

But let's leave the miracles for now and observe that no matter what actually happened to produce those astonishing reports, they show as plainly as possible that Jesus Christ was the ideal bearer of compassion.

GOOD FRIDAY: THE DEATH OF JESUS

Jesus' cruci-
fixion is *the*
hot potato
The cause of Jesus' crucifixion has been a hot potato — *the* hot potato — from the early days of Christianity right up through today.

The old medieval view, alive until these post-Holocaust days, boiled down to this: the Jews did it. Christ spoke a message of love and compassion to them, but it threatened their temple and their vested interests. So the Jews got rid of him, their priests leading the charge. There is a partial truth to this. Certainly a group of temple priests found his attacks on their institution and on some of their teachings to be alarming. Christ threatened to cut the jugular vein of some of their theology. But to say the Jews did it, as the Christian churches have generally said until recent times, would be to speak a half-truth.

The more recent approach in assigning blame for Christ's death, an approach influenced by the post-Holocaust world's revulsion against anti-Semitism, is to declare that the Romans did it. They regarded Jesus as a potential revolutionary against their rule. Their spineless and anti-Semitic governor, Pontius Pilate, got him out of the way for reasons of state. This second view, which whitewashes the Jews — as the older view whitewashed the Romans — is popular today. It is also politically correct. Its high-water mark was the movie *Jesus* that was made in 2000 for American television, in which, when Jesus says from the Cross, "Father, forgive them, for they know not what they do," the Roman centurion shoots back: "No, Lord, we know exactly what we are doing."

A third view of the cause of Christ's death comes from old Protestant teachings on original or universal human sin, according to which *everyone* crucified Christ. This is because we all have it in us to call the good bad and to demonize just men. This appeal is summed up in verse two of a 1630 hymn for Good Friday entitled "Ah, Holy Jesus," by the German Protestant poet Johann Heermann:

> Who was the guilty? Who brought this upon thee?
> Alas, my treason, Jesus, hath undone thee.
> 'Twas I, Lord Jesus, I it was denied thee;
> I crucified thee.

In other words, all of are part of something, the human world, that annihilates the good and muffles the wise.

These three possible answers to the questions Who did it? and Why did he have to die? weave in and out of Christian history. The most persuasive answer theologically is the last. This is because it reflects life as it really is: a repeating cycle of unfairness in which only the good die young. It also avoids scapegoating — scapegoating either the Romans, who don't count anymore, or the Jews, who count very much today. So the third is theologically both true and ultimately kind. I accept it.

It was Jesus' *teachings* that led to his arrest and death

But we need to go one step further in explaining the cause of Christ's death. It was his *teachings* that touched off the negative reaction, in all quarters, that led finally to his arrest and death.

Why do I say that? Well, as we have seen, Christ preached God's Grace over against the Law of Moses: "The men of old said to you . . . I say unto you . . ." Jesus presumed the superiority of his words to the founding words of Moses. He also attacked the Sabbath's blue laws (i.e., rigorous regulations regarding commerce, amusement, and personal conduct) and threatened the whole cycle of life that surrounded them. He directed the finger of blame at the inside of a person, not at its infinite potential object outside the person. This was threatening. Christ also spoke of the kingdom of God as if he were on a first-name basis with the Deliverer. And by his exorcisms, he seemed to indicate that he himself was the Deliverer.

Christ's teachings put him on an inevitable

collision course with the vested interests of his surroundings. It is no wonder that Christ got into very serious trouble enunciating such thoughts in a world governed by the laws of Second Temple Judaism and imperial Rome.

In his thirty-third year, on a day Christians call Palm Sunday, Jesus entered the city of Jerusalem, riding on a donkey. Palm Sunday is so named because many people, observing his humble procession, spread palm branches in front of him as a mark of honor, hailing him as the Messiah, the Son of David.

Palm Sunday

Christ then proceeded to the great temple, where he became offended by the sight of merchants engaged in the petty commerce of selling animals for sacrifice. In righteous indignation, he overthrew their tables, causing much consternation among those gathered there. Things moved quickly during the next few days, as many in the city thought Christ could be the Messiah *and* it was Passover time, the great religious holiday at which the presence of Jewish males was generally required. The city was packed!

Jesus' teachings and his quite dramatic symbolic actions, such as the Palm Sunday procession and his outburst in the temple, were a huge offense to many of the priests. And when Jesus said that the temple would soon be destroyed (Mark 13:2; Luke 19:43–44), the priests had the ammunition they needed to proceed against him. He could now be arrested as a blasphemer, one who speaks against God; and if the Romans could be persuaded that Christ was also a political threat to them, all the better.

Jesus knew they had him. He also knew what could come next. For this reason, he organized a Passover meal with his twelve students, or disciples.

The disciples or apostles (Matthew 10:1–4; Mark 3:16–19; Luke 6:14–16) (*disciple* and *apostle* are interchangeable terms) were the twelve men whom Jesus invited and summoned to go with him on his ministry. Christ wanted these men to help him, to also befriend him, and to be the inner circle of his teaching and healing work. All are now designated as saints, except for Judas Iscariot, who betrayed him.

They were as follows:

- Peter, who represents the Christian faith at its highest point because he was so personally unstable that he had to trust God
- Andrew, Peter's brother
- James and John, who were also brothers. John is sometimes called the Beloved Disciple because Jesus trusted him especially. John also wrote the Gospel according to St. John and probably the book of Revelation.
- Philip
- Bartholomew
- Thomas, known as Doubting Thomas because he did not believe at first that Jesus had risen from the dead

- Matthew, who was a tax collector and who later wrote the Gospel according to St. Matthew
- James, the son of Alphaeus, also known as James the Less
- Thaddeus Simon the Canaanite
- Judas Iscariot, who was the traitor in the group

These twelve disciples were, with Jesus, the first Christians. They were also all Jewish. Several of them were fishermen. All of them came from humble backgrounds, socially and educationally. They were also mostly from Galilee, the region of Israel that was considered provincial or redneck. Two of the twelve disciples, John and Matthew, wrote Gospels of the New Testament. Mark, who was not one of the twelve but was a very young original follower of Christ, wrote the Gospel ascribed to him. A Gentile doctor named Luke wrote the third Gospel. The authors of the Gospels are called the Four Evangelists.

When Jesus met with his disciples at the Last Supper, he predicted his death. He also put some words of interpretation on this event, which was rushing toward them all like a mighty wind. He connected his death with the experience of the forgiveness of sins and represented this, again symbolically, in terms of the bread and wine of the meal. The bread symbolized "my body which is given for you" (Luke 22:19). The wine sym-

The Last Supper

bolized "my blood . . . , which is poured out for many for the forgiveness of sins" (Matthew 26:28). The disciples would vividly remember this last supper with Jesus. The symbolic connection between the bread and wine and the meaning of what it foreshadowed would forever stamp the future of Christian ritual. The Christian ceremony of Holy Communion is based upon the Last Supper.

After the meal, Jesus and his disciples went to Gethsemane, a garden on the slope of the Mount of Olives, opposite the temple. It can still be visited today.

Meanwhile, one of the disciples, Judas Iscariot, betrayed Jesus, telling the priests where they would be able to find him in an unprotected place, vulnerable to capture. Judas then accompanied a band of temple guards to Gethsemane to arrest Jesus. When the guards confronted him, Jesus ordered his disciples, who owned two swords among them, to lay down their arms and not resist. This was a most unusual thing to do — to do nothing in the face of an illegitimate and actually illegal action. But Christ was clear beyond any question. His disciples complied. The guards then arrested him, and all his friends headed for the hills.

The next act in the drama is a little harder to pin down, because each of the four Gospels gives a slightly different report of what took place. Jesus was taken to the high priest's house and interviewed. Witnesses came forward and confirmed what he had said at the temple. The governing body of the temple, known as the Sanhedrin, thereupon convicted Jesus and sentenced him to death, under Jewish Law, as a blasphemer. However, the Sanhedrin had a problem. It could judge Christ as deserving of death under their law, but only the arm of the state, the Romans, could carry out the execution. Accordingly, the priests of the Sanhedrin awakened the Roman governor, Pontius Pilate, very early on the day Christians call Good Friday. They requested that their sentence of death for blaspheming be converted from a wish to a judicial deed.

Pilate agreed. Why? Pilate agreed because a delegation of Jews from Palestine had recently complained to the emperor at Rome that Pilate was anti-Semitic and that he had reacted with extreme force to a meeting of Jews in the north that had been religious and not political in nature. Pilate was already under a cloud. His superiors back home regarded him as an unsuccessful and possibly corrupt governor. So he had to curry favor with the temple leaders. This he did, after a brief and fruitless interview with Jesus, by confirming the Sanhedrin's sentence. The Romans would now say that Jesus was a rebel against good and orderly government.

Thus, Jesus was executed from the Jewish point of view as a breaker of the blasphemy laws and from the Roman point of view as a pretender against the authority of the emperor. In any

Motivations of Pontius Pilate

event, he was taken out and nailed to a wooden cross, the transverse beam of which he had to carry to the site of execution. The final judgment from Pilate and the judicial killing took place in immediate succession. No last meal!

Jesus was recorded by the few friendly onlookers who stayed by his cross in the final three hours of his life as saying seven things, the Seven Last Words. But he died quite quickly. The Romans would have put him out of his misery by three o'clock anyway, as Jewish Law required him to be buried by sundown. That was because sundown was the start of the Sabbath, when no manual labor of any kind could be done. But Jesus died quickly. The cause of death was asphyxiation, which was due to his chest cavity continually falling forward and then being yanked back again because of the pain from the stress on his nailed hands.

Every single event that occurred during Jesus' last week, known as the Passion of Christ, stayed impressed on the memory of those who witnessed the events, especially the twelve disciples, and had great meaning for Christians in later times.

Two principles to be derived from the Passion of Christ

In retrospect, there are two principles to be derived from the Passion of Christ. The first is that every single event that took place during Christ's Passion came to have significance for the future of Christianity. There were no exceptions. What he *did not do* — for example, his silence at certain points when he could have defended himself — carried weight for the future. And what he *did do* — for example, the seven things he said during his death agony on the Cross — carried weight for the future. Those events are not myths or legends. They actually happened — though there are some gaps and a few inconsistencies in the four Gospels that relate the story. I tell the story here in slightly more detail because all of it came to have importance for the future of Christianity. This is true right up through the present day. Because every breath Christ took during his Passion had implications for the future of the religion, I needed to take some time and space to tell the story.

The second principle of the Passion story is that it illustrates the three great themes of the Christian religion that I stressed at the beginning of the *Primer.* Christ's Passion illustrates the theme of *Grace versus Law,* in that he presented his message as going against the Law of Moses. He was therefore condemned as a blasphemer against God.

The Passion illustrates the theme of *Gospel versus church,* in that the official "church" of Christ's day rejected him massively. It is not that the Jewish people, as such, rejected him massively, for there are accounts of the women of Jerusalem accompanying him on the way to his execution, weeping and wailing in sympathy. But the Gospel leaves no fuzziness about the fact that the priests engineered his betrayal. To be sure, the Romans carried out the actual execution, but members of the Sanhedrin engineered it.

Finally, the theme of *strength in weakness* flows though every cell of the story. Christ is beaten, mocked, whipped, and stripped, and he answers "not a mumblin' word," to quote a Negro spiritual. His goodness is treated as a crime, and his kindness is judged worthy of total scorn. He loses, in the profoundest sense. He dies alone and exposed. He is forced to ask the most uncomfortable question he could possibly ask: "My God, my God, why hast thou forsaken me?" (Matthew 27:46; Mark 15:34) The entire sad scenario sets the stage for every future Christian script of persecution and powerlessness.

Of the seven things Jesus said from the Cross, two were extremely important. This is because they — like almost everything else he did that last week — bore awesome significance for future generations.

The first memorable and unforgettable sentence was "Father, forgive them; for they know not what they do" (Luke 23:34). Jesus asked God not to hold against his executioners what they were doing. This prayer is regarded in Christian teaching as the maximum possible statement of the forgiveness of sins. Christians see the Cross as the greatest miscarriage of justice in the history of the world, bar none. So it is amazing to us that Jesus fully forgave the men who were killing him. The long march of Christlike forgiveness, the long saga of

"Father, forgive them; for they know not what they do"

its practitioners as well as its mockers, begins
here. His "Father, forgive" has stamped every single Christian who has ever lived — even in our
widespread inability to do it or even to pray it.

The second memorable thing Jesus said from
the Cross was "My God, my God, why hast thou
forsaken me?" (Matthew 27:46; Mark 15:34).
This was a remembered verse from Psalm 22 in
the Old Testament. It came to Christ's lips
because it expressed his feelings just before he
died. It is a vast admission for the Gospel writers
to state that their hero really said these words.
This is because these words implied — very
clearly implied — a most tragic sense of God's
abandonment of his Son at the end. We would
prefer him to have said only what he also said:
"Father, into thy hands I commit my spirit!"
(Luke 23:46) But the words from Psalm 22 suggest complaint. They convey overwhelming dis-
appointment. "Why have you let this happen to
me? Why have you not helped me out here?
Where are you? (Anyone home?)" Christ's cry of
dereliction is so plaintive. The One whom he
counted on most had vacated the premises.

The power of what Christ said, however, for
Christians in all future spaces and periods, would
be that the One they adore *has been there, too.*
The divine figure — the human face of God, as
Christians really do esteem Jesus — experienced
the abandonment of unfair suffering to the final
degree. So the defeated human being is not alone,

"My God, my God, why has thou forsaken me?"

at least in his defeat. To Christians, this is the rainbow behind the cloud. His defeatedness gives us heart in our defeats. He has, to use the old language, borne it with us.

To summarize this description of the most climactic moment in Christian history, the death of Christ: He died forgiving but friendless. He was friendless in the worst possible sense. His teachings and distinct emphases had led to this Gothic moment. But once there, it was even worse than he had imagined. He died forgiving but also friendless to the furthest extent conceivable of human isolation and defeat. God was silent.

What did it mean?

He died forgiving but friendless

EASTER DAY: THE RESURRECTION OF JESUS

Jesus was buried on a Friday afternoon. On Saturday, nothing happened. Or rather, nothing was noticed. This is because it was the Sabbath and everybody was at home. But very early on the first day of the week, which was the Jews' Monday but Christians' Sunday, three women, including Jesus' mother, went to the tomb to put spices on the body — equivalent to what cosmeticians do at funeral parlors today. They found the tomb empty. They saw that the large rolling stone that had covered the walk-in entrance to the tomb was out of the way. The entrance to the tomb was completely open. But there was no body inside.

The women were very alarmed. They assumed

that Christ's body had been stolen. So they ran to tell the disciples, who were at that time hiding in a safe house somewhere in Jerusalem because they feared that they themselves were next in line for arrest. Nevertheless, two of the disciples, Peter and John, hurried to the tomb in a state of high anxiety. They found it exactly as the women had said. It was empty. Yet John concluded that Jesus had risen from the dead.

The first fact of Easter was the empty tomb.

The second fact of Easter was the appearances of the Lord to his disciples. In the Gospels, the narrations of these appearances are a little jumbled. Some reports say that the risen Christ met Mary Magdalene, one of the first women at the cemetery, right after his tomb was found to be empty. Some reports say he appeared to the disciples in the "upper room," or safe house where they were huddled in Jerusalem. The risen Christ is said to have visited the upper room twice.

There is a report of Christ's appearing to two of the disciples as they hastily departed from Jerusalem after the Crucifixion. Initially, as he walked beside them, he was unknown to them, but he then made himself known when they stopped to have a meal together.

There are extended reports of Christ's meeting his disciples by the Sea of Galilee several days after his death. He advised them, but in the guise of a stranger, how to catch fish during a slow day. Then he ate some fish with them on the beach. On that occasion he also talked to Peter alone.

The Easter appearances of Jesus are summed up by St. Paul in chapter 15 of his first letter to the Corinthians:

> For I delivered to you as of first importance what I also received, that Christ died for our sins in accordance with the scriptures, that he was buried, that he was raised on the third day in accordance with the scriptures, and that he appeared to Cephas, then to the twelve. Then he appeared to more than five hundred brethren at one time, most of whom are still alive, though some have fallen asleep [i.e., died]. Then he appeared to James, then to all the apostles. Last of all, as to one untimely born, he appeared also to me.
>
> (vv. 3–8)

How St. Paul's listing of Christ's appearances relates exactly to the stories in the Gospels is hard to decipher. No one has ever succeeded in matching up what Paul wrote with every detail of what the Gospel writers wrote. But basically they speak with one voice. Yes, Jesus appeared to several people on more than one occasion; and yes, he appeared to individuals also; and yes, he appeared to one last man — who was not one of the original disciples — well after the others had seen him. Many Christians since then have felt themselves able to identify with Paul, the "one untimely born." This is because Paul, like us, did not know Jesus when he was alive but experienced his appearing both "late," (i.e., after the ascension of Christ), and also spiritually.

Did Christ really rise from the dead? To put it another way, can we know for sure that this miracle of all miracles actually took place? If we could go back in a time machine and set up a video camera outside the tomb of Jesus late that sad and darkened Friday afternoon, would the tape reveal, upon inspection Sunday morning, that the stone had been moved from the inside?

The great question of Christianity

This is the great question of Christianity. It is not too much to say that everything else hinges on the answer.

One school of thought says that you can prove that the Resurrection happened, or try to prove it. This approach emphasizes the number of witnesses St. Paul mentions in I Corinthians 15; the fact that the Gospels agree in the main about the event itself; the knowledge we already have that first-century Jews were not superstitious — far from it; and that Paul himself agreed that Christian faith rises and falls with the bodily resurrection of Christ (I Corinthians 15:14). This appeal — trying to prove that it must have happened — stresses the fact that Thomas, one of the twelve disciples, did not believe Christ had risen until he put his fingers into Christ's wounds (John 20:27). It is true without question that the earliest Christians believed that Jesus had come back from the dead in his body.

Another school of thought in Christianity tries to say that it does not matter whether the Resurrection happened in a historical or scientifically provable way: such an event is beyond proving. Rather, it is a matter of faith. We have to trust God and close our eyes, so to speak. Don't try, in other words, to pin down something scientifically. The miracle is simply above and beyond our rational faculties.

Most everyday Christians combine both these schools of thought. Most Christians believe it happened but are content, in general, to take it on faith.

I lean toward the first view. I wish to entrust myself only to a God who is really there. And when I lay dying, I want to know, and know for real, where I am going. Or at least that I am going somewhere — that when the moment comes, the lights will not simply go out. I am a Christian because I believe that death is not the end of life. Such a hope, as Christians call it, is extremely important to me. Moreover, such a hope is tied directly to the Resurrection of Christ on the first Easter Day.

But there is something more to say. I have stressed so far that one of the most important insights of Christianity is the value it assigns to weakness. This value assigned to weakness is not an end in itself. It is not the idea that weakness, self-effacement, nonresistance to evil, and humility are good in themselves. No, it is rather the idea that the only way to lasting strength and ultimate power in a besieging and hostile universe is to acquiesce to weakness.

Jesus did not die in a shameful way simply to bless shame. Rather, he bore the whole weight of human shame and injustice to neutralize them. If he had stayed dead, the shame and cost would have amounted to nothing. At most they would have added up to one touching example of human resignation to injustice. But Jesus died and then rose. This is what Christians believe.

You will recall that earlier in the *Primer,* I discussed Martin Luther's comparison of a theology of the Cross and a theology of glory — that glory in life is realized first through suffering and innocent affliction. But God raises the dead. He brings into existence things that do not yet exist. He spins gold out of straw, as in the fairy tale of Rumpelstiltskin or, more metaphorically, as in the Disney classic movie *Dumbo,* in which the source of affliction (the poor elephant's enormous ears) becomes his source of escape because they allow him to fly.

I keep a plaster figure of Dumbo on my writing table. It reminds me that the Resurrection is directly related to handicap and loss. The handicap precedes the victory. The little model of Dumbo rests beside a simple wooden cross my grandfather carved when he was old — my grandfather whose chronic depression burdened him almost all his adult life, my grandfather the Protestant pastor. Jesus' life, his teachings, his humble death, and his amazing resurrection:

The Resurrection is directly related to handicap and loss

these unique events in history were shot through with Grace in opposition to Law, with Gospel in painful rejection from church, and with weakness in prelude to glory.

Now we can start to see how these themes began to play out in a new, growing, and also suffering religion. We turn now to the most important interpreter Christ ever had. We turn to Saul of Tarsus, who became St. Paul of the Christians.

†

III
JESUS CHRIST AND
ST. PAUL

PENTECOST AND ST. STEPHEN

In his first letter to the Corinthians, St. Paul gave a short list of the post-Easter appearances of Jesus. Paul concluded the letter with an account of his own confrontation with the risen Jesus on the road to Damascus. Soon after the confrontation, Jesus' appearances ceased, at least in physical form. Exactly why these appearances ceased, why such a unique physical event began to change its character, is impossible to say. However, what the writers of the New Testament came to believe was that Christ had left behind a representative of himself. This representative they identified as the Holy Spirit

What happened to create this conception is this. Forty days after Jesus' last appearance, the eleven remaining original disciples (the twelfth, Judas Iscariot, had committed suicide), plus a new disciple named Matthias, were celebrating a Jewish festival when they were filled with the presence of Christ. The festival was called Pentecost. For that reason, the Christian feeling of being filled with the Holy Spirit was forever after described as Pentecostal.

These men, together with the several women who were also in the group, experienced themselves as being "switched on," filled to overflowing, overcome by the Spirit and presence of God to such an extent that they began to pray in public ecstatically. Their words became *God's* words. The people around them, who came from many language groups other than the local brand of Hebrew, called Aramaic, experienced this as hearing "in our own tongues the mighty works of God" (Acts 2:11). The disciples' prayer language was heard as being a translation of the

Speaking in tongues

varying mother tongues of the different peoples gathered in Jerusalem. This phenomenon of God's words in translation became known as speaking in tongues.

As with so many other phenomena of Christianity, this event, which took place in the founding time of the movement, developed "legs." It developed mighty legs for any number of futures. Even today — now more than ever, in fact — people speak in tongues in Pentecostal churches from Rio to Los Angeles to Beijing.

In Christian theology, this ecstatic experience of the disciples with the presence of the Holy

Birth of the Christian movement

Spirit came to be understood as marking the birth of the Christian church. From that day on, from the Day of Pentecost on, the disciples and their followers began to fan out beyond their communities. They became international witnesses to the Resurrection. They started saying in public what they had seen in private. The Christian movement was born.

Of course, a backlash did not take long to come. The same priests who had gotten rid of the master were extremely uneasy with his students.

The most famous example of the backlash is the stoning to death of Stephen, which is described in detail in chapter 7 of the book of Acts. This event was a major event in the earliest days of Christianity. It is remembered in formal or liturgical churches on December 26.

Stephen, like his master Jesus before him, criticized the great temple as a temple "made with hands," a house unworthy of God's greatness and also a house whose stewards had rejected the One awaited. Stephen spoke with passion:

> You stiff-necked people, uncircumcised in heart and ears, you always resist the Holy Spirit. . . . Which of the prophets did not your fathers persecute? And they killed those who announced beforehand the coming of the Righteous One, whom you have now betrayed and murdered.
> (Acts 7:51–52)

Hearing these incendiary words, Stephen's listeners rushed him and stoned him. Just before he died, he was heard to say, "Behold, I see the heavens opened, and the Son of Man standing at the right hand of God" (v. 56). He also prayed, "Lord, do not hold this sin against them" (v. 60). It was easy for people to see the parallel between the death of Stephen and Christ's own death just a short time before. Stephen died for the same things Christ had died for and in the same way Christ had died. They were both martyrs (the word *martyr* comes from the Greek word for witness), and their deaths set the pattern for all future Christian martyrdoms. The conditions for martyrdom would be external persecution, on the one hand, and Jesus-like meekness — forgiving humility — on the other. This pattern has continued from Stephen right up through present-day martyrdoms in Sudan, Pakistan, and China.

The stoning of Stephen was regarded as a major event for two reasons. One is that Stephen was the first Christian to die for his faith. His death became the model for all future Christian martyrs. His death for the sake of Christ was seen as an unforgettable witness to the power of Christ to make a man stand firm under persecution.

There is a second reason Stephen's "witness unto death" was important: Saul of Tarsus, a man of incomparable importance for the future of Christianity, was there. "Saul was consenting to his death" (Acts 8:1). "Then they . . . stoned [Stephen]; and the witnesses laid down their garments at the feet of a young man named Saul" (7:58).

Saul was a highly educated Orthodox Jew with

a passion for the Torah (i.e., the Law) and a position of total commitment to living it out in every aspect of his life. Saul (now become Paul) wrote later about himself that he had been "of the people of Israel, . . . a Hebrew born of Hebrews; as to the law a Pharisee, as to zeal a persecutor of the church, as to righteousness under the law blameless" (Philippians 3:5–6).

The life and the mind of St. Paul now brings us to a quantum leap forward for the new germinating faith.

A quantum leap for Christianity

Chapter 9 of the book of Acts tells the story of Paul's famous conversion to Christianity. In the same way that Stephen's martyrdom supplied the prototype for all future martyrdoms, the conversion of Saul of Tarsus — by which he became for Christians St. Paul, Apostle to the Gentiles — offered the model for all Christian conversions forever after.

In the aftermath of Stephen's death and the resulting flight of Christians from Jerusalem, Saul embarked on a trip by horseback to the city of Damascus, in Syria, to identify and arrest certain Jews there who had become followers of Jesus. As Saul traveled along the road to Damascus, Jesus appeared to him in the miracle of a bright light and a voice that only he could hear. The voice said, "Saul, Saul, why do you persecute me?"

"Who are you, Lord?" asked Saul, who had fallen from his horse and lay prostrate on the ground in shock. The voice replied, "I am Jesus, whom you are persecuting; but rise and enter the city, and you will be told what you are to do."

So important was the Jewish Saul's conversion into the Christian St. Paul that Paul himself told it again and again to his hearers. The writer of Acts, who was probably St. Luke, included the story three times in his book (see chapters 9, 22, and 26).

Here is a principle that we have already seen in *The Christianity Primer.* The events that begin a phenomenon — in this case, Christianity — define it forever after. Thus, Jesus' humiliating but forgiving death on the Cross became the benchmark for Christians of all future reactions to injustice that plague the human race. Christ's "love to the loveless" became the defining characteristic of Grace in later thought and history. Christ's troubled relations with his church, specifically with the Jewish temple, became typical of countless Christians down through the history of the church.

The same principle was now seen with Stephen and Paul. Martyrdom in the future would always fall along the lines of Stephen's innocent yet extremely faithful and articulate defiance of outward authority. And conversion in the future would always fall along the lines of Paul's, a 180-degree turn from a past position to a new one.

Interestingly, as we move forward through the *Primer,* we shall see over and over again how each new generation discovers for itself the meaning inherent in the original events. John

Wesley will "drop" like St. Paul when he finally hears the convicting and converting word on May 24, 1738. Dietrich Bonhoeffer speaks like Stephen when he is martyred by the Nazis on account of his faith in the summer of 1945.

Christianity at its root is never not radical. *Radical,* which comes from the Latin word *radix,* meaning "root," always describes Christianity. This is because Christianity is always driving back to roots. Among those roots are the first martyrdom, that of St. Stephen, and the first conversion, that of St. Paul.

Christianity at its root is never not radical

THE LIFE OF ST. PAUL AFTER THE CONVERSION

Paul's life, like his conversion, became the paradigm, or model, for every wandering evangelist who has ever lived, from St. Dominic in the Middle Ages to George Whitefield in the eighteenth century. Paul wandered "relentlessly," as his twentieth-century German interpreter Ernst Käsemann used to say, east and west over the Mediterranean world.

Immediately after his conversion on the road to Damascus, Paul fled away for three years of isolation and solitude to absorb what had happened. The shock to his system, that the One he had been persecuting was the One he had been needing all along, had to be absorbed.

I have often wondered how it happened that Paul's conversion stuck. So often with abrupt changes of course, I have seen people reverse the change later in life. Jews who become Christians in their youth often return to Judaism at the end of their lives. Roman Catholics who become evangelicals through a dramatic conversion in late adolescence characteristically return to their church much later. As Sigmund Freud observed, we are ever moving backward, backward to childhood, when we think we are moving forward. Religious conversions of a sudden nature seldom stick.

Paul's conversion stuck. It probably had something to do with his going into seclusion in Arabia for three years, as he reports in his letter to the Galatians (1:17). Paul absorbed the shock of what everyone else could scarcely believe: "He who once persecuted us is now preaching the faith he once tried to destroy" (1:23). When Paul finally surfaced, he seemed to have gained a clear understanding of his major emphases and primary insights. To these emphases and insights, the *Primer* will return shortly.

What Paul first realized about his future was that he would have to stay in touch with the original disciples, several of whom were still at Jerusalem. These included Peter, the disgraced but still chosen leader of the original twelve, and also James, the brother of Jesus. Paul went to these men, and sought and received their blessing.

A problem that needed to be solved before Paul could begin

However, a problem needed to be solved before Paul could begin his principal work. Paul had come to believe, both while he was in seclu-

sion in Arabia and also when he came to know
some Christian believers from *non*-Jewish stock
in the city of Antioch, that Christ was for Gentiles
(i.e., non-Jews) as well as for Jews. The forgiveness of sins that Paul began to preach as the gift
of God in Christ was not just for Jews. It was also
for Gentiles. It was for everybody. This was a
huge step. It was an initially unforeseen and actually wild step forward for the earliest Christians.
It was a leap into the dark.

Jesus himself had spent his life almost exclusively among Jews. His message was heard
almost exclusively by Jews. Yet there was implicit
in just about everything Christ did and said a picture of God that burst the borders of Jewish
Law–keeping. There was an expression of messiahship by Christ that was extremely disturbing to
those who valued the temple. And there had
taken place a devastating conclusion to Christ's
life that had marked the work of God in human
lives as taking place through weakness rather
than strength.

Yet the work had still been among Jews by
blood. It had not taken place nor been received
among Gentiles.

But Paul began to draw an inference, a deduc-
tion. He inferred from his own experience — and
also from the evidence that a few Gentiles as well
as some pagans (i.e., those who were not Christian, Moslem, or Jew) had embraced "the way of
Christ," as it was first called — that Christ had

come for non-Jews as well as for Jews. The inference was that Jesus' message was for everybody.

Paul carried his inference back to headquarters. He traveled to Jerusalem to get the OK for
his new direction. Paul wanted a green light to
pursue his ministry among the Gentiles and
pagans, who were, after all, the vast majority of
people living at the time. Thus in the book of Acts
(chapter 15), there is a detailed report of a meeting between Paul and Peter, James, and the other
apostles, which has been referred to ever since as
The First the First Apostolic Council. Paul received the
Apostolic approval he desired! He was told he could preach
Council to Gentiles and win them to the worship of Jesus
provided that they were asked not to eat meat
that had been sacrificed to idols (i.e., to any other
[pagan] gods but the One God of Israel); that
they not eat meat that still contained blood; and
that they limit their sexual lives to monogamous
heterosexual marriage.

Every other requirement of Jewish Law, such
as circumcision and the dietary laws relating to
kosher preparation of food, as well as the detailed
Sabbath regulations that ruled Jewish life, were
stated to be nonbinding for non-Jews. Except, of
course, the Ten Commandments, which would
later be called the Moral Law.

The approval Paul obtained from the apostles
to undertake his ministry among the Gentiles had
immeasurable impact on the future of Christianity. For one thing, it freed him to start an evangelistic campaign in the cities of Asia Minor (now

Turkey), a campaign that was to experience immediate success.

Paul undertook three missionary journeys, a chart of which used to hang in almost every Sunday School classroom in America, and a map of which can still be located in the back of nearly every Bible. These journeys occurred in ever-widening circles, as Paul founded more and more Christian communities or "churches" in the port cities he visited. I have visited many of these cities. It is easy to imagine, even today, the arrival of Paul, with perhaps one companion, in a bustling town of twenty thousand to sixty thousand people *where there was not a single Christian.*

Paul's three missionary journeys

Paul would first go to the Jewish synagogue, where he would try to interest a few hearers in the idea that Jesus of Nazareth was the famously promised Messiah. Failing there (although he sometimes won over a few), he would go to one of the schools of rhetoric, a feature of Hellenistic or late Greco-Roman culture, which taught public speaking — in those days, the most common form of mass communication. Paul would give a short speech about Jesus and then try to engage a member of his audience in an argument about God and the nature of wisdom. Sometimes Paul won hearers in this school setting, as he did at Ephesus. Sometimes he fell on his face, as at Athens.

The point is, Paul took every possible chance he could find to speak about Jesus, the Christ, and what Christ meant to him. He was not unlike one of today's street-corner or soapbox preachers. What was distinctive about him, however, in addition to his sincerity, was his obvious learning. He was extremely well educated and also conspicuously articulate.

During Paul's three missionary journeys, he wrote a series of letters that were to exert tremendous influence on Christian theology. These letters were all, or almost all, *occasional* (meaning that they were written for a specific occasion, such as to answer a theological or ethical question vexing one of his new churches or to reply to objections that others were making to his ministry or authority).

The following letters are definitely from the hand of Paul: Romans, First Corinthians, Second Corinthians, Galatians, Philippians, First Thessalonians, Second Thessalonians, and Philemon. Other letters that hold a solid kernel of his work are ascribed to St. Paul but may have been written by close students of his. These are Ephesians, Colossians, First Timothy, Second Timothy, and Titus. We shall examine these letters in relation to the other books of the New Testament in the next chapter.

As Paul journeyed from city to city in the Mediterranean world of the Roman Empire, he would often stop in order to strengthen a particular church, correspond with his other churches, and check in with headquarters, the founding Jerusalem church. He enshrined in his life a principle of Christian mission that has never left us:

the idea of staying in touch with one's roots. Christianity has produced many original thinkers and bold pioneers. Almost all of them, however — from St. Francis to William Carey, from Jerome the monk to the painter Andrei Rublev — have felt a compelling, sometimes even a restraining need to stay in touch with the main trunk of the tree. St. Paul started this pattern.

Paul strove continuously to maintain his blessing from the first Christians at Jerusalem. He wanted to be in contact with men and women who had been with Jesus. One way Paul did this was to collect money wherever he went for the needs of the Jerusalem church, which by that time had lost most of its power and influence. It was existing under constant pressure from the temple and was always on the verge of repudiating Paul's breakthrough to the Gentiles and morphing into a sect or variant solely of Judaism. Nevertheless, the church at Jerusalem held a magnetic attraction for Paul. This attraction would become the occasion for his death!

The story is told in chapters 21 and following of the book of Acts. Sometime in the mid-50s A.D., Paul felt a need to return to Jerusalem in person. He was somewhat conflicted theologically about the temple at Jerusalem and planned to bring some "Greeks," or Gentiles, with him into the temple space. He actually required some of them to be circumcised in order to do this. He was clearly making a point. He was trying to reassure his Jewish opponents that his Gentile converts could act like good Jews.

When Paul and his circumcised Greek friends arrived at the temple and were recognized, a riot broke out. The group was rescued by a Roman centurion, who, as it happened, mistook Paul for a zealot or political rebel. The Roman officer's arrest of Paul as the supposed ringleader of a religious riot started a complicated chain of events that led eventually to Paul's being taken to Rome, the imperial capital, for trial. It is a dramatic and also true story.

Paul was a Roman citizen

Now, Paul happened to be a Roman citizen. His identity papers proved that he was a Roman citizen, in good standing — a status that went back to his father's career in the city of Tarsus. Because Paul carried this impressive mark of identity, he had the right to carry his case personally to the emperor at Rome.

What did Paul's case consist of? It consisted of a Jewish charge of blasphemy for having entered the temple in the company of non-Jews and a Roman charge of being the cause of a riot in a very sensitive place. Both charges might have been dismissed locally. Yet Paul saw these charges against him as an opportunity to get a hearing in what was then the most important political center in the world, the city of Rome. We know also that Paul earnestly desired to travel to Spain, the extreme western edge of the empire, to complete, at least in his mind, a circle of witness to Christ Jesus (Romans 15:24, 28). If he could get to Rome, Paul reasoned, perhaps he could hope truly to finish his course and reach Spain. Perhaps then Jesus would return.

What happened is that after several false starts, disasters, and delays, Paul did indeed get to Rome. There he waited, under a fairly relaxed form of imprisonment, for his case to come up. Unfortunately — or fortunately, depending on how you see martyrdom — after Rome's great fire of A.D. 60, the emperor Nero began an aggressive, short-term persecution of Christians. Paul was thus executed at Rome, so far as we know, in A.D. 60 or 61. The tradition (*tradition* here meaning "a report going back for centuries that an event took place in a concrete place and time") is very strong that he died at Rome as a victim of Nero's scapegoating of Christians.

The martyrdom of St. Paul and St. Peter

The tradition is also strong that St. Peter, by an entirely different set of circumstances, was martyred in Rome at the same time. Peter was a member of the Christian community at Rome when Nero's persecution began. According to a famous legend, Peter, fearing for his life, fled the city. On his way out, the Lord appeared to him. Peter asked the Lord, "Domine, quo vadis?" (Lord, where are you going?) Christ said, "To my people in Rome." Peter was so grief stricken to have let the Lord down yet again that he instantly turned and returned to Rome. There he was crucified, upside down, by Nero's soldiers. There is an ancient tomb below the Vatican bearing Peter's name, and this links well with everything else we know about Peter's life.

In Paul's case, the book of Acts tells us he was in Rome at the end, and, according to a tradition that goes back very far, we know that he had a particularly affectionate relationship with the Christians in Rome. Before being beheaded, Paul was imprisoned briefly in a cellar near the Forum.

But what of this Paul in relation to the Lord? What animated him? What accounts for his relentless passion in trying to make the whole world his field of operations? And what did Paul try to say to his first hearers and later to his accompanying students and disciples? These questions bring us to the most important thing about Paul, which is his theology.

The most important thing about Paul is his theology

PAUL'S CHRISTIAN REVOLUTION

When Jesus appeared to Paul on the road to Damascus, a revolution took place in Paul's consciousness. The revolution was this: the evil one whom he had hated with a violent rage was discovered by him to be the very opposite of what he had thought. Christ was the answer to, not the antagonist of, all his hopes. Here again is an example of a classic reversal of position that frequently occurred among Christians from day one of the movement. Jesus himself had said, quoting from Psalm 118, "The very stone which the

builders rejected has become the head of the corner" (Matthew 21:42). This would become a
refrain throughout Christian history. Saul, converted to Paul, was the very embodiment of it.

When you have a stunning "Aha!" moment
like the one Paul experienced, you have to go
back to school! Everything you once thought you
knew is suddenly in question. This was St. Paul's
experience. Everything he thought he knew
was pulled out from under him. So he went back
to school. He really did. For this man in his
midtwenties, school consisted of a three-year
sojourn in Arabia, which effected a complete
overhaul of his thinking. And although not everything was clear to Paul when he returned to
Jerusalem to consult with Peter and James at the
end of that time, a great deal had fallen into place
in his mind.

What were the big themes in Paul's Christian
thinking?

The first theme was fundamental. Paul was
the first person clearly to see that because of
Jesus' resurrection from the dead, Jesus of Nazareth had become the divine Christ. Scholars
have sometimes made a distinction between the
Jesus of history and the Christ of faith. For most
Christians, however, they are the same. Actually,
the distinction between the Jesus of history and
the Christ of faith is a false one. The only truth in
it is the fact that Jesus Christ is no longer bound
to a particular space and time. Unlike Jesus of
Nazareth, Jesus Christ is invisibly present to

Big themes
in Paul's
Christian
thinking

everyone, or, rather, invisibly present to everyone who needs him and asks for him.

Although many of Jesus' teachings, as well as the manner of his death, were bigger than his context, he did not become the universal God-Man whom Christians adore until after his resurrection and ascension. Saul of Tarsus could not help but grasp this as he fell off his horse and lay flat on his face on the Damascus road. This new fact, the magnitude of the man whom he had been persecuting, came home to Saul and gave him a new being. He called this "a new creation" (II Corinthians 5:17; Galatians 6:15). Paul now saw life totally differently from before, because Jesus of Nazareth, whom he once had hated, was become Jesus Christ the Son of God and Messiah for Israel.

Paul's view of Christ is sometimes called Christ-mysticism. It is sometimes called, jaw-breakingly, participationism. This is the idea that being a Christian means being part of Christ. A believer becomes a part of a "body" of which Christ is the "head." There is a duality to this view: the body of Christ is both spiritual and invisible but also real and perceptible. When Paul says, "Now you are the body of Christ and individually members of it" (I Corinthians 12:27), he is applying a mental image to his readers' real life. But it is still an image. The body of Christ is a figure of speech for the family of faith, a family that acts as one in important ways but also contains different, discrete parts. It is a metaphor verging on the literal.

It is a comparison of something invisible (Christ ascended) to something visible (a human body).

As we shall see later, the church made the mistake of overdoing the literal side of the idea and forgetting that it was a metaphor or image. We shall see this especially with the church's later teachings concerning Holy Communion, or Eucharist. The real point here is that St. Paul's Jesus Christ was a massive and omnipresent divine being to the highest power.

If Paul taught that Jesus of Nazareth had become the cosmic Christ of God, Paul now had to apply this idea to everyday people. Specifically, Paul had to apply the idea to himself! How did Paul's former passionate Judaism relate to a divine Messiah who declared that "the old has passed away, behold, the new has come" (II Corinthians 5:17)? We are now talking about the birth of Christian theology.

Paul saw quickly that the coming of Christ had affected the whole way of being religious that was Judaism. In his view, Judaism had been rendered out of date by the coming of Christ. This was very heavy data.

So Paul began to question the Jewish Law! He began to question the Law fundamentally. If Christ's death and resurrection had made all things new, what was the point of keeping the Law? Or trying to keep the Law? There must be a different pathway to God. This pathway, different from the Law, he called faith.

Faith for Paul was simply trust. It was trust in

God to work out a good plan for people's lives. God's promises — the Old Testament word for things he had said he would do for his people over the long run of human lives and history — had to be held onto by means of faith, which meant trust. Works, or obeying and keeping the Law, were not sufficient to activate God's promises. God's promises were tied to people's simple, even childlike trust. Jesus himself had taught this when he said, "Whoever does not receive the kingdom of God like a child shall not enter it" (Mark 10:15).

What I am saying is that when Paul met Christ on the road to Damascus, that fact alone was enough to undo every mechanism and every principle by which he had lived.

This is the birth of a core idea in Christianity, Paul's *novum.* In the words of theologian Ernst Käsemann, "Paul now taught what Jesus had lived." Jesus had gone to those who had received him, mostly to those who were in grievous need or isolation. They had nothing to give him. Yet he gave them everything.

"Paul now taught what Jesus had lived"

St. Paul put this into words. In other words, *Paul put the lifestyle of Jesus into a conceptual framework.*

Paul's framework became known as justification by faith. It is a concept to which Christian people have returned again and again, even when it has been covered over by other aspects of the religion or even been actively denied. Justification by faith has certainly been denied by the Christian churches at different points in their history.

Here is the short form of St. Paul's justification by faith. Human beings try to do what is right on God's terms. God's terms are embodied in the Law. But we fail. We cannot obey the Law. We cannot obey the Law, first, because we are not able to. We are not good enough and are not gifted enough and are not strong enough. Second, we break the Law because we *want* to. There is something about us that when we are told what to do, we immediately desire to do the opposite. So the Law fails. The Law fails to accomplish its work in the human race because human beings cannot do it and also because they will not do it. We therefore cannot justify ourselves. Nothing we do is enough to wrest the verdict that we have done enough and that we have done it right.

St. Paul's justification by faith

Paul glimpsed this fact about the Law when Christ appeared to him, nullifying Paul's past. Thinking on that, he came to believe that what God requires of us is faith, which is childlike trust. This is the only thing God requires of a person. And trust seems to open God's heart, too. Trust seems to be linked to confidence on a person's part that he is heard and at the same time loved by God. Trust conveys serenity, inward peace, confidence in the future, and a hopeful view of life. Trust operates in the middle of trials and tribulations.

Paul wrote this down in a pure form in chapter 5 of his letter to the Romans:

> Therefore, since we are justified by faith, we have peace with God through our Lord Jesus Christ. Through him we have obtained access to this grace in which we stand, and we rejoice in our hope of sharing the glory of God. More than that, we rejoice in our sufferings, knowing that suffering produces endurance, and endurance produces character, and character produces hope, and hope does not disappoint us, because God's love has been poured into our hearts.
>
> (vv. 1–5)

Thus, God has loved the human race in a new way in the coming of the Lord Jesus Christ. This has put faith, which is childlike trust, in place of Law-keeping as the key to relating to God. It has also opened up the possibility of consequences — Paul says "fruits" — such as joy, endurance, character, and hope. Ironically, the very human qualities that the Law considers good — such as truthfulness, long suffering, humility, and kindness — grow *spontaneously* from this faith or childlike trust. Thus the Law of God gets what it originally wanted! It is just the mechanism or means that is different. That mechanism is no longer obedience but rather, simple childlike trust.

Christianity puts faith in place of Law-keeping

This was a new idea in the ancient world, where religion had always been based on something human beings did to satisfy, appease, or please God. All the ancient religions worked that way. But Paul taught that nothing we do in ourselves is ever enough. Nothing we do in ourselves will ever satisfy. God has to work the work of divine loving and initiative. All we need to do is open our whole heart to it.

Another word for this concept is *Grace*. *Grace* means unmerited favor. We don't deserve it. We get it anyway. It is like romantic love that endures. I am loved. That is everything. And belovedness evokes response, which, unfailingly, is love itself.

This core doctrine of St. Paul, which came about initially as the result of a thoroughly blinding and disturbing encounter in the midst of a differently tilted, zealous Jewish life, is the key to understanding the future of Christianity from that time on. The Law, on this teaching, was null and void for Christians. Grace had superceded it. Grace would activate the holy life that the Law had been unable to evoke.

Importantly, Paul never wiped his feet on the Jewish Law as such. Paul used to say, and say often, "The law is holy, just, and good." He just understood that the Law could not make a person obey it. Human nature being what it is, the Law was unable to get people to obey it.

What was the place of the Jewish Law in the new religion, Christianity? The Law was good, yet Christ had displaced it. Christ had displaced it with simple trust. But what about the fact that God had really and historically given the Law to the world?

Here enters the idea of atonement. Paul imported an old concept from Judaism to retain the Law as a factor in Christian theology. Paul said that when Christ died, he obeyed the Law — fulfilled it — in full, so that human beings would no longer have to fulfill it. But *someone* had to obey the Law. It was obvious that human beings did not and could not do this. So an atonement to God through the Law was necessary. Jesus obeyed the Law when he died, so humbly and unresistingly. Christ made atonement for our failures. This is how Paul put it:

The theme of atonement

> For our sake [God] made [Christ] to be sin who knew no sin, so that in him we might become the righteousness of God.   (II Corinthians 5:21)

> We are convinced that one has died for all,
>   (II Corinthians 5:14)

The exact same idea is expressed in another place in the New Testament — by St. Peter, in fact:

> For Christ also died for sins once for all, the righteous for the unrighteous, that he might bring us to God.   (I Peter 3:18)

The theme of atonement, of someone good dying in the place of people who are not good, came out of the Jewish temple system of blood sacrifice. It was an element of ancient Judaism that Christianity, through St. Paul (and also through the author of the book of Hebrews later in the New Testament), carried forward for all time. It has occurred in literature and poetry again and again over the ensuing centuries of the Christian tradition. It hits us straight in the face whenever we see a billboard or roadway sign that reads "Jesus Saves." It is the heartbeat of evangelical religion. It all comes from Paul, who was trying to make sense of his old life in light of the revolution occasioned by his experience on the road to Damascus.

Muslim converts to Christianity often say they were converted when Christ appeared to them in a dream. It took a "direct hit," so to speak, through a dream, or, as in St. Paul's case, a brilliant waking dream, for them to overcome the natural resistance of heritage, family, and education. Paul's epiphany, which is the technical word for a divine encounter, ended up rewriting Judaism and creating Christianity as we now receive it.

Do you see the logic of Paul's thinking? He went from an experience to a rewrite of his Jewish past to a reinterpretation of the Jewish Law to the idea of Christ's atonement. It would be a short hop next, and especially among the next generation of Christians, to the idea that Jesus was God. Because only God can forgive sins, and because Christ took on the sins of everyone by dying upon the Cross, then — eureka! — Christ must have been God. The idea that Jesus of Nazareth was actually God come into the flesh

The logic of Paul's thinking

would hinge on the earlier idea that only God can bear the sins of others.

This is all of a piece. Whereas Jesus was the first Christian, Paul was the first Christian theologian. Yet Paul simply taught what Jesus himself had done.

In theology, there are important issues and there are also secondary issues. There are central issues, and there are subsidiary issues. For St. Paul, the Gospel, the theme of Grace as over against the theme of Law, was the central issue.

But other, secondary issues were related to it. We shall look at these briefly. Before we do so, however, we need to observe that there are some scholars who do not think justification by faith is the hub of Paul's thought. Some scholars regard justification by faith as only one of several themes in the theology of St. Paul. Albert Schweitzer, the famous medical missionary and scholar of earliest Christianity, argued that justification by faith is just a "subsidiary crater" on the lunar landscape of Paul's thought. Schweitzer wanted to emphasize the Christ-mysticism of Paul — images such as the body of Christ, being joined to Christ, and being participants in the body and blood of Christ through the ritual of the Lord's Supper or Eucharist. Schweitzer, who wrote his books almost one hundred years ago, still has many followers today.

The school of thought that *The Christianity Primer* follows understands the Gospel message of justification to be the center, not a subsidiary

Some disagree that justification by faith is the hub of St. Paul's thought

crater, of St. Paul's theology. Everything else, from his doctrine of the church to his hope of the second coming of Christ, flows from that center. I should not hide the fact, however, that some Christians weigh justification by faith as being less important to an understanding of Paul and his thought.

The question of interpretation, or what an ancient text means today, is called hermeneutics, from the Greek word meaning "to interpret." It is an uncommon word, but it is the correct one. The hermeneutic we can apply to Paul's words is the same one adopted by St. Augustine, Martin Luther, and John Wesley, to name just three among the legions of theologians who have studied this concept. This is the hermeneutic: It is the Gospel, the Good News of justification by faith, that resolves the two desperate and primary problems involved in being a human. These are the problems of guilt and of weakness.

As we have seen already, Paul's version of Christianity speaks to both of these problems. God's Grace overcomes human guilt. And God's Grace displays the strength that exists in weakness. Thus, Grace is the organizing principle for understanding all of Christianity, not to mention all of life. Grace preaches! Other themes, such as the Eucharist and the church and the Second Coming, are important. But they do not *preach*. Which is to say, they are abstract, whereas Grace is concrete.

Because of Grace's concreteness and the fact

that it speaks directly to the perceived human problems of guilt and weakness, I believe it is proper and correct to see Grace as the key to Paul's thought. Grace is certainly that element in Paul's thought which has had "legs." It has had considerable *"carry"* over a very long period and has continued to sound contemporary even in the most diverse settings. I have heard former Hindus speak of the application of Grace to their lives, and I have spoken with Muslims and also Buddhists who are attracted to it. A hermeneutic organized around Grace is the hermeneutic embraced by *The Christianity Primer.*

There are other approaches. And in the *Primer,* we shall see them emerging at different points in Christian history. But all approaches have to deal with the same data: the life, death, and resurrection of Christ. All approaches must also deal with the texts, the letters, handed down from St. Paul. It is just that some approaches weigh his concerns somewhat differently and thus prioritize them differently.

St. Paul put Grace at the center of the religion, rather than Law. He put the Gospel at the crossroads of the new faith, rather than the visible church. He put weakness at the pumping heart of Christianity, rather than strength. These three bold and innovative ideas had spin-offs with regard to the sacraments, money, predestination, and the relation of Christianity to Judaism. The spin-offs were "subsidiary craters," to use Albert

St. Paul put Grace at the center of Christianity

Schweitzer's phrase, with respect to the big three. They were not ultimate, as Grace was, but they were just below it in importance.

In fact, the Grace of God — which began for Paul in his shocking meeting with a risen enemy now become his friend — is a good organizing principle for a quick review of Paul's other themes. Each of these themes, though secondary to Grace, had consequences for the future of Christianity.

BAPTISM

Paul once said very plainly that he had come not to baptize but rather to preach the Gospel of God's Grace (I Corinthians 1:17). Paul did believe in baptism, because it was an overwhelmingly powerful sign of the new creation. It signified and acted out ritually a person's dying to his old life and rising to his new one. But the ceremony of baptism, in and of itself, was not of principal significance, in Paul's view. Rather, it was an outward manifestation of the underlying, far more meaningful theological concept. In later Christian tradition, baptism would be called the "outward and visible sign of an inward and spiritual grace" (Book of Common Prayer).

Never confuse the sign with the thing signified! This is a vital truth. Christians have often done exactly that, as we shall observe again and again. For Paul, baptism represented a person's connecting with Christ. This connection was a kind of felt solidarity with the life, death, and resurrection of Christ — somewhat like a marriage. Some Christians like to say that baptism signifies participation in Christ. I find that too abstract and hard to pin down. Here we shall stick with the language of sign (i.e., the ceremony of baptism) and thing signified (i.e., the Grace of God taking control in a person's life rather than the person doing so by willpower).

THE LORD'S SUPPER

Like everyone else in the first generation of Christians, Paul knew about the last supper of Jesus. He knew that Christ had endowed his last Passover meal with high, deliberate significance. The founder had spoken of the bread and wine received at the meal as a vivid representation of his death: "This is my body which is given for you" (Luke 22:19) and "This is my blood. . . , which is poured out for you and for many for the forgiveness of sins" (Matthew 26:28).

Paul knew all that. Even in the first days when he was absorbing his change after the Damascus road encounter, he was considering the meaning of Christ's body and blood. I do not think Paul would have written much about the Lord's Supper had its meaning not been misunderstood in some of the churches he had founded in Greece and Asia Minor. The misunderstanding arose because of the consumption of meat at the meal. In those times, much of the meat sold in the public market was slightly recycled (i.e., had been cut from an animal that had just been sacrificed to one of the Greek or Roman or local gods). Consequently, in these churches the food consumed at the first Christian commemorations of the Last Supper had very possibly been dedicated to a pagan god. Paul himself did not mind that, because as far as he was concerned, it only mattered what the mind-set was of the Christian believer who actually ate the meat. But Jewish Christians did mind, and they unsettled their more heedless Gentile brothers and sisters with their worries.

Paul thus had to tackle the question of ritual meals that were intended to impress on Christians the meaning of what Christ had said on that awesomely remembered Thursday evening. What Paul did was emphasize the aspect of sensitivity and mutual love:

Paul emphasized the aspect of sensitivity and mutual love

> My beloved, shun the worship of idols. . . . [But] because there is one bread, we who are many are one body, for we all partake of the one bread. . . . Let no one seek his own good, but the good of his neighbor.   (I Corinthians 10:14, 17, 24)

The bottom line for Paul was this: When you observe the Lord's Supper, whatever you do, do it with consideration for the others who are present. The purpose of the meal is to solidify and strengthen love among those for whom God's Grace has become the vital principle of living.

> So then, my brethren, when you come together to eat, wait for one another.
>
> (I Corinthians 11:33)

This was straightforward. The Lord's Supper was a "love feast," as it would later be called within some traditions. It presented or rather re-presented the last supper of Christ. But its point was the coming together in love of diverse, born-again people. It was the social yet serious supper of the new creation.

Paul's teaching on the sacraments (i.e., rites of the Christian church considered to have been instituted by Jesus) of baptism and the Lord's Supper therefore stressed the newness of God's Grace in people's lives (signified by baptism's washing away of sin) and the love within the Christian family (furthered and signified by the Lord's Supper).

ESCHATOLOGY AND APOCALYPTIC

Eschatology is a jawbreaker of a word that comes from a Greek word meaning "last things." It is the aspect of theology relating to the end of the world, the second coming of Christ, and the final judgment of God. Eschatology is an important theme in Christian theology. It was very important to Christ himself. It was also important to Paul.

Paul believed that the world would probably

end during his lifetime. One of the reasons he was so eager to reach Spain was his belief that Christ would come back when the entire known world had been reached by the Gospel of Grace. In Paul's earliest letters, known as First and Second Thessalonians, he had to answer urgent questions from new Christians who were upset that some of their company had died before Christ had returned. Paul attempted to reassure them, expressing his own passionate view that the end of the world was on the horizon.

Paul believed the world would probably end during his lifetime

Paul's thought concerning eschatology was so dramatic that we do right to use another big word, *apocalyptic* (i.e., relating to a theory that offers vivid, even weird pictures of what will actually take place when the world ends). You may remember that Francis Ford Coppola entitled his epic film about the Vietnam War *Apocalypse Now* (1979), because some conditions of that war felt like the end of the world.

Paul used apocalyptic images, such as the rapture (i.e., God's pulling believers up into the air to meet Christ there face to face), to illustrate eschatological ideas. Later, when he observed that the end of the world was not coming so fast, he toned down the apocalyptic emphasis. Yet Paul never stopped believing that Christ would return to earth soon. This idea has affected Christianity ever since. It is stated in its most extreme form biblically in the last book of the New Testament, which is called the Revelation of St. John of Patmos, to which we will return.

FREEDOM OF THE SPIRIT
AND FREEDOM FROM THE LAW

The doctrine of the Holy Trinity

To examine Paul's views on spiritual freedom, I think it would be helpful to briefly digress and review the doctrine of the Holy Trinity.

The idea of the Trinity is kind of a hunch that changed into an insight which morphed into a core *doctrine* of Christianity.

The logic of the Trinity is as follows: Jesus Christ was God, because he did things that only God can do. For example, he forgave people's sins (Matthew 9:6; Mark 2:10; Luke 5:24). Thus Christians say that God was in Christ. But this means that God is also separate in a sense, for God existed before Jesus came into our world. There is a distinction, in other words, between Jesus and God.

But now, Jesus is no longer here physically. He left when he returned to sit "at the right hand of God" (Mark 16:19). So where we had one God, we now have two entities or Persons.

But there's more. Jesus said that after he left, the Holy Spirit would come. The Holy Spirit, or third Person of the Trinity, as Christian theology puts it, comes into the world to "bring to . . . remembrance" (John 14:26) the things that Jesus taught us. The Holy Spirit is the presence of the Christian God with us *now*.

The formal expression for the Trinity, then, is "one God in three Persons." Each of the Persons is distinct and at the same time coequal (that is the precise theological word) with God.

The Trinity is sometimes presented as a way of affirming three manifestations or expressions of the One God. The traditional word for that is *modes* and is used to define and affirm that the One God comes in three modes, or styles. That is incorrect. What the Trinity declares is that God exists equally in three absolutely separate Persons, yet together in a oneness. No wonder the Trinity is referred to as a mystery of faith!

Paul believed in freedom. He believed in freedom in two ways. First was *God's* freedom to act in any way that God wished, through the Holy Spirit. Paul believed that Christ was present in the church, but invisibly. He was working in sermons and prayers and with compassionate actions, even in predictions and healings. But you could not control or pin down God. You could not restrain or contain the Holy Spirit. The Spirit goes wherever it wants.

Paul also talked a lot about the gifts of the Holy Spirit. As he saw it, these expressions of God's presence are visible and touchable. They make the invisible God feel visible. Although Paul was a Pentecostal Christian — "I thank God that I speak in tongues more than you all" (I Corinthians 14:18) — he did not fix the Spirit within prescribed tracks or ruts. God was the only truly free being.

The gifts of the Holy Spirit

The second way Paul viewed freedom was in relation to the Christian response to Jewish Law.

So revolutionary had the Damascus road encounter been for him that, as we have seen, he had had to reconfigure the entire role of Law in religion. It was of the highest importance to Paul that Christians not return to the way of engaging with God that was typical of the Jewish Law. Thus he wrote in the manner almost of an outburst:

> Brethren, we are not children of the slave but of the free woman. For freedom Christ has set us free; stand fast therefore, and do not submit again to a yoke of slavery. . . . I testify again to every man who receives circumcision that he is bound to keep the whole law.
>
> (Galatians 4:31; 5:1, 3)

Freedom of the Spirit for Christians was freedom from the Law. Although Paul "choked" a little, from time to time, on his extremely bold idea, and although he panicked when his people actually broke the Jewish Law (especially in the realm of sexuality), he never took back what he had seen so brilliantly at first. "Stand fast in the liberty of the spirit."

"Stand fast in the liberty of the spirit"

MONEY

The long and developed history of Christian thought concerning money takes its cue from things Jesus taught about it and things St. Paul wrote about it. Jesus basically spoke against money: "You cannot serve God and mammon"

(Matthew 6:24; Luke 16:13). Christ's followers generally left everything they owned behind and followed him in faith.

Paul wrote people, asking for money. In Second Corinthians, he offers a whole theology of money in relation to personal thanksgiving. Two full chapters of that letter are given over to what people in churches today call stewardship.   **Stewardship**

Paul was also forever raising money for the poor and for the mother church in Jerusalem. He often referred to the mother church in his letters and asked the other, somewhat more prosperous churches with which he was in contact to contribute to the relief of the Jerusalem Christians. Ultimately, when he made a last trip to Jerusalem to deliver funds for their relief, his actions resulted in martyrdom.

Paul taught that each of the Christian churches needs to take some responsibility for all the others. He taught that God is always on the side of financial generosity. And he said that the motive for giving should always be thanksgiving for the prior gifts of Christ. "Thanks be to God for his inexpressible gift!" (II Corinthians 9:15)

PREDESTINATION

There is a trend in Christian thought that leads directly to the idea of predestination — the idea that God has planned in advance the way that things will actually go in life. God has a bit of "fate" to him. *Predestination* also means the same thing as *election:* the idea that God has chosen or elected the way the cards will fall in a person's life. The idea of election, moreover, includes the idea that God has chosen or elected some people to go to heaven out of the broad mass of the human race. Perhaps — and this is called double predestination — God has even elected or chosen some to go to hell.

Predestination is the ultimate hot potato in Christian theology

Predestination is the ultimate hot potato in the history of Christian theology. Nothing is able to divide a church — to divide friends and neighbors in faith from one another — like the concept of predestination. Many people resist the idea fiercely. Others find it a relief. Some others are driven to despair by the very possibility of it. Whole churches and sects have been founded according to what a particular teacher or minister had to say about predestination.

Although the Old Testament has many passages that point to predestination, it was St. Paul who brought this idea into the foreground for Christians. Paul was puzzled, awed, and at times driven to despair by the fact that his fellow Jews resisted the idea that Jesus of Nazareth was the promised Messiah. How, Paul asked, is it possible that God's chosen people could reject the Lord and his way? The only thing to say would have to be that God himself had somehow planned it that way. The sole cause of the Jews' rejection of Christianity must lie with the same God who "elected" them in the first place. This train of thought is spelled out in the book of Romans (chapters 9, 10, and 11).

It is a common experience in the history of religions, not just in Christianity, that big ideas are hatched in connection with concrete events. Nonviolent resistance in the United States, for example, came to the fore when one woman refused to take a prescribed seat on a bus in Montgomery, Alabama. *Les Misérables* was written by Victor Hugo as a response to a few incidents he had witnessed in the streets and tenements of Paris. Paul's idea of God's predestinating Grace came about because he was thrown out of certain synagogues in Asia Minor: how could God's chosen people reject God's chosen savior? What kind of mystery was that?

We have already said that Grace, as opposed to Law, was the defining theme in earliest Christianity. It is also clear that Grace in relation to the church was a tension. Then there was the continuing theme of weakness in relation to strength. All three of these big ideas have a logic that carries a reasoning person toward some version of predestination. This is because the burden in Christianity is always on *God's* side: his Grace, in other words. The burden in Christianity is always on the good or strength that comes from *outside* a person. If aid in Christianity always comes from the outside — from God, in other words, rather than from us — then the following questions immediately arise: Why does God work in one way but not in another? Why does he work in some people's lives but not in the lives of others? *He must have his reasons!* Therefore, something like predestination must be at work.

The very contentious and famous idea of divine predestination is a consequence of the idea of Grace. Why is it Grace and not Law that changes the human heart? The answer is hidden in the eternal purposes of God. Why does the Gospel and not the church change the human heart? The answer is hidden in the eternal purposes of God. Why is weakness and not strength the value that changes human hearts? The answer is hidden in the eternal purposes of God.

The answer is hidden in the eternal purposes of God

Paul taught Grace; therefore, he taught predestination. The one idea follows the other.

PREDESTINATION AND THE JEWS

Predestination is a conceptual tool for trying to understand why one thing has happened and why another thing has not happened. The reason for predestination's emerging into Christian thought was Paul's shock over the fact that his people, the Jews, had rejected Christ and Christianity.

This theme has sometimes been a dark subject in the history of Christianity. But it has to be noted, if only to recognize the facts. When Paul was converted to Christianity, he thought his fellow Jews would become Christians if they could

only see things the way he now saw them. Paul
was completely unprepared for the possibility
that his fellow Jews might not see things his way.
That is why Paul wrote these words in Romans:

> I have great sorrow and unceasing anguish in my
> heart. . . . [For] they are Israelites, and to them
> belong the sonship, the glory, the covenants, the
> giving of the law, the worship, and the promises;
> to them belong the patriarchs, and of their race,
> according to the flesh, is the Christ. . . . My
> heart's desire . . . is that they may be saved. I
> bear them witness that they have a zeal for God,
> but it is not enlightened. For, being ignorant of
> the righteousness that comes from God, and
> seeking to establish their own, they did not sub-
> mit to God's righteousness. . . . [Yet] has God
> rejected his people? By no means!
>
> (9:2, 4–5; 10:1–3; 11:1)

Here Paul opened a vein of ambivalence, or
double-mindedness, toward the religion of Judaism. This ambivalence has been a part of Christianity ever since.

On the one hand, Jesus was a Jew, and the
Jews are God's chosen people. On the other
hand, the Jews "did not submit to God's righteousness." This means they chose the Law over
Grace. Many modern Christian scholars do not wish
to put it that way. But Paul did. We should not
make Paul into a politically correct writer by current standards. Paul was divided. He recognized **Paul was
divided**

the Jewish legacy right into the bloodlines of the Christ, Jesus of Nazareth. But Paul saw Judaism as flawed in the now, because Grace was resisted.

Because of St. Paul, Christianity has forever existed in tension with Judaism. Yet also because of Paul, Christianity has forever breathed a spirit of thanksgiving for Judaism. When the tension speaks louder than the thanksgiving, anti-Semitism sometimes emerges. Yet when the thanksgiving speaks louder than the tension, Christianity exists in danger of losing its identity. Christianity then starts to sound like a variant of Judaism. These two possibilities — anti-Semitism on the one hand and dilution on the other — attend Christianity always. I believe they always will. This is because a religion, like a marriage, can never escape from its earliest origins. Jesus Christ and St. Paul both had defining emphases. These emphases have never stopped being a part of the religion they founded.

A religion can never escape from its earliest origins

THE PETER PRINCIPLE

Before we finish this survey of the seeds Paul planted, each of which became a mighty tree on the horizon of Christian history, there is one more theme to mention. It is a theme that exists from negation and concerns St. Peter.

Throughout the New Testament, there is a tension between the legacy of Peter and the legacy of Paul. In the Letter to the Galatians, Paul publicly confronts Peter, the senior disciple, and says that Peter is entirely wrong and even dishonest about the Gospel of Grace. This passage (Galatians 2:11ff.) is extremely uncomfortable for readers who want everything in the church to be just nice and right. It is terminally uncomfortable for Christians who wish to believe in a golden age of harmony and love.

Later, St. Peter, or someone writing under his name, got back at Paul. The author of Second Peter says this:

> Our beloved brother Paul wrote to you according to the wisdom given him. . . . There are some things in them hard to understand, which the ignorant and unstable twist to their own destruction.   (3:15–16)

It is amazing that the Christian church allowed its Holy Scriptures to contain this contradiction. The New Testament does not gloss over the fact that there was tension between what Paul taught, which was Grace, and what Peter apparently taught or at least approved, which was Law.

The dispute between St. Peter and St. Paul

The unhidden dispute between St. Peter and St. Paul in relation to Grace and Law is a wonder. Most religions try to whitewash their gods and heroes. There is a natural tendency in human nature to make our heroes perfect and without blemish. St. Peter is not that in Christian tradition.

The Peter Principle in Christianity has two parts to it. The first part is negative: Grace

The Peter Principle

always stimulates its opposite. This is true in the Christian church as well as outside it. The Peter Principle goes back to the very first days of the religion. Grace and Law have been in conflict from the beginning. Where there was a Paul, there was also a Peter. Where there was Jesus, there were also his opponents: the Pharisees and Sadducees.

But the second part of the Peter Principle is positive. It says that God operates through unworthy vehicles, through flawed, mistaken people. This is the ennobling part of the Peter Principle.

St. Peter thought that Christ was being too heavy when he talked about being crucified. Christ replied, "Get behind me, Satan! You are a hindrance to me; for you are not on the side of God, but of men" (Matthew 16:23).

Peter said he would walk on water if Jesus gave him the word. A moment or two after Peter had started walking, he sank like a stone (Matthew 14:28–30). Peter said he would never run away if Jesus were ever arrested (Luke 22:33). Peter actually denied having any knowledge of Jesus three times that very same night (Luke 22:54–62). After Jesus was executed, Peter went back to his old job and sucked his thumb (John 21:2–3). When Christ appeared to Peter by the Sea of Galilee, Peter protested his love for the Lord, only to be told (three times!) that he would himself be crucified in a horrible manner (John 21:15–19).

Later, in Antioch, Peter caved in on a matter of first importance, Grace in relation to the Jewish Law, and re-created a barrier of segregation between Jews and non-Jews (Galatians 2:12). In fact, the tradition that Peter was unstable and faithless was so strong within earliest Christianity that the legend arose that he fled Rome in A.D. 60 to escape arrest by the servants of Nero. This affecting tradition, that even at the end of his life Peter was just as vulnerable to cowardice as he had been during the time of Jesus, is presented in the novel *Quo Vadis* by Henry Sienkiewicz. In *Quo Vadis,* Jesus appears to Peter as he is fleeing Rome, and lifts a mirror up to Peter's craven character. Then and only then is Peter able to do the right thing, at least from a Christian perspective.

The Peter Principle declares, negatively, that Peter, the top leader of the first church, totally failed and specifically denied the idea of Grace, again and again, and then again and again. The Peter Principle also declares, positively, that Christian character is defined by weakness, moral failure, and repeated offenses. Christian character is thus sinful and prone to repeat its sins, over and over again. But from Grace it becomes the gift, selfless and courageous, rock-like (*Peter* comes from the Greek word for rock) and steady. This needs to be emphasized: *Christian character always starts, and has to start again, from failure.*

Peter's tension with Paul and Paul's emphases created the Peter Principle, which was both good

— God works through brokenness — and bad — our weaknesses never leave us entirely.

The next chapter starts the long "yellow brick road" of Christian history after the founding. The first step in the history of the church, after the giant steps — the cosmic strides — of Jesus and Paul, was to put things on paper. The first step was to write down, for posterity, the events that had birthed Christianity. The *Primer* now moves to the creation of the New Testament.

✝

IV

THE NEW TESTAMENT

I n the year A.D. 70, the religion of Judaism was
forced overnight to change forever. Christianity also changed forever after that year.

In A.D. 70, the Romans sacked Jerusalem and
destroyed the Jewish state. The destruction of
Jerusalem was not a surprise. The conditions
leading up to it had been building for at least one
hundred years. Christ himself had fallen victim to
the uneasy relations existing between the religious leaders of Israel (the priests) and its political rulers (the Romans).

The catastrophic destruction of Jerusalem

There were at least two results of this catastrophe. The first was the Jewish Diaspora, or exile.
Starting from their remaining cultural center in
Galilee, the Jews fanned out all over the known
world. They had lost the Second Temple and thus
their physical connection with the Holy City.
Returning to Jerusalem as a people became a distant dream. The dream never died out. It became
expressed in the toast "Next year in Jerusalem."

The Jews also realized that they must consolidate their religious traditions. Because they were
more vulnerable than they had been before, they
had to codify and centralize their traditions for
the sake of the future. This they did, most impor-

tantly, by settling on a final or approved text of their scriptures, what Christians call the Old Testament. At a meeting in Jamnia in Galilee in A.D. 90, the rabbis declared what was officially to be regarded as Scripture and what was not. The same thing would happen soon within Christianity.

The shock of A.D. 70 affected Christians as fundamentally as it did the Jews. The small Jewish-Christian community left Jerusalem just before the final Roman assault on the city and fled north to the city of Pella. The rest of the Christians in the Roman world experienced the death of the Holy City as a break with the Jewish past.

The Jewish past, the Jewish side to Christianity, took an immediate downturn. Remember that Paul had made a conscious, consistent effort to stay true to the Jewish-Christian community at Jerusalem, the mother church. Now the mother church no longer existed. Now the cord was bound to be cut, ideologically as well as physically.

The mother church no longer existed

Like the Jews, the Christians were also forced to begin consolidating their traditions and committing them to paper. Word of mouth was not enough. It was essential, absolutely essential, that the memories of Jesus — as well as the earliest history of the first Christians, not to mention the valued letters of St. Paul, together with the letters of a few others — be preserved. Thus, one of the most important results of the fall of Jerusalem in A.D. 70 was the formation of the Christian scriptures: the New Testament.

THE SYNOPTIC GOSPELS:
ST. MATTHEW, ST. MARK,
AND ST. LUKE

The four Gospels in the New Testament are biographies of Jesus. Three of these, the Gospels of St. Mark, St. Matthew, and St. Luke, are called the *synoptic* Gospels, from the Greek word meaning "parallel" or similar. Mark, Matthew, and Luke have much material in common. Despite important differences, each tells the same story, in roughly the same order. (The fourth Gospel, St. John's Gospel, is not a synoptic Gospel. This is because it is very different from the other three. The differences are so noticeable that it is in a class by itself.)

Although each of the synoptic Gospels tells basically the same story, each of them is different. The differences are in two areas: the area of tone or voice and the area of editing. Many of the same stories appear in each of the synoptic Gospels, but they are told differently, or they are placed at a different point in the biography of Christ, or certain events occur in one Gospel or two but not in the others.

Most scholars think that the first Gospel to be written was that of Mark, possibly as early as A.D. 45. It was probably written by the man who is mentioned (in Mark 14:51–52) as fleeing the Garden of Gethsemane naked at the time of Jesus' arrest. This biography of Christ contains only sixteen chapters, has an abrupt ending, and yet also has a definite, gripping narrative structure. It emphasizes Christ as a somewhat disguised Messiah. It also stresses his exorcisms and physical healings.

Matthew's Gospel came next, although this, too, is not accepted by everyone. The date is hard to know, but the book of Matthew seems to predate the year A.D. 70. This is because Matthew's Gospel seems designed particularly to appeal to Jews, who were, of course, dispersed after the fall of Jerusalem in A.D. 70. A lengthy account of Jesus' moral teachings is contained in Matthew, in particular the Sermon on the Mount (which is included in the appendix to this book on page 303. Jesus is seen as a sort of new Moses, speaking with Moses-like authority as a supremely wise rabbi. Matthew's account of Jesus' Passion is long and detailed. It is also harrowing.

The Gospel according to St. Luke is regarded as the most literary and polished of the three synoptic Gospels. Luke is thought to have been a doctor, an educated Gentile who spoke Greek. He wrote a fluid account of Christ's life, including several details of character and personality that are unique to Luke. The Holy Spirit is a featured actor in Luke's high drama of Christ's life.

The theologian (and later, bishop) Marcion of Sinope considered Luke the most graceful and hence the least legalistic of the synoptic Gospels. Marcion was particularly impressed by the beautiful parable of the prodigal son (15:11–32).

Luke's profile of Jesus is of a gentle, compassionate pastor, seeking out the lost and desperate.
Interestingly, Marcion, who found several books
of the New Testament to be too "Jewish" or
"legalistic," considered Luke's Gospel to be by
far the best of the Gospels. So he cut the other
ones from his authorized version of the Christian
scriptures.

St. Luke the Evangelist wrote a second major
book of the New Testament, the Acts of the Apos-   **The Acts of**
tles, which immediately follows John's Gospel.   **the Apostles**
In this almost novelistic masterpiece of ancient
literature, Luke created the first history of Christianity, which is the Christian movement after
Easter. The main character in Luke's post-Res-
urrection history is the Holy Spirit. The Spirit is
constantly sending an apostle here, driving an
apostle there, shaking the building where the disciples are praying, extricating the Christians from
trouble, and propulsively driving forward and
outward the movement of the church. Luke himself is among the cast of characters in Acts. At one
point, the missionary travels of St. Paul, whom
Luke accompanied for a period, are narrated in
the first person. Thus, "when we had parted from
them and set sail, we came by a straight course to
Cos" (21:1).

Luke's Acts is so literary and even so artful
that parts of it fall into an ancient literary form
called the Hellenistic romance, or novella. It is a
work of refined literary portraiture, civilized yet
bearing a passionate message.

The synoptic Gospels — Matthew, Mark, and Luke — together with the Acts of the Apostles are one of the two major building blocks of the New Testament. The second major building block is the letters of St. Paul.

THE LETTERS OF ST. PAUL

Paul's letters, as we have seen, were inspired occasional correspondence written to respond to specific occasions or situations. They were written to comfort or criticize and to answer specific questions that had been put to him.

The original Pauline letters, or Epistles (which is the older word), are Romans, First and Second Corinthians, Galatians, Philippians, First and Second Thessalonians, and Philemon.

The text of Romans, especially the first eight chapters, is the closest thing we have in the Bible to a systematic theology.

First and Second Corinthians, which may in fact contain three letters, address several diverse problems that came up in the life of the Pentecostal-style Christian church in the Greek city of Corinth.

Galatians is the direct answer to Jewish Christians who were seeking to persuade Gentile Christians to become more Jewish.

Philippians links with Galatians in rebutting the Jewish Law in relation to the Grace of Christ. Philippians also contains a short, important summary of Paul's early life.

Second Thessalonians is the earliest book in the New Testament. In First and Second Thessalonians, Paul tries to reassure first-generation Christians concerning their Christian brothers and sisters who had died before Christ's return.

Finally, Philemon, which is only one chapter long, makes a personal request concerning a runaway slave.

All these letters were dictated by Paul to a secretary or scribe. They were then carried personally to the local church and read out loud during a church meeting or service. This means they would have been read in someone's home. They are an invaluable "you were there" commentary on life among the first generation of Christians. For most Christians today, the original letters of Paul breathe with marvelous conviction and, for me, with inspiration.

Five other letters in the New Testament are ascribed to St. Paul but were possibly not written by him.

Colossians was written to a Christian community that is otherwise completely unknown to us. The site has never been fully excavated. Some parts of the Letter to the Colossians sound very much like Paul. Other parts are more "cosmic" or metaphysically "out there" than almost anything else Paul wrote. I believe Colossians probably comes from Paul, but I am not sure about it.

Ephesians, on the other hand, which is also ascribed to Paul, reads too "high church" to have been written by him. Ephesians puts us both "high up in the heavenly places" and also in the here and now. Ephesians makes much of the church and lays it on thick with celestial adjectives. Quite a bit of Greek, or Orthodox, Christianity takes its cue from Ephesians. But the cartwheeling, free-floating ways of the Holy Spirit of Christ, which we hear about so clearly in First and Second Corinthians, are absent in Ephesians. Ephesians must have been written by a high-flying student of St. Paul's who still wanted to stay in touch with Paul's Grace teaching. Fortunately, the Grace teaching exists in Ephesians alongside the high church metaphors.

Three other letters, short but full of substance, are assigned to Paul in the New Testament. These are First Timothy, Second Timothy, and Titus. These letters are called the pastoral Epistles because they speak in a mentoring and fatherly way, hence pastorally (i.e., literally like a shepherd), to two students of Paul — Timothy and Titus. Questions of church order, such as who should be ordained, or set apart for official leadership, and how discipline should be administered, are the main focus.

The pastoral Epistles are sometimes regarded as expressions of early or growing "catholicism" in the church. Although the word catholic in this context means universal, or general, by catholicism I mean a trend toward institutional religion and a tendency, natural in second-generation religion, to pin things down.

First and Second Timothy and Titus were

written in a different atmosphere from that of Galatians and the Corinthian letters. They deal with questions that postdate Paul, who died in A.D. 60.

The pastoral Epistles contain several memorable passages such as this one:

> I am reminded of your sincere faith, a faith that dwelt first in your grandmother Lois and your mother Eunice and now, I am sure, dwells in you. Hence I remind you to rekindle the gift of God that is within you through the laying on of my hands; for God did not give us a spirit of timidity but a spirit of power and love and self-control.   (II Timothy 1:5–7)

Note the three generations that are mentioned. Note, too, the gift of faith that was given "through the laying on of my hands." This is a reference to something similar to the rite that later came to be known as confirmation, or possibly even ordination. This tends, mildly, toward the development of a hierarchical structure (i.e., organization of a group of persons by rank, as in the Catholic church). Note also the sublime opposition of Christian power, Christian love, and Christian self-control in relation to worldly fear. Many scholars of the New Testament, though not all, see the pastoral Epistles as products of a successor to St. Paul writing about twenty or thirty years after Paul was martyred.

"Laying on of my hands"

It is important to realize that *even in the New Testament, there is evidence of the three tensions that marked the ministry of Christ.* There is evidence of Grace versus Law in the arguments that Paul made in opposition to some Jewish Christians. There is evidence of Grace versus church in the observable tendency of the later letters ascribed to Paul to speak in institutional terms. And strength versus weakness is a theme as the church appears to become more vertical in structure and less spontaneously democratic.

At the 1963 World Conference on Faith and Order, the New Testament theologian Ernst Käsemann argued in a lecture that the several different interpretations of Christianity that have marked the history of the church can all find their founding concepts and charter in the diverse New Testament itself. Thus, Protestants can find their charter in the six original letters of St. Paul and in sections of the Gospels; Catholics have a place to go in the pastoral Epistles (First and Second Timthy and Titus), and also Second Peter and James; and the Orthodox can look to Ephesians and also the entire text of St. John's Gospel, with his exalted doxological (i.e., high praise) language, the language of glory and mystical transcendence.

THE GOSPEL AND LETTERS OF ST. JOHN

The next big section of the New Testament is the books that were written by St. John. John was "the disciple whom Jesus loved" (John 21:20). Of the original twelve, John, together with Peter, was the closest to the Lord. After Easter, John took Jesus' mother, Mary, with him to the coast of Anatolia (or Turkey) and became the leading elder or minister in the Christian community at Ephesus, which was founded by St. Paul.

In Ephesus, John wrote his Gospel. It is a long *interpretive* life of Christ. John's Gospel has been a place of shipwreck for New Testament scholars for hundreds of years. In comparison with Matthew, Mark, and Luke, there are obvious and important differences in John's portrait of Jesus. For one thing, John's Jesus speaks more than he acts. He gives long speeches, or discourses, as they are called. He speaks in riddles sometimes, and often in circular arguments, which can torture a strictly logical person. Certain events take place in John that take place nowhere else in the New Testament, such as the healing of the blind man and the turning of water into wine at the wedding in Cana.

A shipwreck for New Testament scholars for hundreds of years

Christ in John's Gospel appears to be more divine than human. The old question among the theologians is this: Do the feet of John's Jesus really touch the ground? The word *docetic,* from the Greek word meaning "to seem," is often applied to the Christ of St. John. This is to say, John's Christ seems to be human, but he is really not. John's Gospel is rich, complex, and full of beautiful images and metaphors. Jesus is compared to a vine, to a door, to a gate, and to a good shepherd.

The Roman Catholic and high church doctrine of the Eucharist has its roots in John (chapter 6).

Some people even think that Christian anti-Semitism has its origin in St. John's Gospel. This is because John pits Christ against "the Jews." In John's Gospel, *the Jews* becomes the generic term for the opponents of Christ's appearing.

John's Gospel is powerful and brilliant. It is well worth a lifetime, many lifetimes, of study. It has been a primary resource for meditation in the Christian church for two thousand years. It is also the source, with Paul's letters, of Christian Christology, which is the doctrine of Jesus' identity.

In addition to his Gospel, John also wrote three letters, called First, Second, and Third John. They accord in tone with John's Gospel and contain beautiful, treasured sentences, such as "There is no fear in love, but perfect love casts out fear" (I John 4:18). Each of John's letters was written when John was a settled church overseer at Ephesus.

"There is no fear in love, but perfect love casts out fear"

Under the emperor Domitian, about A.D. 93, a persecution of Christians began throughout the empire, resulting in John's having to flee Ephesus for the safer haven of Patmos, a remote island close to modern-day Greece. On Patmos, John wrote the book of Revelation.

REVELATION

When I first studied theology, it was generally assumed that the St. John of Patmos who wrote Revelation was a different person from St. John the Evangelist. This assumption was made primarily because the style of and the intention behind the two books are different. I now believe that the two books were written by the same man. I changed my mind when I visited Patmos, at which time I realized that the conditions of violent and uprooting persecution under Emperor Domitian were sufficient to explain the changes in tone between the two books. Also, the extremely vivid visual imagery of Revelation coheres with the symbolic and metaphorical character of John's Gospel.

The book of Revelation, which is the last book of the New Testament, has sections that appeal to fanatics and even to mentally ill patients. It is also the source of several schemes for predicting the future, schemes that have emerged again and again in Christian history as grounds for hope and comfort when times were bad for Christians. Revelation was written for Christians suffering persecution. This explains its extreme illustrations and also its strong threats.

HEBREWS AND THE "CATHOLIC" EPISTLES

There are two other bodies of work in the New Testament: the book of Hebrews and the block of so-called catholic Epistles — First Peter, Second Peter, James, and Jude.

No one knows who wrote Hebrews or exactly to whom it was written. This is why it is called a *general* Epistle. But it was evidently written to

Christians who were Jews by birth and education. The author of Hebrews spends a lot of time demolishing the rituals of the temple system of Judaism in favor of the once-and-for-all sacrifice of Christ on the Cross.

The Protestant Communion services of the sixteenth-century Reformation period are based on the theology of Hebrews. This is especially true for English speakers, given that the 1549 and 1552 editions of Thomas Cranmer's Book of Common Prayer for the Church of England were formed based upon the book of Hebrews. Famous treasured phrases such as "a full, perfect, and sufficient sacrifice, oblation, and satisfaction, for the sins of the whole world" are derived from Hebrews.

I referred earlier to the Peter Principle in Christianity, which consists of two ideas: one, Peter's gravitation toward the Law as over against Grace, as a recurring theme in Christian history; and two, the idea that Peter's consistent failures embed Christian leadership forever in the soil of human weakness. In the case of Peter's two letters in the New Testament, both sides of the Peter Principle can be seen.

On the one hand, there is strong emphasis on the Law in Second Peter. It is as if Peter were writing to reverse Paul's focus on Grace. On the other hand, there is the penetrating black-and-white statement of the Gospel in Peter's first letter: "Christ also died for sins once for all, the righteous for the unrighteous, that he might bring us to God" (3:18). Peter is clearly aware of his need for a full and perfect atonement.

The apostle James composed the third catholic letter of the New Testament. This letter is celebrated in Christian theology partly because the Protestant reformer Martin Luther could find little Grace in it. On the other hand, the later Christian philosopher Søren Kierkegaard found much in James over which to rhapsodize.

It is no wonder that James is controversial. This is because he takes on Paul's teachings about Grace versus the works of the Law directly. In a much-quoted paragraph, James asks:

> What does it profit, my brethren, if a man says he has faith but has not works? Can his faith save him? . . . So faith by itself, if it has no works, is dead. . . . Show me your faith apart from your works, and I by my works will show you my faith. . . . You see that a man is justified by works and not by faith alone. . . . For as the body apart from the spirit is dead, so faith apart from works is dead.   (2:14, 17, 18, 24, 26)

That is an astonishing passage in the history of world religion. It expresses an argument, publicly displayed in founding scriptures, between two creators of Christianity. James is refuting, or trying to refute, the concept of Grace as the core of religious experience preceding works of practical obedience. It is remarkable that the Christian church should have left uncensored, for all future generations to see, an internal argument of such importance between two revered religious leaders. Christians can be glad that the letter of James is in their Bible, for it witnesses to the honesty of the Bible's account of Christian origins.

Finally, a note on the letter of Jude, called famously by the English novelist Thomas Hardy *Jude the Obscure*. Jude has some bleak images, especially one concerning heretical souls that are "waterless clouds, carried along by winds; fruitless trees in late autumn, twice dead, uprooted; wild waves of the sea, casting up the foam of their own shame; wandering stars for whom the nether gloom of darkness has been reserved for ever" (vv. 12–13; Jude has only one chapter). Like First and Second Peter and James, Jude is a catholic Epistle because it is supremely worried about Christians who have supposedly turned Grace into an excuse for sin.

Christianity carries within its cargo some ancient baggage

Christianity carries within its cargo hold some very ancient baggage. The tension between Grace and Law is vividly portrayed in the letters of Peter. The tension goes back to Peter himself, who struggled with Grace at Antioch and failed fundamentally to sustain it. It was Paul, not Peter, who saved the Gospel for Christianity in the earliest days.

St. James' letter also struggles with Grace. James fears that the Grace of God will lead to lawlessness and licentiousness. James fears that Grace will result in antinomianism, which is the word in theology for illegal behavior supposedly deriving from the belief that God will forgive you no matter what you do. Actual antinomianism shows up quite seldom, for forgiven people almost always steer away instinctively from the behavior that required Grace in the first place. But legalists — people who believe that the Law holds the power to change people's bad habits and correct them — like to claim that the teaching of Grace produces antinomian fruit. The American Episcopal Church, known as ECUSA, is a contemporary instance of an actually antinomian church.

Together, James and Peter represent the "Catholic" as opposed to the "Protestant" version of Christianity. From their view of the Law, it is a short step to the second continuing tension in Christianity: the tension between Gospel and church. James and Peter lend support to a kind of religion that is more hierarchical and institutional than Paul's. They are worried more than Paul about dogma as such, whereas Paul wants to know what the Spirit is saying to the churches.

The "Catholic" versus the "Protestant" version of Christianity

If Jesus was the first Christian, Paul was the first "Protestant" and Peter and James were the first "Catholics."

People on the Protestant side of Christianity tend to say that the New Testament gave rise to the church. The Word preceded the institution, in other words, so Bible is prior to church. The Bible brought about the church. People on the Catholic side of the faith tend to say that the church produced the New Testament. In other words, the institution gave rise to the Bible.

Both these ways of putting it are partly true. The texts themselves preceded their being collected into one place. Yet the church approved what was finally collected.

The evidence, however, is more on the Protestant side than on the Catholic side, at least in this point. The New Testament writers were inspired by God, Christians say, to put their thoughts on paper. The church later simply ratified what was already in existence and what had already become valued for itself. Everyone knew, for example, that Paul's letters spoke with power. This had become self-evident. Everyone knew that some later literature, such as the Letter of Clement or the manual on church life called the Didache, was good but not as good as St. Paul's creations. Distinctions were made by the church, yes, but only on the basis of prior popularity and acceptance. Thus it is true to say that the New Testament preceded the church's confirmation of it as holy.

Influence of Marcion of Sinope

What, then, caused the Christian scriptures to take the specific form they now have: the New Testament? It was the pressure of one man, the aforementioned Marcion of Sinope. Marcion was a theologian of Grace — and a flawed genius — who came from the Black Sea coast of what is now northern Turkey. He was uncomfortable with books within the recognized Christian scriptures of his time that seemed to de-emphasize

Paul's and Christ's focus on Grace or even replace their emphasis with teachings rooted in the Law. Thus Marcion did not think that either Matthew's Gospel or the letter of James should be in the Bible. In fact, Marcion edited his own Bible, keeping only Luke and most of the letters of St. Paul. This compilation was one-sided. It also failed to acknowledge some very Grace-filled elements within John's Gospel, within the book of Hebrews, and also within First Peter. However, and even though Christians often raise their hands in appalled horror when his name is mentioned, there was some good in Marcion. His intentions were good. But he was somewhat adolescent, or overly schematic, in his rejection of much that contained insight.

Marcion's importance in Christian history has as much to do with the reaction against him as it does with his teachings themselves. The so-called fathers of the church, especially a North African writer named Tertullian, realized that they would need to construct a written alternative to what Marcion was proposing.

Therefore, in response to Marcion's attempt to pare down its content, within a few decades of Marcion's death the bishops of several Christian areas had approved the text of the New Testament as Christians know it today. From St. Matthew to the book of Revelation, the Christian scriptures were codified. Although the weight of New Testament teaching is on the side of Grace and not on the side of Law, the final canon, as it is called, came to be a collection that held within itself the tensions we have already observed. Thus a "Catholic" Christian could find himself within the text. And a "Protestant" Christian would later be able to find himself within the text. An "Orthodox" Christian could observe himself in John. *The New Testament is theologically diverse.* And the fact that this is so is the result of Marcion. Had Marcion had his way, the Bible would be thinner and also more homogeneous. Yet even in Luke and Galatians, Marcion's desert-island (i.e., absolute favorite) books, there are still traces of the Law and moral exhortation. We can thus see that no early Christian document was free of the tensions we have described. The problems of Grace versus Law, of Gospel versus church, and of weakness versus strength shoot through the history of all Christian thought and experience.

†

V

CHRISTIANITY IN THE ANCIENT WORLD

The founding events of Christianity, Pentecost being the last, were now in the past. The implications of all the events remained to be fully understood.

The founding texts of the religion were now complete, too. Their implications were just coming into view.

What now began was Christian history. This is often called church history, but I prefer the term *Christian history,* to distinguish between Christianity and the church. Christianity and church are not indistinguishable. They are not the same, although it has appeared that way at several points in history. Great events of Christianity took place outside the visible church. They still do.

Christianity and church are not the same

Christian history, like most secular or other histories, is a coming together of ideas and personalities. The ideas of Christianity were alive. They existed independently of their spokesmen. Yet they required spokesmen, and every generation raised up new ones. Context, of course, as well as cultural and economic circumstances, had its effect on the direction things went. But in Christianity, it was principally the ideas that raised up personalities, usually through conversion, in differing contexts. Individual men and women were seized by convictions that sprang from the radical origins of Christianity in the life of Christ and the first disciples. This impelled a person, as St. Paul observed in Second Corinthians (5:14) to become creative, perform a mighty deed, or make an awesome journey, all in the name of Christ.

It is remarkable how every generation of Christians is marked by the appearance of at least a few transforming personalities. We shall see this again and again.

THE PARTING OF THE WAYS WITH JUDAISM

After the fall of Jerusalem in A.D. 70 and the city's total destruction by the Romans, Christianity's parting of the ways with Judaism went quickly. What had been incipient or pregnant within the relation of the two religions became visible. Most significant was the instant Jewish dispersion north to Galilee, where many rabbis found refuge and were able to continue their studies. In reaction to the catastrophe of A.D. 70 and to the growing pressure of Christian ideas in the region, the rabbis sought to consolidate their intellectual position. Thus they set in final form their scriptures, what Christians still call the Old Testament.

The writings of the rabbis from the period after A.D. 70 reveal considerable evidence of

Christianity. Christians (or Nazarenes, as they were then called) are referred to as heretics, and Jesus himself is obliquely mentioned in the same terms. The separation from Christianity is also implicit in the hardening — or rather, clarifying — exegesis, or analysis, by the rabbis of the old texts. Also, a lot of storytelling, mainly concerning popular rabbis in post–A.D. 70 Galilee, entered the literature. The ancient religion of Judaism began to become Judaism with a very specific understanding of itself; with the development of a unique Jewish identity; and with the construction of buffers against a harsh and threatening world. From the codification of rabbinic tradition in Galilee, Judaism began to look like the Judaism of today, as opposed to the earlier Judaism of temple, prophecy, and the Bible nation of promise, Israel.

After A.D. 70, there was no way that Jews in large numbers would be attracted to "the way." Especially on the Jewish side, the walls went up. The Jewish no to Jesus' messianic identity became a pillar of Jewish identity. This has not changed.

Especially on the Jewish side, the walls went up

Meanwhile, the original Jerusalem Jewish-Christian church refused to support the rebellion against the Romans that culminated in the catastrophe of A.D. 70, and moved to the town of Pella, in the North. By the end of the first century, Christianity was spreading far beyond Palestine, and mostly among non-Jews.

WHY DID CHRISTIANITY SPREAD?

The short answer to the question Why did Christianity spread? is one simple word: Grace. The longer answer is two words: home church.

Daily life for the overwhelming majority of people living in the period we know as late antiquity, the period in which Christianity came into the world, was extremely hazardous and vulnerable. The working man and the farmer and their families rarely had any form of financial security. For thousands, slavery, which was unpaid domestic service, was preferable to trying to make a living on your own. This was because financial security was rarely possible to guarantee. The insecurity of most people was mirrored famously in the inability of the average family to make satisfactory arrangements for the burial of its dead. Unless you had the money to hire a guard or could bury your dead in a mausoleum or temple area, the chances of your loved one's body being robbed of its funeral garments and jewelry were almost one hundred percent. I use this example to show how exposed the average person was.

The average family could not bury its dead properly

The Roman writer Apuleius, a contemporary of the early Christian movement, made much of this particular and scandalous illustration of the average family's being at the mercy of a society that was in many ways predatory, impersonal, and uncompassionate. Late antiquity made less allowance for sufferers and victimized people than other eras of human history. Compassion was a blind spot.

The early Christians were compelling conduits for the divine Grace that had touched their lives. They saw themselves this way. In community, Christians proved to be a mirror for Grace, for what we today call unconditional love. The specifically Christian property of unconditional love came to the fore in the welcome that converts found in what were referred to as house churches in the first and second centuries.

House churches were extended families, or communities, of Christians who met at least once and sometimes twice a week in the house of a wealthy person. Twenty-five to sixty or more Christians would gather in the open courtyard of a Greco-Roman house, sing "hymns and spiritual songs" (Colossians 3:16), listen to Bible readings, hear an address given by the leader or teacher of the group, and celebrate, regularly, the Lord's Supper. When a member of the house church died, it fell to the group to raise the money for a proper burial place and then maintain it. The need for secure burial was also met by the digging of catacombs, a series of underground tunnels, to construct hidden burial chambers. These early Christian catacombs can still be visited today outside the city of Rome. They convey the communitarian provision among the early Christians of a need that had not been met by their society in any other way.

House churches were extended families

It is the house church, rooted in Grace, rooted in "love to the loveless shown," that caused the spread of Christianity. No wonder slaves and sailors and career soldiers in the army and women without protection were attracted to Christianity. We know they were.

The critics of Christianity regarded the house churches as secretive, centers of possibly sordid or criminal activity, attended primarily by people in the lowest social classes. This was not true, as almost every house church had a mix of classes and types. We know that the rich met with the poor in these intimate churches. This was new!

Love is a powerful force for change

No wonder the house churches were popular. They offered a community of love, and love is a powerful force for change. When it is sincere, it is almost always received. Roman society, so stratified and hard for its millions of unintegrated service workers and unprotected women, was in some ways a pushover for the Christian message sincerely conveyed.

EARLY CATHOLICISM

The trend to centralization in religion is a fact of life in Christianity, as it is in all world religions. It is a must to avoid. We have already seen a trend toward hierarchy and order in the New Testament letters of Timothy and Titus. But the centralizing trend picked up more steam as the direct memories of Christ and Paul receded. Polycarp, an Anatolian (i.e. Turkish) bishop and martyr, was a much more controlling and forceful figure than his predecessors. St. Clement of Rome revealed an attraction of tradition to a particular and mighty geographic place, the imperial capital. Local Christian bishops started to act like prelates — with real power over people — in the second century. In the third century, bishops began to challenge kings. Steel masculine leadership began to be exercised by bishops and their assisting priests.

In the third century, bishops began to challenge kings

The bishop of Rome attracted unique prestige. This was because Peter had died in Rome and was buried there. Violent street battles took place in Rome, right up to the fifth and sixth centuries, between the supporters of rival pretenders to the Vatican see, the top episcopal job in Rome. Militant bishops, ruling over large geographic areas in which many Christians were living, achieved reputations and power. The transformation of Christ's and St. Paul's Grace model into autocratic governance of the faithful continued without a break until the religion of Christianity had become the charge almost entirely of a single institution.

Early Catholicism, ever visible in the New Testament, never let up. Its seemingly inexorable trajectory to victory in the governance of Christianity was not to be challenged effectively or decisively until the Protestant Reformation of the sixteenth century, despite many courageous, unsuccessful pleaders against Catholicism in this sense — from the Celtic Irish to Origen to the

Montanist Pentecostals, right up to St. Francis of Assisi, St. Catherine of Siena, and Jan Hus. None of them, however, succeeded in derailing the ever-rolling train of Catholicism. That would wait until Martin Luther.

THE POSITION IN 312

Believing as I do that ideas connect with transformed personalities to create the main elements of Christian history, I also have to concede that climactic external events, such as the fall of Jerusalem in A.D. 70, can also have big impact.

Christians tend to excise from secular history events that have to do uniquely with divine revelation to the world. Such events include the exodus of Israel from Egypt, the giving of the Law on Mount Sinai, and the crucifixion and resurrection of Christ. These events exist at a different level from historical watersheds like the Battle of the Boyne (1690) or the Emancipation Proclamation (1863). But some non-salvation events, such as a battle that occurred in 312, did have important consequences for Christianity in history.

The position of the Christian church in 312 was as follows: Hundreds of thousands of Christians lived within the Roman Empire. They had grown to such high numbers primarily because of the attraction of house churches. The house churches had welcomed atomized, alienated people and had sustained them, especially in relation to comfortless penurious death. Persecutions of

Christians had also occurred on several occasions, first under Nero (A.D. 37–68), later under Domitian (A.D. 51-96) and Marcus Aurelius (A.D. 121-180), and then again under Julian the Apostate (331-363), who hated Christians. These persecutions had strengthened the church.

Also by this time, the wall between Judaism and Christianity had become almost impregnable. The two religions existed in different worlds.

The Christian movement had also become closer in appearance to a human organization. Bishops in many jurisdictions were monarchical prelates. This was not so everywhere, but it was true in most places. The Catholic or catholicizing trend was irresistible.

As we shall see in the next chapter, distinctions were being made in theology that shaped an increasingly complicated thought world. Heresy, or unsound teaching, was a factor. It would soon become a huge, absorbing factor.

In 312, the Roman Empire was mainly Christian in population. This demographic fact had been true for some time. It was what today is called a "fact on the ground." However, this state of affairs had not been recognized officially or legally. The church was not yet legally tolerated. But what occurred at the Battle of the Milvian Bridge in 312 would dramatically alter the status of Christianity in the Roman Empire.

The battle of the Milvian Bridge

What occurred is this, although the records are somewhat mysterious. The night before he was to fight a crucial battle against Maxentius (the Roman emperor in the East), Constantine (the Roman emperor in the West) had a dream. In the dream, he looked up at the sun, but he said it could have been the sun's reflection on a bronze shield. In any case, he saw something that looked like the Roman letters *IHS*. A voice spelled out the words and said, *"In hoc signo vinces,"* a Latin expression meaning "By this sign you shall conquer."

Constantine, like most ancient people, believed in omens and portents, in acted-out signs of what would happen in the future. So he received the words *In hoc signo vinces* as a good omen, pure and simple. His mother, Helena, later St. Helena, was also already a Christian. So when the emperor won the battle the following day, thus uniting a previously divided empire, he immediately attributed the victory to Christ. There and then Constantine became a committed Christian.

Constan-
tine's
conversion

Great things followed from Constantine's conversion in 312. Within a year, he declared legal toleration and official recognition of all Christians in the empire. No more persecutions! Within a few further years, Christianity became the official religion of the whole Roman Empire. This meant that Constantine played a direct role in overseeing the church, that Christian services were held at court, and that Christian bishops became chaplains at court. For the church, the timing was good, because a serious heresy called Arianism was at the time threatening to tear it in two, as we will see in chapter 7.

The point is, empire and church became united. It was a move that proved extremely fruitful for the evolution of Christian civilization in Europe. From another perspective, it was a disaster.

Constantine united church and state

When a situation goes from implied (i.e., the position of Christians in 312) to explicit (i.e., the position of Christians after 312), many things change. Although much that was beautiful and good would flow from Constantine's first step in the direction of the unity of church and state, some things came with it that could hold back human progress. If Constantine had not won at the Milvian Bridge, the great deconstructing and dismantling that occurred during the Protestant Reformation also would not have happened.

✝

VI
THE BIRTH OF
CHRISTENDOM

I t is often said that Christendom came into existence with the conversion of Constantine. He offered his protecting and sponsoring power to serve the church. The emperor protected the church, even from itself, as we shall see. He also sponsored key initiatives, such as the Council of Nicaea in 325, which furthered both the peace and the growth of the institution.

But the big idea that Constantine brought to the foreground in Christian history was the union of church and state. The first Christian movement had lived in tension with the political order. The Romans, together with the temple authority in Jerusalem, had executed Christ. The emperors Nero, Domitian, Marcus Aurelius, and Julian persecuted Christians for almost three centuries. The Christians themselves more or less conquered their oppressors by means of meekness.

The appearance of an emperor, an unquestionably supportive emperor, on their side was new. Constantine sponsored the erection of church buildings. He took an active and perceptive interest in theology. He prayed for the well-being of the church. He disempowered the few remaining

The Union
of church
and state

old aristocratic families who still resisted Christianity because of their Roman Republic values, their old attachments to the Roman hearth gods, and their all-important nuclear families. Constantine united the good interests of the Roman imperial state with the Christian church.

Forever after — until, that is, a liberalizing wind blew across western Europe after the Thirty Years' War of the seventeenth century — church and state would be united. The state would safeguard and promote the interests of the church, and the church would help the people become good citizens. Not only did church and state become one, but at various points, the church determined the operation of the state.

For example, a celebrated encounter took place in the year 1076 between Pope Gregory VII and the Holy Roman emperor Henry IV. The emperor, Henry, sought to appoint his own bishops against the will of the pope. But it was Henry who had to give in. He gave in by means of a high-profile form of apology. Henry knelt in the snow for two, some say three, days in front of the gates to the pope's mountaintop castle at Canossa. Only then did Gregory VII "forgive" Henry. Church won over state in January of 1077. So far had the tide come in.

Twenty-first-century Americans have no experience of this union of church and state. Our country came into existence as a direct result of the Glorious Revolution of 1688 in England and Ireland, together with our reaction at the time of the

American Revolution to the union of church and state as it was practiced in England. The English king and bishops, after all, had forced the Puritans to emigrate to America in the early seventeenth century.

But until the American Founding Fathers, who were almost all conscious Christians in some form or another, were forced to write down what they really thought about Christendom, the union (not the separation) of church and state was the rule.

Constantine and his successors created the model for what is known as caesaropapism. This is the specific form of church–state union by which the bishops of Rome, the popes, became political and military leaders, and little, or sometimes big, caesars. There were several warrior popes in the Middle Ages and the Renaissance. The pope appeared indistinguishable from a successor to the Roman caesars.

A high-water mark of church–state union was the coronation of Charlemagne, the French king, in St. Peter's Church, Rome, on Christmas Day 800. Taking his cue from Constantine, whom Charlemagne looked upon as a sort of supreme example, the king of the French had himself crowned by the pope as a sort of new Constantine. Charlemagne saw himself as both the religious and the political leader of the people.

The coronation of Charlemagne

The union of king and governor of the church was reflected in the coronation rites of all new kings. It is reflected still in the coronation service for the English sovereign.

Much later, in 1641, King Charles I of England set off a war with Protestant Christians who would not accept the notion that the king was God's appointed and special messenger for their highest good.

If caesaropapism is rooted in Constantine's conversion in 312, the divine right of kings is the later expression of it. Superstitious as it is — and the idea that a human being has divine properties by virtue of his political office has got to be regarded as a form of superstition — the union of state and church proved enormously influential, enduring, and even creative in Western history.

Interestingly, this idea is still acted out in the religion of Islam. At this moment, King Mohammed VI of Morocco, who is understood to be a direct descendant of God's holy prophet Muhammad, carries the title Commander of the Faithful. The king of Morocco takes that role more to heart than any other part of his duties. When I visited Morocco, I think I understood why the English king Henry VIII's title, Defender of the Faith, meant so much to him. It is still in the English coronation oath, despite its politically incorrect message.

The later logic of the Protestant Reformation, which was anti–institutional church in favor of the theological core of church, was in the direction of breaking up Constantine's Christendom. But the reformers, especially Martin Luther, could not free themselves from the inherited idea that the king or duke or royal was supposed to protect the true interests of the church. Thus Luther leaned heavily on Frederick, duke of Saxony, his noble protector. It is also true that the Reformation could never have succeeded without the vigilant "air cover" of monarchs and nobles who protected it from Rome and Rome's long-armed political fingers.

A famous phrase that speaks of the revolution inspired by Constantine's conversion in 312 is the expression *cuius regio, cuius religio*. This translates as "Whoever is king in a place determines the religion of the place." Thus, if the king of Denmark is Lutheran, the people of Denmark will be Lutheran. And if the Holy Roman Emperor of Austria is Catholic, all the people of Austria shall be Catholic. When Europe fell apart, exhausted, after the wars of religion that followed the Reformation, this concept was hatched. If you were in England, you would have to be Protestant. But if you were in Spain, you would have to be Catholic. The result was a patchwork of local religious loyalties in Europe, all hinging on the specific form of Christianity adopted by the person in charge locally.

Cuius regio, cuius religio

The trouble with Constantinian Christendom is that it runs counter to two of the three most important insights of basic Christianity. It runs counter to the idea that power is resident in weakness, as in the abdication of power represented by Christ's refusal to fight on the night he was betrayed in Gethsemane. Uniting the Christian movement with political power removes faith

from its necessary position on the down and ener-
vated side of life. The unity of church and state is
contrary to the theology of the Cross. It strays
unavoidably into a theology of glory. True Christianity rejects this.

Constantinian Christendom also runs counter
to the suspension of Law by the operation of God's
Grace. When church and state become yoked,
the possibility of using force to achieve the aims
of the church becomes a factor. This impregna-
tion of force as potential for realizing religious
aims is what created all the injustices of the
Christian church. It led to the burning at the
stake of Joan of Arc. The church could "do nothing with her," or with any other given heretic, so
it turned her over to the secular arm to execute
punishment. This was horrible. It still is horrible.
Force is opposed to Christian freedom. St. Paul
said this plainly in Galatians, Luther proposed it
in his lyrical tract entitled *The Freedom of a
Christian Man*. John Milton gave voice to such
freedom in several inspirational tracts.

Force is opposed to Christian freedom

The point is, Constantinian Christendom crippled Christian freedom. It existed in opposition to
it. It could never finally carry the day. The Christian world now rejects it, and almost universally.

†

VII
HERESY AND THE
FATHERS, TRINITY
AND THE COUNCILS

A lmost as soon as Constantine declared for
Christianity, he was faced with a crisis —
one of the biggest crises the Christian church had
ever faced. This was a controversy concerning
the Incarnation, or the embodiment of God
in the human form of Jesus. It stamped Christianity forever.

Concerning the incarnation of Christ, there
were two schools of thought at the end of the third
century. The school of thought associated with
the city of Antioch emphasized the humanity of
Jesus but did not explicitly deny his divinity. The
school of thought associated with the city of
Alexandria emphasized the divinity of Jesus but
did not explicitly deny his humanity.

A theologian named Arius argued that Christ's
human nature made him Son to the Father but
not equal to the Father. Christ was thus subordi-
nate to God. Arius was gifted, persistent (tireless, The
in fact), patient, and courageous. His teaching, this doctrine of
doctrine of Arianism, effectively made Jesus into Arianism
a very great man and was logical and consistent.

Arius was opposed by a theologian named Athanasius. Athanasius, who was even more gifted than Arius and equally as persistent and courageous, had studied at Alexandria. Athanasius said that Christ was equal to the Father. Christ was God, in other words. Now Athanasius' idea, that Christ was God, was a stretch, because it is stated explicitly only in the Gospel of St. John. But it is the clear inference of the New Testament. Christianity required the affirmation of Athanasius to become a world religion rather than just a memorial to a revered teacher.

The Arian heresy

The Christian church was ripped in two by Arianism, or, as it later became known, the Arian heresy. (Heresy is a wrong idea about God, as opposed to orthodoxy, which is a right idea about God.) Today, Arius is considered a heretic. Conversely, Athanasius is considered orthodox.

Yet who is to decide who is heretic and who is orthodox? That is always the question.

The Council of Nicaea

To restore peace to the church, in 325 Constantine convened a great council — known in church history as a general council — of bishops, theologians, and priests in a city called Nicaea (in what is now northwestern Turkey) to consider the question. After sharp discussion, the participants ratified the view of Athanasius as orthodox. They confirmed Athanasius' view as being truly catholic, or "to be believed in all places by all people." Athanasius was declared to have been right, and the Arians lost, one hundred percent.

Much later, Reformation-era followers of Arianism, called Socinians after a sixteenth-century teacher, would surface again. These later Arians would birth what was later known as the Unitarian Church. The Unitarians do not believe that Christ was divine.

Incidentally, the famous Nicene Creed, which is still recited in liturgical churches on Communion Sundays, came out of the Council of Nicaea.

There were other councils and other heresies. In the period 325–787, seven great general councils were convened. In each of these, it was believed that such a great gathering of bishops and scholars from the entire Christian world could reach a conclusion concerning the mind of Christ and the position of the Holy Spirit. These general councils were regarded as unerring. Yet the expectation outpaced the reality.

From a Protestant point of view, the councils are correct only to the degree that their findings accord with the Bible. From a Roman Catholic point of view, when or where do the councils ever end? Apparently there is no end to such councils over time. However, most Christians today recognize as orthodox, or true and right, the six general councils that took place between 325 and 681. The seventh, Nicaea II as it is called, which was summoned in 787 to rebut the doctrine of iconoclasm (i.e., the banning of images for religious reasons), is accepted only within the Eastern Orthodox churches.

The further history of heresy in the first centuries of Christianity is a history of individuals —

single theologians who put forward one specific idea or another about Christ in relation to God or about the three Persons of the Trinity in relation to God's oneness.

Some of these Christian thinkers, especially if they came out on what the councils decided was the right side, became known as fathers of the church. Some preceded Nicaea, so they are called the Ante-Nicene Fathers. Others came during the six general councils held after Nicaea, so they are called the Post-Nicene Fathers.

The Ante-Nicene Fathers from the Western Roman Empire were St. Clement of Rome, St. Irenaeus, St. Hippolytus, and Tertullian. The Eastern Ante-Nicene Fathers were somewhat more metaphysical and cerebral than their Western counterparts. They included Justin Martyr, Clement of Alexandria, and Origen. The books written by these Ante-Nicene Fathers became a resource library for future Christian thought.

Three other individuals are worthy of mention for the important contributions they made during this period: Sabellius, St. Jerome, and St. John Chrysostom.

The second general council was held in 381 at Constantinople and was summoned to combat renewed Arianism, together with the concepts of Macedonianism and Apollinarianism. Both of these concepts were condemned by the Council of Constantinople. Yet a third heresy, Nestorianism, was condemned by the third general council, which took place at Ephesus in 431.

The terms of debate during this long march of theological controversy were dense. They are hard to follow today. The ideas were hard enough for even the original protagonists to understand. Remember that the issue was always one of two questions: How could Jesus be fully human and fully divine? and How can three divine Persons exist in full independence and equality within the absolute oneness of God? To safeguard the Incarnation, which is the orthodox answer to the first question, and the Trinity, which is the orthodox answer to the second question, theological definitions of breadth and also precision had to be given. They were given.

The most important of the general councils after Nicaea was the fourth, the Council of Chalcedon in 451. This was the meeting for which Pope Leo I wrote a famous letter called the *Tome*. Leo wrote that in Christ, human nature and the divine are distinct, yet also united. Leo was opposing a man named Eutyches who had been teaching something called Monophysitism. Leo's contribution was to affirm the two-ness of the natures and simultaneously the oneness of the Person in which the two natures are joined. The *Tome* of Leo sealed the church's historic teaching on the incarnation of God in Christ.

Pope Leo I and his Tome

The six general councils took place over three and a half centuries. They established concepts that were never formally challenged again in mainstream Christianity. They were all focused on the internal relation of the divine and the human in Christ, and therefore in the Father; and also Christ's extension in the Spirit. Luther and the reformers accepted all the findings of the six great councils.

To us today, the results of the councils, and also their methods, sometimes sound like hairsplitting. But the concepts they affirmed are held, in theory at least, by orthodox Christians in all places.

If you overemphasize the humanity of Christ, he becomes no longer a saving figure, and you thus lose everything. If you overemphasize the divinity of Christ, he is no longer with us, here, our Friend. The councils' decisions guarded the *with*-ness of Christ, his sympathetic humanness with us; as well as the *for*-ness of Christ, his effective saving function as divine redeemer of the fallen world.

We might wish the councils had taken place over 50 years rather than over 350!! It took *three and a half centuries* to settle these questions of metaphysics. It seems like a lot of lives and deaths and travel expenses and exile and lost time and killed causes. And it was! I used to think it a poor excuse of a movement that could give its whole life to purely intellectual questions. And it is true that questions of salvation — the connector of Christian theology with living, needing individuals — took the backseat during the period of the general councils. But we can also see how important the result was. Jesus' divinity, crucial to his impact on the world, was deduced from Scripture, from the memories of the people who had been there. And his humanity, that point of fellow feeling so needed by sufferers, was never for a second given up or conceded. He was a saving figure. "Who can forgive sins but God only?" (Luke 5:21) But Christ was also "a man of sorrows, and acquainted with grief" (Isaiah 53:3). The councils secured the proper Christocentrism of Christianity. The church will always be in their debt. The world will always be in their debt. Nothing can take away from the labor of love and the courageous struggle that was the life of St. Athanasius and his passionate students and followers.

The church will always be in debt to the councils

†

VIII
MONASTICISM

I n the mid-1960s, Dr. Timothy Leary invited
the world to "turn on, tune in, drop out." He
called on establishment people to get high and
turn their backs on convention. Thousands heeded
his call. Without exalting Leary's psychedelic invitation, it is certain that he tapped into a feeling
many people have of wanting to exit the rat race
of competition and production in favor of a qui-
eter, more peaceful life.

Monasticism, which is a chronic theme in
Christian history, is the religious form of withdrawal. All world religions have it. The Christian
religion is no exception.

How did it come into being and develop?

Monasticism (which comes from the Greek
word for celibate or solitary) was an idea, or
movement, that began in Egypt during the fourth
century. St. Anthony was the first leader of the
movement, in which individuals retreated into
the desert to live entirely alone with God. These
anchorites or "desert fathers" were Egyptian
Christians who pursued with their whole being a
lonely relationship with the Lord.

The foundation of monasticism

The foundation of monasticism was the memory of Christ's forty-day fast in the Judean wilderness at the start of his ministry. For like every

other aspect of Christianity's development, the seeds of monasticism were planted in the earliest days of the religion — specifically, in the days of Christ himself. Monasticism went back to Christ's own example. And there is no question that solitariness is a part of what we today term *spirituality*. We know that most people hide their true needs and inner hopes beneath a cover of busyness and casual relationships. Monasticism is a denial of such behavior.

The problem with the anchorites' form of retreat from the world was that they could easily became unhinged. Self-denying in every way, such a lifestyle produced extreme mental instability and also a degree of misanthropy.

The anchorite or solitary tradition has been strong in Christianity right up through the present day. Irish monks a few centuries after St. Anthony became famous and admired for their spartan and solitary stone houses, which can still be seen in the western part of Ireland.

Cenobitic monasticism

Cenobitic monasticism was the next phase of the movement. Cenobitic (from the Greek *kionos,* or "common," and *bios,* or "life") monasticism is life in community. So many solitary desert fathers had lost their moorings and slipped into a sort of quiet lunacy that St. Pachomius gathered monks around him and required they submit to a "rule of life" in community. The origin of the monasteries and nunneries that evolved later in the Middle Ages — and that still exist today, from Holy Cross Monastery on the banks of the Hudson River in New York, to the missions of Southern California, to St. Catherine's Monastery at Mount Sinai — is with Pachomius and his students. They sought God through their rejection of the world, but they did it *together.*

A majority of the leaders in theology, both in Eastern Christianity and in the Western Catholic church, were monks. Most were celibate, or unmarried. Almost all came to live in forms of community, often moving from one common-life center to another.

It is an extraordinary but authentic and dramatic fact that the period from the early fourth century to the late fourteenth century demonstrated the continuing, contagious appeal of Christian monastic life.

How can we explain this? Well, life was extremely hard for the average person in those times. The monastery was an escape from the rigors of scratching out an existence. Like becoming a eunuch in Asian or Islamic societies, becoming a monk could also open the doors to careers and social-class breakout. If you wanted something better for your life, and especially if you hungered to read and get an education, the monastery was just about the only way open to you — the only way, that is, unless you were born into the ruling or noble class. Additionally, monasteries performed the valuable functions of preserving ancient texts and were centers of learning.

There are three outstandingly important figures in the history of monasticism. The first is

Three important figures in monasticism's history

St. Benedict

Benedict of Nursia. St. Benedict, the founder of the Benedictine movement, was an Italian nobleman who wrote a "rule of life" that was accessible and, in its way, profound. A Benedictine monastery was governed by an abbot, who was the unchallenged ruler of the monks. Included in the rules of the Bendictine monastery were several safeguards against mental health problems and internal divisions. Almost all contemporary forms of Christian monasticism have their roots in Benedict's achievement. As a matter of fact, so-called Benedictine spirituality is again popular among Christians today. Everyone wants someone to tell them what to do! For a time.

Benedict founded the monastery of Monte Cassino, halfway between Rome and Naples. Exactly fourteen hundred years later, it was the site of a horrifying battle between Americans and Germans toward the end of World War II. In fact, movie director John Huston's documentary on that battle, shot during the siege of Monte Cassino itself, may be one of the best antiwar films of the twentieth century. St. Benedict's monastery was completely destroyed during the siege.

Of all the many and moving manifestations of the monastic impulse in Christian history, I prefer a subset of Benedictinism called the Cistercian movement. The Cistercian movement, a "lean and mean" puritan form of St. Benedict's movement, was founded in 1098 by Robert of Molesmes, a Frenchman. Cistercian churches, which can still be seen from North Yorkshire to southern France to Jerusalem, are extremely simple, auditory (i.e., favoring the preached word and solo chanting), and user-friendly, both to the monk and to the outsider.

When I stand within a Cistercian church — and you rarely sit down in one — I feel close to the spirit of Protestantism. The Cistercian movement, like Protestantism in its ideal manifestation, was a triumph of substance over form. I invite the reader to make a pilgrimage to the Cistercian buildings of France. Some are now museums; some are still working churches. They are a witness to the power of simplicity and weakness in the formal act of prayer.

A second, fruitful voice in the history of monasticism was that of St. Dominic. Needless to say, St. Dominic founded the Dominicans. Dominic understood preaching to be the "one thing needful" in Europe. Confronted with a wild and popular heresy in southwestern France known as Catharism, he threw his heart and soul into trying to win back the thousands who had been attracted to that somewhat magical school of thought. Dominic won, at the expense of several thousand lives. His preaching order of Dominican friars became attractive to the hierarchy of the Catholic church. Dominic's order, the Dominicans, is still alive within Catholicism.

St. Dominic

The third and by far most famous person in the history of Christian monasticism was St. Francis of Assisi. Francis founded the Franciscan order, which is also alive and well today, even

St. Francis of Assisi

within non–Roman Catholic churches such as that of the Anglicans. Francis' gifted and devout coworker, St. Clare, founded the Poor Clares, or Sisters of St. Clare. Together, Francis and Clare brought an infusion of life to monasticism that has never fully run out.

Francis brought to his monastic order an integrated and unassailable moral commitment and character. He possessed a spirit of love that reached out to animals, especially to birds; and even more so, to his fellow men and women. So Christlike in personality was Francis that he is believed to have received the stigmata, or visible wounds of Christ, on his hands and feet. Although stigmata are usually fake — the psychosomatic result of an hypnotic state of mind — I would not be surprised if this phenomenon actually occurred in Francis' case. Francis, like Mother Teresa of Calcutta in recent years, was the genuine article!

To his credit, Francis was utterly unimpressed and also unintimidated by grand or beautiful buildings. He was a true friend to the poor. He was also completely unfazed by worldly rank or status. Part of this was because he came from the privileged class and had nothing to prove.

But there was a problem with Francis in relation to the Law. Francis believed that use of the imperative — Just do it! Be conformed to Christ — was sufficient in itself to obtain the desired effect of holiness in a person. There is therefore a grimness to some of Francis' writings — the spirit of a "commander of the faithful," to use an Islamic phrase.

I do not believe that Francis' understanding of paralyzing sin within the human condition went deep enough. He inevitably became an example, an example too awesome for the many who are inclined to say, "What would Jesus [or Francis] do?" I am concerned by the truculence of Francis' attitude in relation to human resistance to change and human paralysis. We can regard him as the best and the brightest of what monasticism offered the world. But surely there had to be a better way.

The monastic movement was constantly degenerating and falling into chaos, then having to be pulled back to ideals and first principles. This was what St. Francis was all about. As in all Christian enterprises, human nature would taint the original core within a generation or two. Then an inspired leader would emerge to conduct a "back to basics" campaign. Such was the mission of Francis.

At the Protestant Reformation, however, the cycle was finally broken. Luther and the reformers did not believe in retooling the old machine. They did not desire to pump up a flat tire. They came to regard the whole idea of monasticism as false, self-deceived, and corrupt; and to believe that monasticism was corrupt by nature rather than by development, mistaken in its motive and in its core drive.

As we shall see later, Luther rejected the idea

of a group of people making concentrated efforts to be holy. Luther had a different concept of personal holiness, a concept of holiness that was both wholly unattainable — because only Christ himself had been intrinsically holy — and at the same time wholly attainable — because God regards trusting sinners as totally holy by *Grace,* not effort, received through faith. This sounds very theological, I realize, and I shall explain Luther's exact ideas later. The point is that the Protestant reformers saw the spring of monasticism as being wound wholly in the wrong direction. They wanted to emphasize God's initiative toward man, not the initiatives of monks and nuns toward God.

Monasticism took a strong knock in the sixteenth century. Beginning in the early sixteenth century, monasteries in Protestant areas were suppressed. This was because Protestant theologians saw them as fruitless communities of self-deceived religious people whose minds were ignorant of the Grace of God. Also, the political and business leaders of the day saw in the monasteries' inherited wealth and real estate an opportunity for gain and investment. Monastic lands and possessions were confiscated and awarded to noble families close to the king or held in trust for later political reward. However, in Germany and Switzerland, the focus of a number of monastic foundations was changed to education, especially the training of Protestant pastors, schoolteachers, and civil servants.

Protestant reformers saw monasticism as being in the wrong direction

Monasticism died in Protestant countries because of theological objections and also because of political and economic considerations. The human urge to form communities in pursuit of God did not die, however. I wish it had. That is because in Christianity, there are no privileged classes or privileged personal pilgrimages. We are all absolutely equal before God. Monasticism distorts that equality.

But the urge to form communities in pursuit of God did not die. It returned, in fact, with intensity and fervent vigor. It returned in the form of the Jesuits. **The Jesuits**

As we will examine in more detail when we discuss the Protestant Reformation, it was inevitable that forces would arise to counter it. Suppression always increases the force of the thing it tries to suppress, following Isaac Newton's law of physics that every action produces an equal and opposite reaction. Case in point: the Counter-Reformation (the term for the Roman Catholic reaction to Protestantism) and the Jesuit order!

Ignatius Loyola, a converted Spanish noble- **Ignatius** man who wished to offer his entire energies and **Loyola** creativity to the service of the pope in Rome, answered the call of the pope to form a community of priests to re-evangelize territories that had been lost to the Reformation. Loyola and his spiritual brothers, who became known as the Society of Jesus (another name for the Jesuit order), became a SWAT team to recoup the Pope's losses connected with the Protestant suppression of the monasteries.

Unlike earlier monastic movements, the Jesuit order was elitist. For in its recruitment, it majored on the brightest and the best. Jesuitism encouraged a high level of education and scientific training. Thus men like Francis Xavier, the Apostle of Japan, were cultivated by the order. The Jesuits' participation in the Counter-Reformation was a substantial factor in the Catholic church's being able to turn back the Protestant tide; and the Jesuits also carried Catholic Christianity to India, China, Japan, and South America.

The success of the Jesuits was a new thing in the history of Christianity. Never before had a monastic order attracted such human talent, been so intentionally trained, and been so rough-and-ready. The secret was their recruitment policy and the entire subordination of their candidates to authority.

You can now see the range of monasticism over time. From the first communities of gathered hermits in Egypt, to the early Benedictines of Italy, to the "renewed" and puritan Cistercians of France, to the Dominicans who first anticipated the style of the later Jesuits, to the Franciscans who imitated in a fresh cycle the humility of Christ, to the Jesuits who exploded with the fury of Counter-Reformation: the beat goes on!

There were further renewals of monastic zeal in the seventeenth century, such as the Jansenists of Port Royal, who because of their ideological link with Protestantism are a special case that will receive special treatment later.

Various Protestant religious communities also had some common ground with Catholic monasticism. The most important example of Protestant monasticism would be the community at Herrnhut, near the German border with the Czech Republic. This community was founded in 1722 by Count Nikolaus Ludwig von Zinzendorf. Zinzendorf, a Lutheran in theology, held high aspirations for whole families to live communally. The Herrnhuters still exist today, and their daily Bible study guide is read throughout the world. They founded the city of Winston-Salem, North Carolina.

Monasticism has always failed over time. Yet it has also almost always reemerged over time. The most famous monk in the twentieth century was Thomas Merton. Merton's writings and spiritual autobiography again brought huge attention to the monastic ideal.

Monasticism has always failed over time

In the later nineteenth century, there was a further development, a development that shed more light yet on the undying urge of Christians to form separated communities. This was the emergence of the Anglican orders of religious brothers and sisters. The background of the movement is this. The Counter-Reformation of the seventeenth century was a reactive moment, grasping back for monasticism what the reformers had taken away. But there was a second Counter-Reformation in the nineteenth century, by which Catholic ideas entered Protestantism by

Emergence of the Anglican order

means of a Trojan horse. At that time, English people and Americans became enamored with the Middle Ages. They began to view the Middle Ages as a unique age of faith. This trend of looking backward on something with rhapsodic longing is called romanticism.

In Christianity, the romanticism of 150 years ago produced a rebirth of religious communities within Protestant countries, especially in England, and particularly within the Church of England, or Anglicanism. These religious communities included men's orders, such as the Society of St. John the Evangelist (known as the Cowley Fathers), and women's orders, such as the Society of St. Margaret. These orders, which were composed of sincere and committed people, held a fascination for the upper or educated classes in particular. But they took place in *modern* or post-Reformation times. Thus they were usually more liberal, sometimes without even knowing it, than the medieval models they imitated.

Liberal catholicism, as this school of thought is now known, was a fascinating and also influential trend in Christian thought. Liberal catholicism had a particular interest in monasticism. It rebirthed it.

The problem with monasticism   The principal problem with monasticism is that it fosters an overly high view of human nature, which in turn nurtures false and ultimately always disappointed hopes among monks and nuns. There is also the question of whether monasticism fosters a spiritual class system. How can mere mortals attempt it?

It is helpful to interpret Christian monasticism against the background of the three themes that the *Primer* has stressed from the start. First, monasticism emphasized Law at the expense of Grace, always turning back to the "rule of life" of St. Benedict or like-minded followers, and offering a full-service menu of lifestyle prescriptions. Second, monasticism was at times in tension with the church. Even though the pope sometimes used the monastic orders, especially the Dominicans and the Jesuits, for his purposes, he could also suppress them, as he did the Jesuits in 1773. And although the monastic impulse usually lived quite well within the church, sometimes — as in the case of the first Franciscans, and certainly in the case of the Jansenists — the orders were on the edge of the church. Third, although the orders almost always did try to start from weakness (they majored in poverty, celibacy, and humility, and their greatest strength was their commitment to the question "What would Jesus do?" [today shortened to "WWJD"]), their problem was simply that human beings could not do it. Every second generation failed to live up to the ideals of the founder, such as Dominic or Francis. The whole movement shipwrecked — and shipwrecked over and over again — on an overly confident view of human nature.

Which leads us to the noblest pessimist in history, St. Augustine of Hippo.

†

IX
ST. AUGUSTINE

S ome people believe that Christianity turned dark under the influence of St. Augustine. There is a school of thought (now associated in part with a Princeton University professor of religion named Elaine Pagels and to some extent with Dan Brown, author of *The Da Vinci Code*) that sees Christianity after St. Paul, but before Augustine, as a time of optimism about human nature — a time when there existed relative equality of the sexes, a good deal of mystery concerning the sacred teacher Jesus, and a thoroughly less bloody view of the Cross, Crucifixion, and atonement. In this view, St. Augustine is regarded as a pessimist, a misogynist, a Calvinist before Calvin — *the* Calvinist before Calvin — and a generally cruel thinker, capable of consigning babies to purgatory and almost everyone else to hell. This view of Augustine, who was in fact dubbed by the popes as a doctor of the church, is incorrect. Although commonly, almost universally, held today, it is a journalistic, misinformed view, fueled by a culture in denial concerning the human condition.

At a unique moment in world history, the fall of Rome, Augustine interpreted the recurring facts of human lameness in terms of the wisdom

Some believe Christianity turned dark with St. Augustine

But this is a misinformed, incorrect view

of St. Paul. Augustine also thought systematically and was able to get his ideas across clearly. Augustine also *changed his mind* and had the courage to admit it.

Augustine grew up in North Africa. He later fathered a son through an early love affair and never forgave himself for it. What happened to the woman no one knows. Augustine's mother was a devout Christian whose prayers for her son were answered when he became a Christian later in Italy. The story is told in some detail in Augustine's famous book *The Confessions*. *The Confessions,* which is often placed on lists of the world's great classics, is generally overvalued. What is more, it reveals little about the man in a human or psychological sense. Like another classic of Christian autobiography, that of John Bunyan, *The Confessions* is repetitive and extremely "religious," yet fails to reveal much about the inner workings of the mind of its author. Moreover, *The Confessions* very rarely mentions Christ. It is all about God, but it seldom speaks of Christ.

Early in his career, Augustine came under the influence of a Christian teacher and bishop named Ambrose, who perceived young Augustine's promise. In assisting Augustine's conversion to Christianity, Ambrose helped to wean him from a school of thought called Manichaeanism. Manichaeanism, which originated in the country now known as Iran, is a view of the world that sees life and history as divided between good and bad, light and dark. The word for this is *dualism.* Everything has two sides. There is a war going on between the shadows and the sun. Now, Christianity has always had dualism in it: Grace versus Law, Gospel versus church, weakness versus strength, truth versus error, and so on. But dualism cannot be taken too far, for God is ultimately over all things and Christ is Lord of all. As in the annual reenactment of the Battle of the Boyne in Scarva, Northern Ireland, the *outcome* of the Christian battle is never in doubt. So although dualism is an aspect of Christianity, it should not destroy our confidence that Christ has won, and shall win.

Augustine went on to become the Catholic bishop in Hippo in North Africa, an area that is now exclusively Muslim. I say "Catholic bishop" because there were two Christian jurisdictions in Africa at the time: the (Roman) Catholic and the Donatist. (That is another story and not of vital importance for the *Primer.*) Suffice it to say that there were two competing and overlapping Christian bodies in Africa, and Augustine was part of the one that would triumph — until, that is, it was felled by Islam.

Augustine wrote many books and treatises. Several of these concerned abstractions, such as the nature of time and the relation of the three Persons within the Trinity. These treatises are works of theology. They do not constitute the main contribution of Augustine to Christian thought and to the world.

Nor does his supposed masterwork, *The City of God,* constitute his main achievement. That particular work, which is a kind of mammoth panoramic interpretation of world history in light of the fall of the Roman Empire in the early fifth century, is impenetrable to most people today. Despite the reputation of *The City of God* as a world classic, I defy anyone who is reading this *Primer* to finish Augustine's book. Or to get even a third of the way through it! Augustine is so driven by his intellectual context, by the world of Greek and Roman ideas as engaged by Christianity, that the book is not universal. St. Augustine's *City of God,* like his *Confessions,* is a sacred cow.

St. Augustine's contribution to world thought

No, Augustine of Hippo's contribution to world thought is not to be derived from his early or even his middle period. Augustine's contribution to world thought comes, rather, from his later period. At that time, he encountered Pelagius and Pelagius' follower Julian of Eclanum. These encounters led to a late but rich flowering of Augustine's thought in his interpretation of St. Paul's insight concerning predestination. Augustine's engagements on these two fronts — against Pelagius, on the one hand, and in favor of the idea of election, on the other — are, unlike *The City of God* and *The Confessions*, extremely important. They are not only important in relation to the Reformation, to Luther, to Calvin, to the Puritans, and to the whole development of thought concerning free will and determinism; they are also important in and of themselves.

Pelagius was a British monk who taught — and taught forcefully — that a human being could choose to be good and be like Jesus. He taught that a human being is free to do what is just and right. He taught that a man can by his own efforts accomplish the good in God's sight. *Pelagianism,* as this view came to be known, *is the most familiar heresy or untrue teaching in the history of the Christian church.*

The false view of Pelagius

Augustine read what Pelagius was saying and reacted sharply. His sharpest response came in relation to the version of Pelagius' theory that had been adopted by Pelagius' follower Julian of Eclanum. Augustine's response — which may well be the best piece of Augustine's theological writing — was a series of tracts entitled *Against Julian.*

Today, many people are uncomfortable with strongly antithetical statements. It is generally viewed as inhumane and aggressive to say no to one idea in favor of another idea. But Christianity has almost always depended on controversy. Every yes has beneath it a no. Every assertion carries within itself a negation. Thus Augustine was performing the world a service. He was rebutting a false view, as he saw it, in support of a true view.

Augustine understood the human being as paralyzed in relation to his ability to do good.

Man is
unable to do
right, unless
he is aided
by God to
do so

Man is unable, by nature, to do right. Instead, man inevitably chooses the wrong. Unless, that is, he is aided by God to do the right.

Augustine's formula for his view was this:

1. Man in his initial situation is unable not to sin (*non posse non peccare*).
2. Man tries to be able not to sin (*posse non peccare*), but he fails.
3. The result of God's Grace is to form in man the response of Grace by which he becomes, to the degree he is in the Grace of God, not able to sin (*non posse peccare*).

To put it another way, man cannot help himself in his initial situation. He will always sin. After all, did not one hundred percent of the people on Good Friday vote against Christ and for Barabbas? The Christian tries not to sin, but he fails, and miserably. But when God's Grace comes into the picture, the fruit of the Holy Spirit begin to grow spontaneously. Then goodness becomes natural.

Augustinianism is the name in Christian tradition for this perspective on original sin. We cannot save ourselves. We cannot find a way out from our compulsion to do the wrong thing. It is correct to say that Augustine's view of human freedom — or, better expressed, the failure and lack of human freedom — is St. Paul's, as expressed in the seventh chapter of the Letter to the Romans: "For I do not do the good I want, but the evil I do not want is what I do. . . . Who will deliver me from this body of death?" (vv. 19, 24)

Augustine's teaching, so wise and penetrating, and so in accord with truest human experience, was somber and dark. It was pessimistic, yet nobly so.

Augustine's refutation of Pelagius has never been refuted. It is borne out by human experience. The condition of humanity does appear to be irretrievably damaged. A follower of Pelagius need only attend a meeting of Alcoholics Anonymous to discern the brokenness and the futility of human strivings after control.

Toward the end of his life, Augustine reflected on some fairly cosmic implications of this theory of human nature. He wondered: if we can do nothing to merit God's Grace and contribute to our moral significance before God, then how, and also why, is God working in the world to save *some* by his Grace but apparently not *all*? In other words, Augustine pondered how and why God works, or appears to work, *selectively*. Everyone is limping, that is clear. But not all become Christians. Not all are snatched from the world's general holocaust of failed lives and burst dreams. What explains the way of God among and within the human race?

Augustine saw that God's way had to concern the question of the will. What is the will that acts behind the events of the world? It has to be God's will. And God, by definition, is the only being with a *free* will. That is because God, by definition, is the only essentially free being.

Thus Augustine moved, as all theologians of

God's way had to concern the question of will

Grace have always moved, in the direction of pre-destination. God is in charge. God is divine. God, to use the terminology of kings, is also sovereign. It is worth taking a little time within these pages to stress the importance of Augustine's development in this direction. That is because such a development happens again and again within the history of theology. It happened in Paul, as he moved to a predestinarian view of God's action at the end of the Letter to the Romans. It even happened in the ministry of Jesus, when Christ damned the fig tree (Matthew 21:19) and when he spoke of the mystery of accidents and unearned afflictions (i.e., the tower at Siloam [Luke 13:4] and the man born blind [John 9:1–5]). The move toward wonder and mystery and bewilderment peaked in the cry of Christ on the Cross: "My God, my God, why hast thou forsaken me?" (Matthew 27:46; Mark 15:34) Jesus Christ understood *all* will, the cause of *all* events, as residing in the mind and intention of God.

Grace, whether in its presence, to the drowning man who is saved, or in its absence, to the drowning man who goes under for the third time, is problematic. This must be said. Grace is problematic. How does God's Grace work? How is it "allocated"? Why does it operate in the lives of some but not in the lives of others? Why him and not me? Why me and not him?

Augustine — like Jesus and St. Paul and, later, as we shall see, like Luther and Calvin and

Thomas Cranmer — moved in the direction of predestination. Augustine came to believe that God had decreed before the beginning of time the fact and event of salvation in the lives of some, but also the fact and event of damnation in the lives of others. This became known as double predestination.

St. Augustine's Augustinianism is the profoundest word on human experience that has ever been given to the Christian church after the Bible. That is, short of Luther, who was equally profound. The Augustinian strand has always existed in tension with more optimistic views of God's creation and of man, the summit of God's genius. To say, as we used to say in the 1970s and 1980s, that "God don't make no junk" is entirely un- and anti-Augustinian. It sounds good, to insist that man is good and properly equipped to fly right. But it is not true. The human capacity for self-improvement is a myth.

Augustine's view, on the other hand, is true to life. His anthropology, or view of humanity, is the one empirically verifiable Christian doctrine. Human history and our lives demonstrate it. It is wholly sufficient and satisfactory all along the line of actual experience.

This short chapter concerning a very great thinker concludes with a brief survey of what happened to Augustine's legacy. For what happened to his legacy is instructive, hauntingly instructive.

St. Augustine moved towards predestination

After the Bible, the most profound word on human experience

Initially, things went well for the anthropology of St. Augustine. Pelagius was condemned at the Council of Orange, and Augustine's views were sustained. His status as a doctor of the church remained unquestioned throughout the Middle Ages. The monastic order of Augustinians kept the teachings of the master alive and more or less well.

However, some considerable erosion occurred in the late Middle Ages, when the role and force of man's efforts were accorded a somewhat higher status within the thought of the theologian Thomas Aquinas. But the church was committed in theory to upholding Augustine's view. In theory, man was impotent and God sovereign.

Augustine's legacy was eroded in the Middle Ages

The late Middle Ages, with their popular ideas that prayer and pilgrimage could earn points with God, eroded the Augustinian legacy. The legacy became an ideological memory, valued in theory and principle, but vanished in practice.

Martin Luther, an Augustinian monk, came famously to terms with Augustine in the light of Luther's study of St. Paul. The Protestant Reformation took up Augustine's diagnosis of human sin and determinism. The Reformation bloomed from it. The inner spring of Augustine's work — the essential insight concerning human nature — came to the fore again as a result of the Reformation.

But his insights came to the fore again with the Reformation

Now, given that Luther and Calvin and their colleagues at the forefront of the Reformation took the Augustinian view, what happened to Augustine's legacy within Catholicism? The answer is simple. Augustine's star declined rapidly. It was a matter of guilt by association. If Luther and his partners had derived so much from Augustine's books, then there must be problems with Augustine. And after all, had not Augustine changed his mind toward the end of his life? Had it not been Augustine's later work that had been so influential with Luther? Maybe the Doctor's final ideas were also wrong. In short, the mature Augustine, his view of man and his view of God, was put on the back burner of the Catholic Church. "Do not open until Christmas". Better, don't open at all!

Then something strange happened. In the late sixteenth and early seventeenth century, a Dutch Roman Catholic bishop named Cornelius Jansen began to read St. Augustine again, especially his mature works. Jansen discerned the power and loftiness of Augustine's scheme. He began to measure the post-Reformation teachings of his church against Augustine's teachings. He was appalled! Jansen observed the post-Reformation Catholic church's shelving of the doctor's approach and wished to bring his wisdom back. He became a full-service Augustinian.

A complicated series of events, a chain reaction, now took place. Jansen's followers — all French, as it happened — sought to call the French Catholic church back to its Augustinian roots. The Jesuits, who were fighting the Protestants and were highly suspicious of the Augustine–*Calvin* connection, saw the Jansenists as crypto (i.e., hidden)-Protestants. The Jesuits decided to eliminate them.

Because the Jesuit order had the ear of the king of France, Louis XIV, they succeeded in destroying the Jansenist group. Even though as mighty a mind as the famous philosopher Blaise Pascal took the Augustinian-Jansenist position,

The defeat of the Jansenists

and argued brilliantly for it, the Jansenists did not have the political power to win. The Jansenists were utterly defeated. In 1711, as a way of demolishing the followers of Jansen, the pope actually put a ban on the teachings of Augustine. He did this in a deceptive way, suggesting that the Jansenists were wrong about Augustine, rather than that Augustine was wrong himself. Yet the effect was to nullify the insights of the doctor — to erase them — concerning Grace and salvation and election and predestination.

Consequently, since 1711 the Roman Catholic Church has not been Augustinian in theology.

The views of Augustine remained current in Protestantism, however, even though John Wesley rejected some of them toward the end of his

Every Protestant is an heir of St. Augustine

life. Every Protestant who has ever stressed the blinding, binding nature of sin and the total need of men and women for God's Grace is an heir of the very great St. Augustine of Hippo.

✝

X

ROME AND CONSTANTINOPLE: THE GREAT SCHISM AND THE ESTABLISHMENT OF WESTERN AND EASTERN CHRISTIANITY

Almost everything big begins from something small. And if you wish to find out why a particular thing or person has turned out the way it has, you should always go back to its origins.

This principle is true in every part of life. It is certainly true in religion. As we have discussed in the previous pages, for something like the first thousand years of its existence, the Christian religion was Roman Catholic (the word *catholic* means "universal," or "to be believed in all places by all people"), and governed by the pope in Rome. All this was to change as a result of disagreements that began to arise between church leaders in Rome and those in the East, headquartered in Constantinople. These disagree-

ments, which took place between the ninth and
eleventh centuries, culminated in what is now
called the Great Schism (or "splitting") of 1054.
In that year, the papal ambassador to Constantinople placed a letter on the high altar of the
famous cathedral Hagia Sophia in Constantinople, excommunicating its patriarch (bishop). This
letter proved to be the final step in separating the
Christian religion into two establishments: the
Roman Catholic Church and the Eastern Orthodox Church. How could such a fault line in Christianity have opened up?

It all started as early as the Gospel of St. John.
John, who was Jewish but was influenced by
Greek philosophy, said quite a few things about
Christ that were speculative or metaphysical: "I
am in him, and he is in me, and you, my disciples,
are in me, and I am in you," and so on and so
forth. St. John wrote about Christ in ways that
had a lot to do with *being* rather than doing. This
reflected an enduring Greek interest in essences
(or the intrinsic qualities of a thing), or what in
philosophy is called ontology (the science of
describing things in their being rather than in
their effects). You could almost say that Greek
thought interested itself in the inward, whereas
Jewish thought placed more stress on the outward. Jesus had criticized Judaism for this.

In any event, the Greek world of thinking
about essences and individuals affected Christianity in one direction, while the Jewish world of
weighing deeds and their value affected Chris-

tianity in another direction. You can see this throughout the long age of the councils, when the entire Christian world got turned in on essences and attributes, as we have seen. The world of the councils is the world of Greek thought.

Thus the Orthodox churches of the East have historically been more interested in mystery and transcendence, the otherness of God, while the Catholic church of the West has stressed the re-offering of Christ's sacrifice here on earth again and again in the form of the Mass. Roman Catholicism has also tended to focus on the Cross and the atonement — the darker side, you might say; whereas Orthodoxy has stressed the Resurrection — the exultant or glorious side.

Eastern Orthodox churches also wished to declare icons (sacred paintings of Christ, Mary, and the apostles that were believed to possess properties of God's own self) to be mediators for God. Whereas Catholics located God and his Grace in the Mass and in baptism, Orthodox Christians believed that God was present in the icon. (Protestants have also sometimes seemed to make a similar claim in reference to the visible words of the Bible.) Eastern Orthodoxy was more upbeat, you might say; more purely visual; and more up in the clouds.

There were other differences, too. They came to a head in the year 863 when Pope Nicholas I refused to agree to the selection of an individual named Photius as the patriarch of Constantinople. Trouble had been brewing between the two

Differences between the Catholic and Orthodox churches

men, partly because the pope, although he had no external political base, kept increasing his profile as the divinely appointed head of the church, both East and West, as well as the state. The patriarch, who was himself controlled by the Eastern Roman Empire, resented this terribly, as did his political counterpart, the Byzantine emperor.

Photius, a strong character, fired five charges of heresy against the Catholic church. They were as follows:

1. The policy of fasting on some Saturdays. In Eastern Orthodoxy, this was thought to diminish Sunday, the Christian Sabbath.
2. The eating of milk, cheese, and eggs during the season of Lent. Orthodox Christians thought that Roman Catholics had compartmentalized Lent, or made it too easy, by advocating only abstinence from meat eating.
3. Compulsory celibacy for the clergy. Eastern Orthodoxy allowed married priests, although its bishops were unmarried and were usually selected from among the monks.
4. The separation of baptism and confirmation. In the Orthodox churches, baptism and confirmation were both presided over by a priest, who used holy oil blessed by the bishop. In the West, confirmation was performed by the bishop only. Orthodox

Christians did not magnify the office of bishops to the degree the Catholics did. This is important, because it points to a pattern of central control in Roman Catholicism that is not present in the East, nor (as we shall later see) in Protestantism.

5. The West's change of the third paragraph of the Nicene Creed to ". . . the Holy Spirit . . . proceeds from the Father *and the Son.*" This charge of heresy was the most important of the five. The "and the Son" (*Filioque* in Latin) phrase was added without the consent of the Eastern Orthodox bishops. Some later theologians have made much of the distinction suggested by the *Filioque,* but you have to look hard to find what it is. Whatever the cause, the East was offended that the West had proceeded without them.

There were a few other differences, but this controversy between the two branches of the Catholic church boiled down to differences of cultural ethos, to a difference of worldview based on the strong stratum of philosophical theology that had always existed in the Greek-speaking world, and to differences of geography. Constantinople and Rome were simply far apart physically.

The Great Schism became hard and fast in 1054. It remains in place. The Eastern Orthodox have never budged in relation to the pope's authority. Thus, a turf battle is taking place even now in Ukraine, where the governance of some parishes is being hotly contested by Roman Catholic and Eastern Orthodox parishioners. Christian disunity is not limited to America's Southern states or the British Isles. Centuries of separation are, humanly speaking, hard to live down.

Has there been internal development within the Eastern Orthodox Church? Have there been fresh emphases or new projects connecting with culture? The answer for the most part is no. The very attraction of Eastern Orthodoxy for Western Christians is its unchanging character. Every year a number of Protestants, together with a few Catholics, "go Orthodox." They love the mystery and admire the uncompromising stands of Eastern Orthodoxy. They believe it helps them to better connect with God. Almost no one disagrees that the appeal of the Orthodox way is its unshakeable verticality. It is a very religious expression of Christianity.

Appeal of the Orthodox church is its verticality

There is another branch of the Orthodox way: the Slavonic churches. These churches are the churches of Central Eastern Europe, primarily Russia. They were founded initially by St. Cyril and St. Methodius — joyous, courageous evangelists who translated the Bible. When the grand prince of Kiev, St. Vladimir, became baptized in 988, he insisted that his people be baptized with him. However, Christianity did not take a firm hold in Russia until the Mongols invaded 250 years later. At that time, the Russian people were sustained by their faith. Mother Russia, notwithstanding the Communists, has never really left the Orthodox fold.

The reader will note that Eastern Orthodoxy gets less air time in the *Primer* than Catholicism and Protestantism. This is only so because after 1054, Orthodoxy went into a time capsule. Like Islam after the period of the Crusades, there was not much inward development in the church, and certainly not much outward contact, until the Western world of communication and access changed things in the twentieth century. It may be that Russian Orthodoxy in the aftermath of Communism's fall will find a fresh, renewed identity or voice. Similarly, now in relation to the imperviously secular European Union, Greek Orthodoxy may rejuvenate itself. Incidentally, Greece was the first nation to protest vigorously against the exclusion of any reference to God or Christianity in Europe's new constitution. So we may see the pressures on the Eastern Orthodox Church driving it to take new initiatives. I hope so. But there is no question, no question at all, that from 1054 to quite recent times, the Eastern Orthodox Church has gone its own serene and ageless way.

After 1054 Orthodoxy went into a time capsule

XI
TRINITY AND THE SEED OF ISLAM

A principle in the history of religions is the way that gaps in one religion are filled by another. This works out quite clearly when one religious perspective is in close engagement with another. The one sees its own questions *answered* in the assertions of the other.

Nowhere is this mirror principle — this experience of one religion answering another when they confront each other — more obvious than in the birth of Islam during the first half of the seventh century. What we find especially is how the birth of Islam forced (and still forces) Christians to see the mote in their own eye.

The facts of Islam's birth, as it relates to Christianity, are as follows: Muhammad was a prophet who saw unblinkingly into the confusion and superstition of the religion of the indigenous tribes of the city of Mecca, in what is now Saudi Arabia. Their religion was marked by the worship of stones and trees. Muhammad regarded the worship that surrounded him as fruitless, false, and ultimately cruel. At that time, he had also become disillusioned with Judaism and then Christianity, seeing in them false worship.

The birth of Islam

Muhammad writes the Holy Qur'an

Receiving words from the angel Gabriel during a trancelike state, Muhammad began to write a document that would become known as the Holy Qur'an (Koran), the sacred text of Islam that claims the world for the One God, Allah.

Although his message against the idols of Mecca had themes in common with Judaism and Christianity, it was sharp and polemical, making no compromise whatsoever with the entrenched paganism of the region. Consequently, it was not received well. In 622, Muhammad was forced to flee the city of Mecca and find refuge in the city of Medina. There the Prophet's word was accepted and adopted.

Muhammad continued to write chapters of the Qur'an (called suras), during most of the Medinan period. Unlike the Meccan suras, which are mostly prophetic assaults on false worship and reflections on the world's rejection of the One God, the Medinan texts are more focused on the nascent Islamic community, on human society and on social values under the One God. The Meccan sections of the Qur'an read like the prophets of the Old Testament; the Medinan sections read more like the Torah, the Jewish Law of God's covenant people.

In Muhammad's lifetime, most of the majority-*Christian* Middle East came under Islam's rule, *Islam* meaning "submission (to the will of God)." At the time of his death in 632, Muhammad was making plans to send his armies into Syria and Palestine. By 732, Muslim Arabs ruled from Spain, across North Africa and the Middle East, to the borders of China and India, and hundreds of thousands of people had converted from Christianity to Islam.

Because Christianity lost so much ground to Islam (a fact that Christians have seldom considered seriously enough as a form of self-criticism), and because the world situation today is so gripped by Islam as a last holdout in the face of American cultural values and globalization, it is essential that we ask, What did Muhammad say that revealed important faults within Christianity? What did his critique of Christianity communicate about Christianity? What was wrong in Christianity and what was right with it? The rise of Islam forces us to take the temperature of our own religion at this point in the *Primer.*

Islam's rise forces us to examine ourselves

No one has ever been able to establish the precise antecedents of Muhammad's thinking. Muslims believe there were none. They believe the Qur'an was dictated, word after word, by an angel from heaven. Most Christians do not think in that way. They understand the "humanness" of God to have existed within the humanness of Christ. Therefore, divine truth is mediated, at least a little, in Christianity. Thus we insist on the right to ask ourselves: Did anything external, from the world around Muhammad, contribute to the Prophet's emphases? Why did his critique of idolatry take the form it did? The agenda behind these questions is our interest in Muhammad's critique of Christianity, for he critiqued core aspects of our religion. He did so unapologetically and with the idea of changing our way to a better and better-informed way.

It is usually assumed, though without solid evidence, that Muhammad had encountered Christianity in one of two possible forms. Either he had encountered an extreme form of Monophysitism (the idea that Christ's humanity is swallowed up in the one divine nature of God) or he had encountered Arianism (the idea that Jesus is not the equal of the Father but is his Son in the sense of subordination rather than identity). That is a mouthful!

Muhammad was aware of Christianity

But do you realize how important it is? If Muhammad's contact with Christianity was with Monophysitism, which overemphasizes Christ's divinity at the expense of his humanity, then no wonder Muhammad came to believe that Christianity was the false worship of a human man. If, on the other hand, the Prophet knew Christianity in the form of a denial of the Godness of the Son, no wonder he pushed for the subordination of Jesus within his own scheme of things.

Sadly, no one knows the facts concerning Muhammad's first encounters with Christianity. All we know for sure is that Muhammad knew something about Christianity, because he refers to it quite often in the Qur'an.

Where the protest of Muhammad against orthodox Christian theology is important for Christians is in the light it shines on the weak points in our religion. Islam criticizes four emphases in Christianity. As we look at these criticisms, we are able to view our own failings.

1. *Islam opposes the Trinity.* The Trinity, the Christian doctrine that there are three equal Persons within one God, struck Muhammad as a form of tritheism, the belief that there are three gods. It is all well and good to say, as Christians have always said, that the Trinity had been insufficiently explained or represented to Muhammad. But Islam's opposition stands: Show us how the Trinity does not destroy the unity of God! How does the Trinity advance the cause of the perfect creator God who *alone* is over all things and beings? Christians need to feel the thrust of Islam's critique: Why the Trinity?

   Islam's four criticisms of Christianity

2. *Islam opposes the Incarnation,* which is the coming into flesh of the wholly other One God in the historical person of Jesus Christ. On this score, Islam wishes to safeguard the transcendence of God against its compromise within the God-man Jesus. Islam's rejection of the Incarnation leaves a gulf between the unapproachable God and the helpless human being. Christianity denies such an impassable gulf. Unlike the Trinity, which is a philosophical construct, the Incarnation is a *need* we have. Without the Incarnation, the human race is stale and burned. The human race is toast.

3. *Islam rejects the crucifixion of Christ.* Muhammad understood that Jesus was opposed by worldly men. Muhammad knew that Christ's prophethood was, like his own, not received. But Muhammad was not prepared to believe that it could be true of God's perfect way that Christ, God's prophet and perfected messenger, would accede to his humiliation, torture, and execution. In Islam, the category of God's being and the category of failure and humiliation do not coexist. They cannot coexist. Thus, in Muhammad's view, Jesus could not have been crucified. At the last minute, suggests the Qur'an, the Jews crucified another, probably Judas, while Christ returned to heaven. This is the quarrel that Muslims and Christians will probably always have in relation to the Cross. For Christians, the Cross is God's solidarity with sufferers, and his vanquishing of human suffering through his identification with it. For Muslims, God's suffering is an impossible thing, ruled out by the core definition of God himself.

4. *According to Islam, the Jewish and Christian Bible — the Old and New Testaments — was superseded by the Qur'an.* This is because the Qur'an corrects and fulfills the Bible. It corrects and fulfills the Bible because the Bible of the Jews and Christians really points to Muhammad, God's

final revelation of his truth to man. The Jewish-Christian Bible missed him who was to come.

Christians have to take this criticism of their Bible seriously. Are the Law and the prophets, together with the New Testament as added to the Old Testament by Christians, enough? Christians and Jews, from differing perspectives, would both say yes. For Christians, the suffering Son of Man and Prince of Peace are enough. He is the conclusive fulfillment of God's own "personality" in the life of the world. For Muslims, such a Christ is too close to a failure. In their view, the manifest success of the Prophet's cause, by which his religion won victory after victory in its first appearance, is much closer to the true way of God with man.

In Christian eyes, the Islamic critique of the Christian Bible is wrong not because it claims the New Testament is incomplete. The Islamic critique of the New Testament is wrong because it does not appreciate the profundity of Christ's weakness and freely chosen pain. So the question of text here has to do with *substance*. Christians are satisfied that the account of God's Being as rendered by the Passion of Christ is perfect. It is enough.

Why Christians believe the Islamic critique is wrong

The phenomenal growth of Islam in the seventh century reflected something extremely important about Christianity in that era. Christianity was vulnerable, and proved itself vulnerable, to the Islamic protest. It was vulnerable because it had spent huge energies *for almost five centuries* on a philosophical concept, the Trinity.

Although I myself fully accept the Trinity as a unique insight concerning God in relationship to man, and although I see the point of the Trinity and confess it with my lips Sunday after Sunday, I am aware that the fixation on it in the Eastern Christian world from early in the third century to midway in the seventh century proved to be a weakness. Had our focus on the Trinity not held Christianity back from engaging other more gut-level concerns of people, Islam would probably not have grown as rapidly and extensively as it did.

We do not have to give up the Trinity to take seriously Islam's rebuke. We do, however, need to order our priorities so that *preachable* concepts, such as power in weakness and Grace in tension with Law, become the first ones articulated.

✝

XII

THE DARK AGES

A large number of modern historians are revisionists who are always trying to revise the opinions of earlier generations. Apparently they feel the need to show up their fathers in the profession as being ignorant and unsubtle. Thus, revisionist historians today are uncomfortable describing the period between the fall of Rome (410–476) and the building of the European cathedrals (the mid-eleventh century and following) as the Dark Ages. The old term sounds negative to them, too judgmental and too black and white. Surely human history is more ambiguous than that, they say. Surely human history is more nuanced, to use the contemporary term. We know there has never been a purely "dark" age. So how can we label a whole period of almost six hundred years as dark?

In this case, however, the old view is correct. For the Christian West, the centuries from Rome's dissolution to the age of the cathedrals were indeed dark. Very little light was given off anywhere. These were sad, struggling years for Christianity. The glorious achievements of Rome and Greece became victims of an overwhelming impenetrable amnesia. In Europe — which was

Very little light was given off

then Christianity's primary sphere — living conditions were primitive, life was hard, and there was no leisure time for arts and literature. Moreover, in the Middle East and North Africa, the once thriving Christian world had been displaced almost completely by Islam. The Dark Ages really were dark, at least from the point of view of the Christian church.

Here are the basic facts:

Barbarian tribes had been pressing hard against the northern borders of the Roman Empire since the middle of the third century. They pushed down against the western edge of Rome, which was Britain, and against all the territories of Germany and the Danube.

By 312, much of the Roman Empire had become Christian. But Christianity did not serve and strengthen the Roman military. In fact, Christianity probably weakened the resolve of the military. The English historian Edward Gibbon famously blamed the Christian faith for the cancerous weakness of Rome, by which the boundaries of the empire were increasingly and effectively squeezed by the tribes of the north. In part, Gibbon was right. Christianity is normally too critical of secular, economic, and political values, if not indifferent to them, to be a massive rallying point for national and imperial interests.

The Roman Empire lost its coherence

In any event, the Roman Empire lost its coherence. The empire gradually lost its will to fight for itself. The Germanic tribes, themselves pressed by the Huns to the east, came down from

the north and conquered Italy. The Vandals conquered Spain and entered North Africa. The
Vikings attacked Britain. The old governing
power emanating centrally from Rome broke
down into dozens of tribal regions. What we today
call the infrastructure of the empire fell to pieces.
Bits of it can still be seen in ruined cities from
Italy to Libya to Lebanon.

At the same time, the Catholic church, centered at Rome because of Peter's tomb, took on
some of the symbolic meaning of the old empire.
By the sixth century, the Catholic church had
become the lone unifying power in Europe. The
French king Charlemagne took the giant step
toward reimagining the Roman Empire by per-
suading the pope himself to crown Charlemagne
as Holy Roman Emperor in the year 800.

You might say that the Dark Ages were a retro
time. During this long siesta from culture and
criticism, Europeans looked back solely to what
had once existed. Charlemagne's famous action
at Rome epitomizes the spirit of his time. Charlemagne sought to baptize Christianity as the only
hope he knew of recapturing the grandeur that
had been Rome.

The four great themes of the Dark Ages are **Four great themes of the Dark Ages**
the rise of the pope's influence over western
Europe; the notion of a political or temporal
empire to mirror the power of the pope's spiritual
empire; the role of the monasteries in preserving
the ancient texts of Greek and Roman antiquity
as well as the Bible; and the failed competition of

so-called Celtic Christianity with the Catholic church at Rome.

Christianity's three enduring tensions were also present

During the Dark Ages, the three enduring tensions of Christianity that we are tracking in the *Primer* were also present. Law versus Gospel came into play in the confrontation of Roman Christianity with Celtic Christianity. Gospel versus church appeared concretely in that same conflict, pitting dispersed local Christianity against centralized Roman Christianity. Human strength versus human weakness was also a central issue in the rise of the papacy and its blessing of political emperors in the much-reduced guise of Charlemagne's Holy Roman Empire.

The conditions of daily living during this long period made anything like an avocation, such as the adornment of life with beauty or music or theater, almost impossible, even for the very few ruling families who had leisure. A combination of life's realities — the sheer exhaustion of survival, the poor diet, the complete ignorance of the germ theory and thus the overwhelming vulnerability of the population to contagion of any type — made for an extremely low life expectancy. These conditions also made for extremely low life expectations. That is why the forward movement of human progress, of virtually any kind, took so

Pace of change was extremely low

long. The pace of change, any change at all, was slow beyond anything we know today.

Within Europe during the Dark Ages, development or progress as we understand the words was almost nil, on every front you can imagine.

Illiteracy was a huge factor. The written word of the past, the Bible in particular, had a meager audience. This meant that there was also little receptivity to new ideas. There was zero openness to criticism, because few could read texts that might engender criticism.

A further setback for European culture, in the form of a counterrevolution, took place in the sixth and seventh centuries in the British Isles. There, the end of Roman-Christian civilization had come with the overrunning of the islands by Saxon and Scandinavian invaders in the fifth and sixth centuries. Christian priests and monks were able to escape the invasion, during which their monasteries were sacked, only by fleeing west. Consequently, the west coast of Ireland — the furthest possible land mass away — became the sole safe haven for Christians. An authentically original Christian culture survived on a small scale in Ireland. However, it was not as thorough or as extensive as modern enthusiasts of what is called Celtic spirituality like to imagine.

In Great Britain only western Ireland was safe

But it was real. Sometime in the late fourth or early fifth century, a British boy who was a Christian was captured by marauding Irish pirates and imprisoned for six years in what is now Northern Ireland, or Ulster. After he became free and went over to France, this boy felt called by God to go back to the place of his captivity. He felt called to preach the Gospel to the very people who had wronged him. Thus did St. Patrick start his famous mission to Ireland, through which the

Celtic
Christianity

land was authentically converted to Christian faith. Patrick's non-Roman style of evangelism and church planting matched almost ideally the Celtic style of Christianity that still existed in the extreme western area of the island.

The result, which Christians would call providential, was an effective movement of Christianity from west to east, from Ireland to Scotland and England, then later to northern Germany and Frisia (now Denmark). Evangelists such as St. Columba, St. Aidan, and St. Chad were able to carry the Gospel east. They established centers of worship and learning wherever they traveled.

Authentic literary remains of these adventurous Christian saints are few. But enough is known about them to establish that a fairly dispersed and nonhierarchical Trinitarian and Christocentric form of Christianity was their motivating force. The Celtic saints were also iconoclasts. They confronted the pagan gods of the people they sought to reach and, by sheer strength of conviction, overcame the priests, mostly druids of hill and stone and yew, who met them. Because of Patrick's vigor and personal history, Celtic Christianity became a sort of first-generation evangelistic movement, traveling light and without the baggage of institution and structures. It experienced success almost everywhere it went. The few genuine Celtic church sites that have been discovered are tiny to the point of absolute insignificance in worldly terms. Yet these modest sites carried the soul of Christianity for centuries in the wildest sections of the British Isles and the North Sea.

Tragically for the Celtic tradition, the Roman church succeeded in convincing the territorial kings of southeastern England that *its* representatives were the true Christian voice. Thus in 664 at the Synod of Whitby in northeastern England, the English church chose the Roman way. Within decades, the Irish-Celtic style of Patrick and his first followers died out and vanished. Celtic iconoclastic Christianity, with its more communitarian way of forming itself, ceded to the Roman model. Thus the Gospel came again in tension with the institution, weakness losing out to strength.

Before we close the door on this utterly static and also extraordinarily long period of the Christian church's existence, one important fact needs to be stated. It is a miracle that Christianity survived at all during this period. This is because militant political Islam was busily and without resistance conquering the ancient centers of Christianity in the East. Alexandria in Egypt fell, as did Jerusalem. Constantinople held out due to a fluke of geography. Rome was not threatened, but it would have been, had not Charles Martel (Charles the Hammer), king of the Franks, fought a furious battle near Tours in France in 732. Had he failed to defeat the western division of the Mohammedan forces on the plain of Tours, France and Italy — and also Germany and Britain — would probably have been converted to Islam. This book would have had a much-

The Battle of Tours

reduced subject. The point is, the fate of Christianity — or better, the fate of Christian Europe — hung during this sluggish and desultory period on one specific military engagement. At least after Tours the story would continue, albeit at a slow pace.

†

XIII
MEDIEVAL
CHRISTIANITY

Although many historians define the Middle Ages, or medieval period of European history, as lasting longer, I find it helpful to define the period as encompassing the five centuries between 1066 and 1517. You will recall that 1066 is the date when the Normans conquered England, and this was followed by their conquest of most of France, Sicily, part of Italy, and, during the Crusades, much of the Holy Land. William the Conqueror, who became King William I of England, was their most famous king. And as we will be discussing later, 1517 is the date of Luther's inauguration of the Protestant Reformation.

Among Christian theologians, this era of Christian history is sometimes called the Age of Faith, and it is the subject either of contempt or of admiration, depending on where you are coming from. If you admire scientific progress and rational inquiry into things, you probably view the Middle Ages as a time when superstition reigned and freedom of thought was inhibited. But if you value religious faith and humility before the grand design of the universe, you prob-

The Age of Faith

ably view the Middle Ages as glorious and awesome, adjectives that perfectly describe the magnificent cathedrals of western Europe that were constructed during that time. There were fabulous and courageous innovations only in this one vital art of architecture, as one after another dazzling cathedral was built.

First came the cathedrals of Norman design, with their distinctive Romanesque arch. This type is perfectly represented in the church known as Southwell Minster near Nottingham, England. Then during the thirteenth century, the Norman style was succeeded by the Gothic style, which is the typical style of a number of majestic European cathedrals, such as those at Orléans and Poitiers in France.

The Middle Ages were vertical

I may see the Middle Ages as a period of misconceived and misdirected verticality. I may long for the correction to that verticality, which was later supplied by Luther and his friends, who were utterly vertical thinkers, too. But Christian criticism of the Middle Ages should do nothing to detract from the awesome vertical gaze away from the human being to his Creator that the great cathedrals provided to the people at the time. All you need to do is walk into a cathedral such as Chartres or Canterbury and look up, and your breath is taken away by the proportion of the thing: everything, your gaze especially, is directed upward, away from yourself, toward God. The Middle Ages were vertical.

Although there were Christian universities at

Paris, Oxford, and Bologna during the Middle Ages, there was little free thought in the sense that we now conceive of it. Focused thought there was, but almost entirely within the field of theology. The pope's authority was the authority in Europe. That was shown by the assassination of Archbishop Thomas à Becket by the agents of King Henry II in 1170 in England. The king had Becket murdered and then paid heavily for it because of the pope's sanctions. No successor of Henry's would act in such a way toward the church until King Henry VIII in the sixteenth century at the time of the Reformation. And as we have seen earlier, the Holy Roman Emperor had been required to do penance before the pope at Canossa in 1077.

Although contemporary historians sometimes try to underplay the authority of the Roman church during the Middle Ages and speak of a widespread dispersion of authority, when they do this they are not being true to the actual events as they occurred and as they were viewed at the time. Prime authority lay with the church. National kings such as Louis IX of France and Edward III of England were able to do much, but they could not cross Rome. The Middle Ages were almost five hundred years of static power devolved from a central moral and religious — and thus also political — authority: the see of Rome.

Prime authority lay with the Roman Catholic Church

In eighteenth-century England, philosophers and theologians regarded medieval life as stuck, ignorant, bound by the Catholic church, and repulsive to progress — not just technological or scientific progress, but also moral progress. People with this eighteenth-century Whig or liberal view had big reservations concerning the Middle Ages.

But beginning 175 years ago, there emerged in England and America a generation of critics who admired the Middle Ages. These observers (called medievalists), such as John Ruskin and John Henry Newman, saw the Middle Ages as a beautiful thing, an age of God-centered humanity and un-crass humility. When they compared it with the Industrial Revolution of their own century and the decline of refinement and morals that they believed the Industrial Revolution had caused, they despised the times in which they lived. They saw the earlier era as a happier, holier one.

A group called medievalists admired the Middle Ages

What a phenomenon: the different ways in which the past is viewed by consecutive generations. So what then is true? What is the accurate way to look at a thing? We are all so limited by our personal experiences and preconceptions.

We can affirm that from a Christian perspective, the Middle Ages were absolutely tilted toward the dignity of God and the modesty of man. It was truly an "Age of Faith." However, institutions began — even in spite of themselves (and somewhat unconsciously, from a Christian perspective) — to take on the role of God in human affairs, as they had many times since

Christ's appearing. In the Middle Ages, the Christian church and Christ himself were scarcely distinguishable, at least in the eyes of the everyday person. That was wrong. It was untrue to the spirit of Christ.

The grandeur and also the pathos of the Christian Middle Ages are epitomized in an immense failed building, the Saint-Pierre Cathedral at Beauvais, near Paris. Begun in 1227, this Gothic cathedral had the highest roof of any building in Europe until its high vaults collapsed in 1284. The nave was never completed. The masons and engineers who worked at Beauvais, many of whom were killed in the infamous collapse, did not possess the science to realize their dream. Nevertheless, a section of the roof and its supports survived, and the remaining structure is spectacular. When you walk into the cathedral and look up, your eyes never stop. You then look to your right, where a massive blocked wall shows where the nave arches once rose. The Saint-Pierre Cathedral presents in visual form the failed but noble aspirations of the Age of Faith.

THE PERIOD'S TWO GREAT BLOTS ON CHRISTIANITY: THE SPANISH INQUISITION AND THE CRUSADES

Most people now condemn two series of events that began under the leadership of the Roman

Catholic Church during the medieval period: the Spanish Inquisition and the Crusades. The Crusades spanned a period of less than two centuries, ending with the eighth Crusade in 1270. The Spanish Inquisition lasted far longer, even beyond the time of the Counter-Reformation, whose emphasis on greater discipline within the Catholic church actually served to reignite the fervor of the inquisitors.

The Spanish Inquisition
In response to a revolt by several groups of Roman Catholics, Pope Gregory IX created a special court in 1231, called the Inquisition, to investigate and punish those whom the church deemed to be heretics (persons opposed to the church's teachings). The proceedings of the Inquisition were conducted in secret and were usually administered by Dominican and Franciscan friars, who acted as judges. The accused had none of the rights we associate today with fair judicial proceedings; he was forced to testify against himself, he could not confront his accusers, and he had no right to counsel and no right of appeal. Punishments were harsh: life imprisonment for heretics who confessed and repented, capital punishment for those who did not. In addition, all property of the accused was confiscated. The courts of the Inquisition operated primarily in France, Italy, and, most infamously, Spain. During the fourteenth century, abuse of

the Inquisition process by local administrations led the church to institute reforms. Thereafter, in most of Europe the Inquisition courts became relatively benign.

This was not so in Spain, where by the end of the fifteenth century the Spanish Inquisition had become independent of Rome and was being administered by secular authorities. It was truly a monstrous institution. Typical of the Inquisition were the actions of the notorious Tomás de Torquemada, who had been appointed the first inquisitor general by Queen Isabella. He instituted the horrifying punishments and tortures for which the Spanish Inquisition became infamous, including *strappado,* or stretching of the body; *aselli,* or water torment, in which water was poured into the mouth to induce suffocation; and *auto-da-fé* ("act of faith"), or death by burning.

A monstrous institution

The Spanish Inquisition began in 1478 and officially ended in 1808.

It is recorded that the Spanish Inquisition was responsible for the burning to death of 323,352 people, including Protestants, Unitarians, and atheists — but a great number of that deplorable total were Jews.

The Crusades

The Crusades were wars undertaken in the name of Christ the Prince of Peace with the intention of taking back the holy city of Jerusalem from the Saracen Muslims who had conquered it. The

Saracens had closed the city — and thus the Church of the Holy Sepulchre, the holiest site in Christianity — to Christian pilgrims. To Christians this was a blasphemous act. It would be today if it were to happen again.

In response, Pope Urban II called on the Christian Kings of Europe to recapture Jerusalem. Thousands answered his call, and the First Crusade began in 1095.

Originally called armed pilgrimages

Originally, the Crusades were called armed pilgrimages. Many crusaders sewed the cross of Christ on their clothing (the word *crusade* comes from the Latin word *crux,* or "cross"). To "take up the cross" meant to become a crusader.

Of a total of eight Crusades, there were three great Crusades that took place between 1096 and 1192. The first of these was successful. Jerusalem was recaptured, the holy sites were reopened to Christian pilgrims, and the Latin Kingdom of Jerusalem was founded. However, within a short time, this new Christian kingdom became a political football for England, France, and the Holy Roman emperor or the German emperor and their vassals. Thus their common cause — to preserve the official Christian presence in Palestine, especially Jerusalem — quite rapidly became the victim of political rivalries and vendettas. Weakened by internal strife, the Latin Kingdom of Jerusalem collapsed and was reconquered in 1187 for Islam, albeit a relatively tolerant expression of Islam.

The Crusades were not as notorious as they are now portrayed in these politically correct times. They began as a fair protest against the Muslim shutdown of sacred Christian sites that had always been accessible to visitors. The Crusades did not result in bloodbaths of Muslims. In fact, the worst atrocity they unleashed was a massacre of Eastern Orthodox *fellow* Christians in the city of Constantinople during the Fourth Crusade. Cecil B. DeMille got it more right than he knew in his 1935 film *The Crusades,* which begins by showing Muslim spoliation of Christian sites in Jerusalem.

Nevertheless, the Crusades went on much too long and became linked to the political dramas of soldier-kings who governed countries far away from their homes. Do you remember Prince John, the villain of the Robin Hood story? He ruled in the temporary place of King Richard I (the Lionheart), who was captured and held captive during the Third Crusade — not by the Saracens but by another Christian prince. The Crusades, which began in fact as a defensive action, degenerated into a perilous mess through which Christianity itself as a religion became linked with religious oppression and martial intolerance. To this day, massive castles of the crusader knights can be seen in Syria, Lebanon, and Palestine. The Cistercian Church of Saint Anne in Jerusalem is a unique and evocative monument to the crusaders' presence in the Holy Land.

The argument can be made that Crusades were justified, at least in their initial phase, as a defensive attempt by Christians to free Jerusalem's holy sites that had once been open to all but had been arbitrarily and suddenly closed by one particular Islamic ruler. One cannot say that the Spanish Inquisition was justified.

HIGH OR LOW POINT OF CHRISTIANITY?

The era can be viewed under two possible lenses

As I said at the start of this chapter, a person can view the Middle Ages under two possible lenses. The Middle Ages was either the most vertical moment in all Christian history, a time when men and women aspired to love and know God, or it was an unending period of torpor and fog, during which the faculties of human beings were channeled into a very narrow funnel. Where was scientific observation of the natural world? Where was science in any form? Where were medicine and good hygiene? Where were the rights of man? These were things not yet heard of and trumped utterly by the needs of the cathedrals and the church.

Unquestionably, the Middle Ages was a time that expressed the beautiful and ennobling primacy of God, as demonstrated by its majestic cathedrals. But it did not engender a better world. Human living conditions remained stagnant. Nothing changed. The governing philosophy of the age — the ruling ideas that govern the way things worked — was an unsuccessful mix of biblical concepts and tradition, along with some Greek philosophy.

Let's look now at those ideas and try to understand why they failed. Why did the Middle Ages, so long in duration, pass away?

Why did the Middle Ages pass away?

✝

XIV
SCHOLASTIC THEOLOGY

H ans Holbein was a Swiss painter whose gifts came to public attention during the early years of the Protestant Reformation. Holbein created a woodcut that went to the core of theology's problems during the Middle Ages. In the engraving, Jesus is depicted holding aloft a torch whose light serves to intimidate the Greek philosopher Aristotle. Aristotle, accompanied by the cowled figures of monks and priests, is seen scurrying away into the darkness. The idea of this symbolic picture is that the pure light of Christ banishes the lesser light of the scholastic theologians — or Schoolmen, as they were called — along with their ringleader Aristotle.

Holbein's perception of scholastic theology, a term referring to the whole system of ideas that fueled and drove the intellectual life of the Middle Ages, is harsh. But it is accurate. It reflects what had happened to European civilization after the collapse of the Roman Empire. The development of culture came to a complete halt, bringing on the intellectual vacuum of the Dark Ages. For the several centuries of the Dark Ages, this did not really matter. The conditions of life were so hard that there was no leisure for academic life

and theorizing. But in the Middle Ages, as kingdoms and regions began to stabilize, universities —
or schools, as they became known — came into
being. Settled places of learning, or faculties, came
into being. In the Christian world of the Middle
Ages, theology became the "queen of the sciences."

Two
thinkers
came to be
recognized
as the best
Initially, two philosophical thinkers came to be
recognized as superlative, the best of the best.
These were Anselm of Canterbury and Peter
Abelard of Paris. Both of these men focused on
the Cross and the atonement, asking, What did
God accomplish through the death of the Son,
and how did it relate to human beings now?

Anselm proposed an *objective* view of Christ's
atonement — namely, that something universally
valid had been achieved by the sacrificial death of
Christ. We could, so to speak, look a just God in
the face and understand ourselves to be totally
forgiven for our sins. Anselm discerned that what
Jesus did on the Cross moved the monkey of the
past off our backs.

Abelard, on the other hand, proposed a *subjective* view of the Cross — namely, that Christ's
self-sacrifice became the goal and model for human striving after excellent moral living. Abelard
saw Christ's work as establishing a moral norm,
as in "What would Jesus do?"

In the thirteenth century, ancient philosophical texts by Aristotle, which had been preserved
by monks and Islamic philosophers in Spain,
came back into circulation in western Europe. In

Spain, Christian and Islamic thinkers had been pursuing certain ideas in parallel study, especially questions of epistemology (i.e., how do we know what we know?) and system (i.e., what data belongs in this category but not in that category?). The Islamic philosopher Avicenna and the Jewish philosopher Moses Maimonides were both medieval students of Aristotle.

What Aristotle did for western thinkers, especially western Christian thinkers, was to teach them how to think. Aristotle did not supply them the substance of their thought, but he did provide them with the tools of thought. Although other Greek philosophers are important, Aristotle was *the* unique master for western Christians who for the first time in several centuries were attempting to organize the data of the world around them.

The influence of Aristotle

A number of men came forward as students of the Aristotelian method, such as Robert Grosseteste, John Duns Scotus, and William of Ockham. Their senior in every way was the systematic theologian and philosopher Thomas Aquinas. Thomas, who taught at the University of Paris, was the great synthesizer. A thoroughly orthodox Christian who also knew the Bible well —this was rare in a period when church texts like Peter Lombard's *Books of Sentences* was more available and studied than the Old and New Testaments. Thomas Aquinas sought to speak about all aspects of the world in the light of Christian ideas of God and Aristotle's organizing categories.

Aquinas organized what he knew and speculated about what he did not know. After Aristotle, he was the second most influential theology professor in history. He is definitely the most quoted and admired academic in the history of Roman Catholicism. Interestingly, he is thought to have become disillusioned at the end of his life concerning the grand edifice of his thought. Was it all "straw"? he is said to have asked.

Most of the Protestant reformers later came to regard Aquinas and all his students as individuals who were operating from the wrong organizing text — that of Aristotle. Because the Bible was assumed as an authority but rarely ever read, whereas Aristotle and literature deriving from his thought world were explicitly engaged with and never just assumed as authorities, the Bible was always in second place.

Thus the Protestant reformers — for whom
Scripture was always the starting place for all thought, and theological thought most of all — rejected Aristotle. They contended that Aristotle's book, *Nicomachean Ethics,* asserted a view of the good by which a human being was the sum of his works. Luther observed, rightly, that Aristotle taught justification by works rather than justification by Grace. There is no question that Aristotle's ancient ethics proposed a view of the achieved good that is entirely contradictory to Paul's notion of God's Grace.

The scholastic theology of the Schoolmen was

arid. Later, scholastic theology grew one-sided, interested in verbal and philosophical distinctions that were removed from actual life and experience. It was not just cerebral or abstract. It was actually way over on one side of genuine inquiry into the nature of things. This is why the genuine scientific method, as it came to be developed in the Reformation period by minds such as Galileo and Kepler, so outpaced scholastic theology in insight. Like linguistic philosophy in the twentieth century, scholastic theology got bogged down in overly systematic and uncreative verbal distinctions. This was its fatal flaw. It was academic in the negative sense of the word.

Martin Luther, who was trained strictly in the thought world of scholastic theology, came to reject it almost completely, for two reasons.

The first of Luther's objections to scholastic theology was to its hermeneutic, or interpretive principle. Luther observed that scholastic theology assumed rather than engaged the Bible directly. Aristotle's ideas, not the Bible's ideas, were the ideas that were being worked over. Concerning the limits of human reason, Luther objected to the use of Aristotelian reason without criticism based on biblical ideas. He believed that Aristotle's method assumed that human reason was somehow not sinful and self-serving, and thus not self-deceived. You see, Luther was much less optimistic than Aristotle had been concerning the capacity of human beings to attain wisdom.

Martin Luther's objections to scholastic theology

Luther and the other Protestant reformers were
not opposed to reason; they just thought philosophers should understand themselves to be humble before God's wisdom, which was by definition
higher than theirs and superior to it. Interestingly, Luther's view of reason as under the mind
of God seems to have freed people to learn the
scientific method. There was an explicit humility
to Luther's view of reason that actually freed
people to reason!

The second of Luther's objections to scholastic
theology was to its view of the Law or the judicial
(i.e., legal) principle in life. Luther recognized
that Aristotle, like almost all ancient Greek
philosophers (including the grand master of them
all, Socrates), claimed that to know what is right
is equivalent to being able to do it. If I know what
is best, Aristotle said, I shall invariably and certainly wish to do it. But on the other hand,
Luther understood that St. Paul, as we have
seen, held a different view. "For I do not do what
I want, but I do the very thing I hate. . . . Who
will deliver me from this body of death?"
(Romans 7:15, 24)

In his view,
the ancient
Greeks
were wrong
Luther believed that St. Paul was right and
the whole teaching of the ancient Greeks was
wrong. So when the Schoolmen implied that
human beings were capable of being and becoming morally good in themselves and in the sight of
God, Luther blamed their adherence to Aristotle.
Aristotle had claimed explicitly that a man

becomes good by doing good deeds. Luther was convinced that the Gospel said just the opposite. The Gospel says that a man is pronounced good by God only when he comes to the end of his (failed) efforts; that the whole point of Christianity is God's forgiveness of our failures, not his approval of our (so-called) successes.

Thus Luther rejected Aristotle and the moral premise of Greek philosophy. He cut the nerve of scholastic theology and parted company from it entirely. He was in agreement with Hans Holbein's vision that the word and light of Christ dispelled the darkness, the prime representation of which was Aristotle.

Even so, today scholastic theology is once more, for Roman Catholics and for some high church Protestants, an important strand of thought.

For some it is still an important strand of thought

✝

XV
THE PROTESTANT
REFORMATION

Fifty years ago, the Protestant Reformation
was seen as a mainly religious change in
Western civilization that had huge consequences
for almost every other aspect of life. Thirty years
ago, the Reformation was understood more as a
political, social, and even economic movement
that had a patina of religious words and connota-
tions. Twenty years ago, under the influence of
a school of thought known as postmodernism,
Reformation came to be seen as a misnomer altogether. At most, according to this view, reforma-
tions took place, but so did many other things.
The postmodernist view is dominant today. But it
will not last. Fashions of interpretation come and
go. Just in 2004, the eminent and senior English
historian Patrick Collinson published his "last
word" on the subject, titling it *The Reformation*
— definite article, singular noun. As I write this
Primer, the pendulum is swinging back to the old
view of the Reformation.

My point is that things happen, events take
place, yet their interpretation changes from era to
era, even from decade to decade. This is true of

all history. Interpreting the events of history has everything to do with the interpreter. There is a saying that scholarly attempts to picture the historical Jesus as he really was are based on the faulty assumption that ancient history is like a deep well into which the historian can discover the truth by lowering himself foot by foot (or century by century). But when he reaches the bottom of the well and looks down into the water, what he sees is himself! The interpreter has become the object of interpretation. Everything is subjective.

Of course, there *were* other big changes in Europe in the sixteenth century, but in Christian history, the Reformation was the watershed, the decisively influential event, equaled only by the coming of Christ.

The watershed event

The Reformation was led by Martin Luther, a Catholic priest and professor of biblical theology at Wittenberg University in Saxony (now east central Germany) in the early sixteenth century. Through his study and the experiences of his ministry, Luther became convinced that the church's view of how Grace works in the believer's life was untrue to the Bible and untrue to human experience as it really is. Luther was in his own body and psychology a "patient of great importance for Europe," in the words of Danish philosopher Søren Kierkegaard. The pain of Luther's personal crosses, his anxiety and extreme conscientiousness, could not be relieved or removed by the theology he had received from his own church.

ERASMUS AND THE NEW LEARNING

We now have to back up for a minute. The Roman Catholic Church had been sharply criticized by social commentators in the decades right before Luther's breakthrough. For example, Desiderius Erasmus, a caustic, subtle scholar and generally learned man, had seen through the vulgarity and materialism of the church. He recognized that the church had allowed superstitious ideas about relics of Christ and the saints to become money pits into which gullible sufferers poured their money in false hopes of cures and relief. Erasmus' book *In Praise of Folly*, published in 1511, criticized the church for permitting those pitiful but profitable charades of the truth to take place. Erasmus frayed ecclesiastical nerves that were already hypersensitive because of earlier similar criticism by such reformers as the Englishman John Wycliffe, the Bohemian Jan Hus, and the Italian Girolamo Savonarola.

Erasmus' In Praise of Folly

At the same time, a resurfacing of ancient literary texts had taken place in connection with the new learning or Renaissance, which first occurred in Italy during the fourteenth century. A passion for ancient texts, hence for ancient languages, had been stimulated in Europe. Ancient

Greek had become known again, and even Hebrew to a much more limited extent. The original text of the Bible had become accessible to scholars like Erasmus, and also to Luther. The Bible became an object of study, rather than a historical document simply to be taken for granted. Luther wanted to pore over it. He had the tools to do so.

Gutenberg's invention of movable type

Also, in the mid-fifteenth century, Johannes Gutenberg invented movable type that made printing practical for the first time. Printing was to have a powerful effect on the dissemination of knowledge. Whereas before, literacy had been to confined to monasteries, churches, and castles, where only monks, clergy, and the nobility had access to single handwritten manuscripts, now for the first time books could be printed in multiple copies and circulated to the general public. Now, what a man thought in Kraków, Poland, could be read in Tübingen, Germany, or Cambridge, England. Men and women began to read the Bible and compare what they read there with what they saw with their own eyes in the church. Erasmus and his many convinced readers began to attack the visible church as an unsatisfactory embodiment of what it was supposed to be, at least from the standpoint of the Bible.

LUTHER'S BIG IDEAS

Luther was a deeper and more integrated thinker than Erasmus. He was also more courageous. He saw that the whole edifice of the church was wrong because the idea behind it was wrong.

Here was the reformer's breakthrough, one of those rare central insights into reality that has proved to be universal. The church taught that the holy God forgave sinful men and women but that a person had to do something to get the forgiveness rolling. The church taught that a person had free will and could cooperate with God in God's desire to renovate a man. If a man would only come to Christ, Christ would come to him. Christ would then aid the person, and together, the two would create a righteous life. God was needed, but a man had to get his act together.

This doctrine is called semi-Pelagianism. We have seen it before. The Catholic church did not teach that a man's salvation depended on his own efforts alone, but it did teach that God needed man's help to get the job done. But what frequently happens with *semi*-Pelagianism it that it becomes perceived and thus experienced by most people in practice as full-blown Pelagianism. Pelagianism is the doctrine that man has the capacity, *operating alone,* to conform to the Law and lead a moral life.

The doctrine of semi-Pelagianism

In other words, what starts as a cooperative effort at moral improvement between man and God (semi-Pelagianism) is heard, by desperate and needy people, as a summons to do it themselves (or, in modern jargon, to take control) — and thus ends up being Pelagianism. Human beings are so poised to wish to take charge of their lives that they translate the semi-Pelagian idea into full-fledged Pelagianism.

That is what happened in the medieval church. The idea of human limits on achieving salvation or moral innocence — the idea of inhibiting and crippling sin — had been neglected. It had become lost. Augustine's concept of the fallen or lamed human will had become lost. Thus people believed that through special prayer and special acts of devotion and generosity, they could find the serenity that everyone who has ever lived wants to have.

Luther's rejection of indulgences

Luther's specific point of criticism had to do with the church's popular teaching that by giving money toward the erection of a new church in Rome for the headquarters of the pope, people could lessen the time endured by their departed loved ones as they waited for an entrance to heaven in a holding pen known as purgatory. Things came to a head in 1215, when Pope Leo X authorized Boniface, the archbishop of Mainz, who in turn authorized a monk named Johann Tetzel, to sell indulgences. For Luther, this idea summed up all that was wrong in the teachings of the Catholic church.

Luther himself was in touch. This is to say that his personal emotional receptors were extremely sensitive. Nothing but real felt peace would do. Luther struggled with the church's teaching because it did not give him the inward satisfaction he craved. Thus, when he became

stuck on a verse in St. Paul's letter to the Romans
that quotes from the Old Testament prophet
Habakkuk and declares that "the just shall live
by faith" (Romans 1:17; Habakkuk 2:4), Luther
found the resolution he craved for his own restless
sense of self- and divine accusation.

What Luther heard in this until then "buried"
verse is that *freedom from self- and divine accusation comes from trust in God* (i.e., faith) and
not from self-improvement, or what Luther called
works. Acceptance, or the status of serenity
before God, would come as Luther trusted the
gracious, unconditionally accepting God. God had
done it all in the atonement of Christ on the
Cross, and nothing we do can either add or sub-
tract from that. *The Grace of God, which is the
prior acceptance by God of a human being as
beloved by him without reference to anything the
person is or has done, is the gift of life.* The gift
is received at the time of desperation, when a
helpless sufferer trusts God. God is seen at the
point of human desperation not as an accounts-
reckoning, justice-distributing God. Rather, he is
seen, at the point of desperation, as a wholly loving compassionate Father.

Luther understood the Christian Gospel to say
that we do *nothing;* God does everything. If there
is a step or action on our side, it comes only from
simple trust at the point of need, and the very act
of trust itself is a gift from God. Luther's insight
— and it was a single insight — is often called jus-

Luther's
great single
insight
tification by faith. What this really means is justification by Grace received through faith.

When Luther perceived this, everything
changed for him. Christianity became a religion of
Grace and no longer a religion of Law. The
Bible's power to address him in concrete personal
terms instantly increased geometrically. The
Cross became understandable, no longer just a
talisman. The church became the vehicle, rightly
understood, through which the Good News of
divine peace was intended to be preached. The
sacraments of baptism and Holy Communion
became expressions or liturgical enactments of
God's Grace, but not carriers of it in an objective
or chemical sense. They pointed to Grace. They
were not in themselves Grace. The Good News
Good News
trumped
the church
trumped the church — a theme we have seen over
and over again in the *Primer,* when man's weakness becomes the occasion of God's Grace, not an
obstacle of which to be ashamed. Everything
changed for Luther by means of his hold on one
ancient verse, first gleaned from the seventh-
century prophet Habakkuk, for use by St. Paul
in a first-century Pauline letter, and now resur-
rected by Martin Luther in the early sixteenth
century.

Luther combined his new (but really very old)
insight from Scripture with self-analysis, to oppose
a local campaign being conducted by the monk
Tetzel to raise support for the construction of a
new Vatican in Rome.

On All Saints' Eve (our Halloween), October 31, 1517, Martin Luther nailed to the door of the Wittenberg castle church (the city's bulletin board) a list of his arguments in opposition to Tetzel's proposal that people donate money to the Catholic church in exchange for an indulgence. This famous document, now known as the Ninety-five Theses, made the door immortal. *The Ninety-five Theses* More importantly, it announced to the world Luther's single insight, his doctrine of justification by faith, which became the founding, fueling, resourcing engine behind the whole Reformation. Yes, it touched a nerve concerning freedom. Yes, it rallied German nationalism against the distant avaricious power of Rome. Yes, it tapped into the peasants' resentment of their masters. Yes, it was early fodder for the means of mass communication: the printing press. Yes, it enabled local dukes to take charge of an institution, the church, that had always been able to escape their control. And yes, it gave greedy families who wished to be upwardly mobile the chance to take land and treasures from the monasteries to enrich their heirs for generations. *But it all turned on a single insight:* the action of God's Grace toward the desperate, needy human being. And it turned inevitably against the church, which had lost fundamental contact with the one idea it had been entrusted with. The Reformation rallied vast and unconquerable strength from the weakness of one solitary individual.

The Augsburg Confession

Enabled by Luther's 1522 translation of the New Testament, the Reformation movement spread, culminating in what is known as the protest of the Lutheran Nobles at Speyer in 1529 and in the Augsburg Confession (the basic statement of principles of the Lutheran Church) in 1530. In almost every section but the southeastern corner of the country, Germany declared for Luther. Luther was dubbed the German Hercules. The northern cantons, or states, of Switzerland declared for the Reformation. France was strongly affected, and by 1572, almost half of France's noble families had turned Protestant. Central Europe, including Poland, Hungary, Czechoslovakia, part of Yugoslavia, and also Romania, became Protestant. England and Scotland changed religion, too, as did the countries of Scandinavia. Even northern Italy and Spain were affected.

TWO OTHER BIG IDEAS

Before I discuss the Reformed or Calvinist/Presbyterian version of the Reformation, as well as the English or Anglican expression of it, here is a further word on the ideas behind those movements. For ideas are everything in Christianity. Popular movements rise and fall with the appeal of the ideas that lie behind them. Luther's thinking touched on two other extremely important ideas. These two ideas had big implications for the future.

The first idea was the idea of church. How was "church" to relate to Luther's insight concerning Grace? The immediate fighting ground for the tension between the Gospel of Grace and church proved to be the Mass or Eucharist — what Protestants call the Lord's Supper. For Luther and almost all his contemporaries, the question was urgent: Where is the Gospel in the Mass?

Luther's intellectual followers, such as Huldrych Zwingli of Zurich, discerned the implications of Grace theology for the Eucharist. Zwingli hugely subordinated the Mass in favor of the Gospel of Grace. He depreciated the old Catholic liturgy of the Eucharist and wanted to call it simply a memorial.

Luther himself, having become the radical of all time in relation to the question of Grace versus Law, lost his nerve on this point. Having courageously deconstructed the heart of the church's teaching on the soul's relation to God, he timidly stopped at the foot of the next step in reasoning. He feared for his own mental health if he followed to its conclusion the full logic of the Grace idea that he had rediscovered from the writings of St. Paul.

Luther decided, rather, on a view of the Mass known as consubstantiation. Consubstantiation is the concept that the bread and wine remain merely bread and wine, yet also with (i.e., *con*) or in parallel simultaneous existence with Christ's real body and blood. (This is in some contrast to the Catholic doctrine of transubstantiation, which holds that every crumb of the bread and drop of the wine of the Mass become the physical body and blood of Christ.) Luther's theology of the Mass was, then, simultaneously a no and a yes. It was a form of words, you might say, that still managed to preserve a strong element of the old Roman teaching.

Elsewhere, however, and especially in France and England, the Reformation came to grips more radically with the service of Holy Communion. The English reformers, notably Nicholas Ridley, Hugh Latimer, and Thomas Cranmer, together with many others, notably the first "puritan" Anglican John Hooper, all died because they rejected the Catholic idea of transubstantiation. They were all burned at the stake because they followed the logic of Grace (i.e., the new, spiritual view of the Eucharist) in relation to church (i.e., the old, tangible idea of transubstantiation) and stumbled on that very first "rock of offense," or obstacle, the Catholic Mass. The French Reformation was specifically fought over the Mass. Thus the heat of the day did not light on the Grace teaching of justification. It lit rather on the first presenting *implication* of the doctrine of Grace: the essence of the Mass, the principal Christian act of worship.

The idea of predestination

The second big idea issuing from Luther's Grace project was the theme of predestination, or divine election. This theme, arising from his first principle that God's Grace is the essence and center of all Christian theology, was courageously taken up by Luther. Unlike the Mass, he did not try to walk away from the idea of predestination.

Luther reasoned that if God's word to man is Grace, and we bring nothing whatever to the table, then we also do not bring our will. We are limited by our own inherent defects. We are unable in ourselves to choose him. In actuality, as Augustine said, *we choose him not!* The crowd, hard-pressed, chose Barabbas and not Christ on Good Friday. Our wills are impaired; our choices are not free, as we wish to think they are; and we simply need all the help we can get. This stress on the impairment of human nature, coupled with the full attention paid to Grace, became intertwined in Luther's thought with the idea of the sovereignty of God. The sovereignty of God is the idea that God alone has a fully free will. God alone is sovereign. God is sovereign in that he is the only being who is able to do exactly what he wants to do. *Sovereignty* refers to the free divine will that can do and really does whatever God intends. Unlike us human beings.

Luther's conviction that God alone is sovereign pushed him toward the idea of predestination. Not only did Scripture indicate that God is the prime mover, and only prime mover, in the salvation of the world, as was argued by Paul in Romans (chapters 9, 10 and 11), but the logic of Grace as the sole cause of our salvation put all the emphasis on what God does for us, not on what

God alone is sovereign

we can do for him. This means that all cause is from God. God is the cause of our salvation. Why, then, are not all people saved? Well, that's the way God planned it. He decided to run the world in his way and not in ours.

The Bondage of the Will

Luther's big book on this subject, published in 1525, is called *The Bondage of the Will*. He wrote it as a defense against an attack by his earlier companion on the way, Erasmus, who had come to see Luther's Grace insight as too radical. Luther argued that whereas man is bound — he cannot do what he wants and really ought to do — God is not bound. God predestines or elects those whom he wills. Uniquely, God is able to do what he wants.

Like others in the first generation of reformers, Luther was reluctant to say that God damns people as well as saves them, which is referred to as double predestination. St. Augustine had taught double predestination at the end of his life. And surely election to damnation is the corollary of election to salvation. But for Luther, Scripture was not entirely clear on this question. So he held back from going all the way, logically, with the sovereignty of God. He and his colleagues, such as the famous scholar Philipp Melanchthon (author of the Augsburg Confession), did not wish to go all the way there!

However, the next generation of reformers — John Calvin and especially his immediate successor, Theodore Beza, among others — bit the bullet. They began to teach that in the same way he chooses some for salvation, God must simultaneously choose others for damnation. Although, in theory at least, all the Protestant reformers embraced the Romans 1:17 insight of Martin Luther concerning God's Grace in tension with God's Law, many of them, especially Zwingli and later the Baptists, went further in relation to the sacraments than Luther was willing to go.

CALVIN AND THE REFORMED VERSION

The second generation of reformers, especially John Calvin and his followers in England, France, and the Netherlands, went a little further than Luther in relation to predestination. The Second Reformation, the Calvinist movement that advanced or added to the Lutheran one, would emphasize especially the divine predestination of the saints or believers. (British and American Puritans would later take this emphasis and convert it to bolster their serenity as well as their anxiety, for they made the doctrine of election a defining characteristic of their church.)

The Calvinist movement

However, the second generation of Protestant reformers actually made their major mark — their identifying, agonizing mark — in relation to a higher doctrine of church than the first generation had preached. This new, higher doctrine resulted from a misstep they took in relation to the Law, a misstep that was very important for the future of Protestant Christianity.

John Calvin was uncomfortable with Luther's claim that like fruit growing from a tree, the forgiven or justified sinner would automatically do the right thing. Luther's insight assumed that the graced person would fulfill the Law but would fulfill it not out of fear or because it was demanded, but out of love. *Belovedness* would engender love. The Law had taught that works of love on our part would trigger love on God's part. The Gospel, by contrast, had taught that God's graceful love would trigger works of love, automatic and unself-conscious, from forgiven sinners.

In fairness to Calvin and his students, it is certainly true that the Epistles of St. Paul abound in moral exhortation. There is plenty of invitation and call to *do* in Paul's work (known as *paraenesis* in Greek). But Luther understood Paul's exhortations to Christians to fly right as being *de*scriptive rather than *pre*scriptive. In other words, Luther saw the calls to holiness that are found in the second half of Paul's letters as a description of the way forgiven sinners actually live. Everything flowed from the Grace affirmations in the first half of Paul's letters.

Calvin, however, was unsatisfied with Luther's explanation. So he hit upon the idea of a third use for the Law. The first use of the Law was to keep chaos from overtaking the human world; it had to do with such things as traffic lights and patent protection and jails. The second use of the Law was the establishment of the perfect standards of

God that would smash to bits all the pretensions of human beings of being or becoming good on their own. This second use of the Law led to repentance in people with destroyed lives, and trust in the graceful and saving God.

But in Calvin's view there was also a third use of the Law. This was the Law for Christians. It consisted of guidelines and models and instruction. It was three-hour quiet times, and fasting, and keeping your door open, and various other warnings and instructions and disciplines for the practical correction of Christians.

In Calvin's view there was a third use of the Law

Luther did not teach the third use of the Law. He never taught it. He believed the first two uses were enough to enable change to take place in human lives and in the world. But for the sake of his churches, Calvin felt it important to teach the third use. And this expresses the big difference between the Lutheran and Calvinist streams of the Reformation. It made the Calvinists declare that there was also a third, discrete mark of the true church in addition to what the Lutherans (and Anglicans too, as we will discuss next) had taught. The Lutherans taught that the true Christian church exists wherever the Gospel of Grace is preached and the two sacraments of baptism and the Lord's Supper are administered in the way Christ commanded. End of definition!

The Calvinists and the Reformed insisted, passionately, that there is a third, indispensable, identifying mark of the church: discipline. Discipline and the way discipline are exercised were crucial to the Reformed. Thus, true Presbyterians, who believe their concept of church discipline to be core to the Gospel in practice, have a higher view of church than most Lutherans and Anglicans. This is because for them, church discipline is vital to church essence.

Forever after, right up through the present day, Reformed Christian thought has stressed, in addition to doctrinal purity, purity in the visible church. This extends to Reformed fellowships and ministries of every kind.

THE CHURCH OF ENGLAND

The Reformation came to England in an unusual and somewhat localized way, in the form of tracts by Luther that were first read by junior academic theologians at the University of Cambridge. These theologians included Robert Barnes, who became an early martyr for Protestantism; and, most importantly for the future, Thomas Cranmer. The Reformation in England was helped along hugely by the work of William Tyndale, who was the first to translate the entire Bible into English. Sections of the Bible had been put into English earlier by the followers of John Wycliffe, but William Tyndale's genius for expressive language succeeded in giving a deep hearing to Bible ideas within the everyday language of the people.

The Roman Catholic Church in England

Barnes, Cranmer, and Tyndale

proved able to suppress Tyndale's Bible and also most of the books shipped in illegally from Germany. Then a historical accident occurred that many Christians saw as providence, or God's intervention. The king of England, Henry Tudor, or Henry VIII, was desperate to divorce his wife, Catherine of Aragon, in hopes of marrying a "true love," Anne Boleyn. (In fairness to Henry, his first wife was a witch.) Catherine had been unable to produce a son, and Henry was fearful that without a male heir, England upon his death would fall into civil war. Henry's urgent needs to end his marriage and sire a male heir intersected with Thomas Cranmer's creative mind. When Henry learned that Cranmer could argue on biblical grounds for an annulment of his marriage to Catherine, he commissioned Cranmer to create a divorce/annulment scenario that seemed to work, at least on paper. This document having been produced, Henry divorced Catherine and married Anne, and by definition the Protestant Reformation in England had begun, or at least the anti-Roman phase of it. Now Henry, and not the pope, was the supreme governor of the church in England.

Henry VIII's divorce

When Henry died in 1547, his *sixth* wife, a convinced Protestant named Catherine Parr, succeeded in tilting the royal succession toward the Protestant side. This meant that now, Protestant tutors would instruct Henry's son Edward, the king's son by his third marriage. Thus Protestant protectors, or regents, came into place.

The reign of Edward VI proved most important for Protestantism, both religiously and politically. The Reformation of the Church of England developed rapidly. However, and unfortunately for the Reformation cause, Edward died young and was succeeded on the throne by his half-sister Mary, who was as firm a Catholic as Edward had been a sincere Protestant. So the Reformation immediately went into free fall. Hundreds of Protestants were burned at the stake, including Archbishop Cranmer himself, while other influential Protestant leaders, including several future bishops, escaped to Switzerland and Germany.

When Bloody Mary, as she became known, finally died in 1558, her half-sister, Elizabeth Tudor, a moderate Protestant, became queen. Now, in the years 1560–1563, the English Reformation was secured and made official. Elizabeth's accession to the throne saw the ratification of the Protestant English Prayer Book and the establishment of the Thirty-nine Articles of Religion as the legal confession or charter of the Church of England. The monarch would now be the supreme governor of the church. After 1560, the Reformation was relatively though not completely safe in England.

The Thirty-nine Articles of Religion

Anglicanism was in some ways unique. It was Protestant, mainly Lutheran, in its theological first principle of justification by faith. It was roughly Calvinist in its teaching concerning baptism and the Lord's Supper. It was Catholic in certain surface things by which it attempted to look like the church that it had once been. The Anglican Church of England was in *essence* Protestant, yet in *form* Catholic. Its somewhat ambiguous character was due to the influence of Queen Elizabeth's own moderate religious Protestantism, coupled with the need for the Church of England to include the whole population of England, which was primarily Protestant by conviction, yet also encompassed a minority of Catholics who were not going to go away.

Politically and culturally, and also religiously, by the end of the sixteenth century England was a Protestant nation, a reality expressed through the trauma and victory of the year 1588, when the Spanish Armada failed to conquer England for Spain and Catholicism.

During the next hundred years, there was much seesawing back and forth between various factions — especially during the civil wars of the 1640s — as delayed reactions to the Reformation of the prior century. The reactionary King James II tried craftily and pathetically to reconvert England to Catholicism. But James was overthrown and forced to leave England by the (nonviolent and Protestant) Glorious Revolution. William of Orange became King William III, under the provisions of the Declaration of Rights of 1689, bringing the lasting imprimatur and seal of official Protestantism to an English constitution that was rooted absolutely in a Protestant view of

The Glorious Revolution

The Battle of the Boyne

Grace and religious liberty. William defeated James one more time at the Battle of the Boyne in 1690 in Ireland, ensuring the stability of the Protestant faith and freedom both in Ireland and in England. British Christians can properly remember with gratitude the defeat of the Armada and the defeat of autocratic James at the Boyne 102 years later. If those two events had gone the other way, Protestant Britain, and likely the United States, would not exist.

✝

XVI
THE COUNTER-
REFORMATION

A s you might suppose, soon after Luther posted his Ninety-five Theses on the Wittenberg church door, the Roman Catholic Church reacted. This reaction to Protestantism become known as the Counter-Reformation. It was a conscious, deeply thought-through response, ultimately proving successful in many ways. It was impressive testimony to the continuing power of Catholic themes in Christian thought and life.

A reaction from the Roman Catholic Church

At first, the pope issued a bull, or official statement, condemning not only Luther's heretical ideas but even his sheer existence. Luther burned the bull, announcing that he would become a Catholic again if the pope would just reorder the church's teaching along biblical lines. Then the pope sent various prelates of the church, including Johann Eck and Cardinal Cajetan of Thiene, to engage Luther in debate in hopes of changing his views. But Luther was determined, courageous, and unstoppable. Even in an audience with the Holy Roman emperor, Charles V, at the city of Worms in 1521, Luther refused to recant anything he had said.

The first comprehensive attempt of the Catholic church to answer the criticisms raised by Luther and resist the Reformation was the convening of the Council of Trent from 1545 to 1563. The Council of Trent reviewed the teachings of Luther, as well as those of several of his students, point by point and created a series of edicts condemning most of them. The theological term for this is *to anathematize,* or to declare an idea as blasphemous and wrong, and hence officially heretical.

The Council of Trent

The Council of Trent was at pains to recognize the institutional faults of the Catholic church and hence to refit it for its mission. But the council was at greater pains to spell out the core error of Luther in propositional, verbal terms. It did not anathematize Luther's view of Scripture, nor his view of the atonement, nor his views on the sacraments, which were quite conservative. It did anathematize Luther's idea of justification, according to which God forgave the sinner while the sinner was still in a state of sin. The Council of Trent did not wish to say that God's Grace extends to sinners before they have been cleansed from sin and have started their way back to a moral life.

This is important for the *Primer.* Luther taught that God forgave the sinner while he was still in a state of sin, imputing to the sinner divine Grace and thus justifying him while he was still a sinner. The Council of Trent taught that a man had to give up the sin and have it removed from him through the church's absolution before he could enter into Grace again. Luther taught that a Christian is sinful and forgiven at the same time (*simul iustus et peccator*), a human condition that never changes until death. The Council of Trent taught that you are either one or the other, either justified or a sinner, and that you should receive the sacrament only when you are in a state of Grace. This led to the church's insistence on confession to a priest, together with the priest's absolution, before receiving the sacrament.

At Trent, Catholicism simply reaffirmed the idea that a Christian could, by intention and discipline, assisted by sacramental confession, defeat the problem of moral failure. Luther, on the other hand, saw the indwelling fact of sin as more severe, more inherently deforming, than did the Council of Trent. This difference concerning human nature and its moral limits has ever since been the main dividing wall between Protestantism and Catholicism.

Rome's Counter-Reformation, anchored in the repudiation of the Protestant doctrine of human nature as bound, could now take place. It was not a rethinking of doctrine, however. It was rather a refit of the institution. It was not a critical discussion of first principles. It was rather a strenuous reapplication, through every aspect of the church's life, of an old idea of the Law. Discipline was tightened up, and a "leaner, meaner" church was the result.

Counter-Reformation was not a rethinking, but a refit

Rarely in Christian history has a negative event had the power or influence to cause the church to think again. This thinking again happened in connection with Christian reflection concerning the Holocaust. Reacting to its failure to resist the Holocaust, the Catholic church has sought to make core changes in theological emphasis. You could almost argue that the Holocaust has changed Catholic teaching in its essence.

The same cannot be said of the Catholic Counter-Reformation of the sixteenth century. I repeat, the Counter-Reformation was not a rethink. It was a refit. Certain institutional changes were made. The religious orders were disciplined; the clergy became better trained and educated; moral and institutional laxity were punished; old ideas were rearticulated and represented. Church buildings were cleaned up; ritual was centralized; regional variations from Roman use were discouraged or suppressed; reading lists were culled; ministries out on the edge of the church were pulled in or silenced.

The Jesuit order   The Jesuit order (as we saw at the end of chapter 8) was accepted and then thoroughly and aggressively employed by the Catholic church to fight heresy in certain areas where Protestantism and Catholicism interfaced, such as Poland, Lithuania, and Czechoslovakia. Jesuits were also smuggled into Protestant regions to say Mass among insurgent Catholic families and to bring in Catholic books that refuted Protestantism. The

Jesuit order did more to advance the Counter-Reformation of the Catholic church than any other agency or person.

Along with the Jesuit initiatives to reestablish Catholicism in Protestant areas, there was a dramatic increase in the size and impressive character of Catholicism as it presented itself to the world. For example, the baroque style of architecture and art was developed to express and evoke power in connection with the church, as grandly illustrated by the great plaza of St. Peter's Basilica, designed by the illustrious Gian Lorenzo Bernini. Filled with magnificent sculpture by Bernini and paintings by Peter Paul Rubens, St. Peter's became one of the grandest church buildings in the world. Complex choral works were composed by such great artists as Giovanni Pierluigi da Palestrina. The Counter-Reformation emphasis was obviously on bigger and bolder.

During the Counter-Reformation, Catholicism was also exported successfully to Central and South America. The Jesuit order proved particularly able at synthesizing elements of indigenous South American religions with elements of Roman Catholicism. Not until the second half of the twentieth century was any other form of Christianity so well received in America's southern hemisphere. Today, however, Pentecostalism and the house churches of evangelical Protestants are finding a wide and deep hearing in that crown

Catholicism was exported to Central and South America

jewel of the original Counter-Reformation, Latin and South America.

The military side   The Counter-Reformation also had a military side. Reconquest was its most effective tool, initially through the forces of Austria (i.e., of the Holy Roman emperor), which later linked with the Catholic army of France and especially with the Spanish armies and fleet of Philip II, to reconquer the Protestant part of Europe. By an apparent miracle, a sudden storm at sea, England and its Protestant faith survived the attack of Philip's Spanish Armada. But the French Protestants did not survive. On August 24, 1572, thousands of Huguenots, as they were known, were massacred as the result of a massive conspiracy organized with the official approval of the French king Charles IX, supported by his mother, Catherine de Médicis. The French Reformation was cut off at the neck! Poland, Czechoslovakia, and Lithuania were reconquered, while the war in Czechoslovakia opened a front that became the Thirty Years' War in the years 1618–1648.

During the Counter-Reformation, much of Germany was recaptured for Catholicism, and central Europe was decimated in population and resources. So terrible, costly, and inhumane was the Thirty Years' War that intellectual Europe had a collective nervous breakdown. Thinking people on both sides of the religious divide lost their nerve and resolved that such a war would never happen again. The Thirty Years' War was the last major European conflict to be fought between factions of Christianity. You could say that Serbia has had such wars in the twentieth century and that Ireland still carries the seeds of such a conflict. But no armed conflict of the magnitude of the Thirty Years' War has recurred in Europe.

I wish to add three important things to this brief account of the issues and events of the Counter-Reformation. This is because the *Primer* needs to show the whole forest, as well as the individual trees. The *Primer* needs to show the interlocking picture of the Christian story to tell its tale.

What was happening within the Eastern or Orthodox expression of Christianity during the long period of impassioned conflict between Catholics and Protestants? Where were the Orthodox churches at the time? The short answer is that they remained untouched, turned in on their own internal politics and independent, ongoing life. I draw attention to the stability of Orthodox Christianity during this destabilized time. However, there was at least one dramatic instance of crossover.

What was happening in the Orthodox churches?

Around 1630, the patriarch of Constantinople, Cyril Lucaris, the leader of the Greek Orthodox Church, was converted to Protestantism. He accepted the Thirty-nine Articles of the Church of England as the result of conversations with English and Dutch ambassadors and in response to specifically Jesuit incursions into Orthodox territory. This is a rarely told story, but Patriarch Cyril came to believe, sincerely, in the Reformation account of salvation and Grace. He became convinced that Orthodoxy needed a reformation and that Protestant or Reformed Christianity held the key to such a change. He even issued an edict calling on his clergy to subscribe to a form of the Thirty-nine Articles of the Church of England. This was a dramatic, awesome, counterintuitive step in the history of Orthodox Christianity.

Unfortunately for Cyril, he was murdered almost as soon as his reformation began. Then a heavy curtain of enforced amnesia fell over the matter, and his name was never mentioned again. Most Orthodox theologians still regard Cyril Lucaris' conversion as an unbecoming, even shameful, incident in the history of their church. The patriarch's portrait, sadly not now on view, is in Lambeth Palace, the archbishop of Canterbury's residence in London. Cyril's story gives the lie to generations of high church Anglicans who have felt attracted by the mystery and mystique of Orthodoxy. For Cyril Lucaris, the only way out of centuries of spiritual sedation was a reformation along Protestant doctrinal lines. In any event, his sad, suppressed story shows us that the Reformation and Counter-Reformation reached all the way to Greece and Turkey.

What about Islam? Now to a second note: What about Islam during this period? The most powerful empire of the world at this time was the Islamic Ottoman

Empire. It controlled what is now Turkey plus large expanses of northern Africa, southwestern Asia, and southeastern Europe. In the sixteenth and seventeenth centuries, the Ottomans attempted to expand into western Europe but were repulsed, first by the navies of Spain, Venice, and the Papal States at the battle of Lepanto in 1571, and then later by the armies of Austria and Poland at Vienna in 1683.

During that time, a meaningful encounter for the fortunes of Protestantism took place at Mohacs, in Hungary, where a battle was fought between Hungarian Catholics and invading Ottoman Muslims. The Hungarians were totally defeated and fled from the area. The Ottomans did not follow up their decisive victory at Mohacs and advance further west. However, they did not want a new Catholic or Holy Roman army anywhere near their area. Now, it happened that a sizable Magyar, or native Hungarian, population of Protestants also lived in that area. So the Ottoman Muslims supported the Protestant Magyars! The Muslims saw the Protestants, most of whom were Reformed or Calvinist, as a buffer against the Holy Roman or Hapsburg emperor. So they not only tolerated the Hungarian Protestants; they encouraged them to thrive. This is why eastern Hungary and western Romania — the area known as Transylvania — are, right up through the present day, Calvinist. I myself believe Count Dracula was a Presbyterian.

We know where Orthodoxy was, on the borderlands of this part of the Christian story. And we have not lost sight of Islam, also on the borders, yet always pushing against them.

What about Judaism?
What about Judaism? Where was Judaism, the ancestor of Christianity? What was Judaism's condition at this point, and where were the Jews? The brief answer is apt for this chapter, because Judaism intersected the Protestant story. The intersection was ugly. It was not as ugly as many contemporary commentators suggest, but it was ugly, and it has never been forgotten.

The background of the controversy is this. At the time of the Reformation, Jews were common throughout Europe, living in countless enclaves, including in Luther's homeland of Saxony. Moreover, Luther had always previously been philo-Semitic, or friendly to the Jews. While Luther was working on his translation of the Old Testament, he invited some Jewish rabbis to help him out with a section of Isaiah 53, the promise of the prophesied suffering servant. As he talked with the rabbis, Luther grasped in a flash of understanding that they did not regard the suffering servant as a representation, or anticipation of Christ the Messiah. No way! They understood the servant of God in Isaiah as representing the historic people of Israel, under oppression but looking forward to future vindication. Luther suddenly grasped that there was his Christian way of reading the Old Testament but there was also a

Jewish way. The second way was completely different from the first.

Luther loved the Old Testament and was also in no denial about Jesus having been a Jew. But he had been misinformed about Jewish interpretations of Scripture. When he realized for the first time the depth and extent, not just historically but also intellectually, of the enduring Jewish protest against the messiahship of Jesus, he was shaken and surprised.

Much later, when he was suffering from gallstones and in chronic pain, he was informed that some Jews were cursing the name of Christ during the Sabbath services in their synagogues. This, too, was news to him. At that point, he wrote two tracts, or short polemical pieces, that he never should have written. These tracts blamed the Jews for the political reversals befalling the Reformation at that time, and even for the advance of the Ottoman Turks. The tracts were white-hot pieces, blaming the Jewish people and their practice of Judaism for the crises of Europe. Forever after, the memory of Luther, and the legacy of the Lutheran churches, has carried the implicit, deadly charge of anti-Semitism. And the fact that most — but not all — German Lutherans did not speak up in defense of the Jews after the rise of Nazism in 1933 has strengthened the charge.

Was Luther anti-Semitic?

The charge against Luther that he was an anti-Semite can be sustained, but only in part. In a theological sense, it is true that some of Christian theology is anti-Jewish. That is, Christianity presents the New Testament of Jesus Christ in contrast to the Old Testament of Moses. There is a relation of promise and fulfillment between the Old and the New, but there is also contrast and comparison. Nevertheless, it is extremely unfortunate that the reputation of Protestant Christianity as the defender and embodiment in human affairs of faith and freedom was tarnished by Luther's two tracts.

†

XVII
THE PROTESTANT
ENLIGHTENMENT

Two "Enlightenments" took place in Europe during the eighteenth century. One was anti-Christian, and one was Christian. One conceived itself as working against the church and the norms of orthodox faith. The other conceived itself as advancing the true interests of Christianity. One took place in France. The other took place in Germany and Switzerland.

The "secular" Enlightenment that occurred in France is a subject for European and American history. The "religious" Enlightenment that occurred in the north is a subject for Christian historians, and thus for the *Primer.*

The wars of religion between Catholics and Protestants that culminated in Europe's Thirty Years' War ended with an uneasy peace. The principle of *cuius regio, cuius religio* (the principle that the religion of the king, be it Protestant or Catholic, would determine the official religion of the people in his country or area) anchored that peace. Thus, William of Orange was Protestant, so the people of England were almost all Protestants. Louis XIV was Catholic, so the people of France all had to be Catholics. This idea, the exact opposite of what Americans regard as the necessary separation of church and state, held a grudging peace in place for about one hundred years. There continued to be echoes of the wars of religion in Europe throughout the late seventeenth and early eighteenth centuries, such as the unending battles between French (Catholic) and English (Protestant) armies in the New World. But all-out or total war there was not.

After the Thirty Years' War, there had developed a deep-reaching disillusionment with religious passion, called *odium theologicum.* (You can see this in a masterpiece of antiwar irony entitled *Simplicissimus,* a German novel about a sort of fool or innocent who gets mixed up in the Thirty Years' War but doesn't know about the underlying issues. The fool, Simplicissimus, is constantly asking the obvious question: What is going on? What are you people doing?)

Another influential early figure of reaction to Europe's religious wars, who became more or less agnostic as the result of his reaction to "God's warring servants," was Michel de Montaigne. He was disturbed to the core by the French wars of religion and undertook to retreat to his quiet tower and compose his reflections on life in his work *Essays.* Something between an amateur scientist and a philosophical Stoic, Montaigne's thoughts about his context spoke for many. "A plague on both your houses," he seemed to say. "Just look at the good earth around you, and

Disillusionment with "God's warring servants"

cease your pointless back-and-forth over uncertainties in any case." Montaigne was thus anticipating the Enlightenment that was soon to flower in France.

The French intellectuals' reaction to the wars waged in the name of Christianity was engendered not by their interest in theology but by their reaction to it. A society of these intellectuals, who became known as the philosophes, produced an encyclopedia of knowledge that was explicitly anticlerical and opposed to the Catholic church. The *Encyclopédie* was also full of carefully investigated essays on natural phenomena and philosophical ideas. The most famous of the philosophes were Diderot, Montesquieu, and Voltaire. It was Voltaire, in particular, who epitomized the attitude of the philosophes to Christianity. He hated it! He gave it exceptionally poor notices. It was not so much that he hated the Christian belief as such, or Jesus; but he hated what the church had made of Christianity. Voltaire's often-repeated cry was *"Écrasez l'infâme!"* ("Eliminate that awful thing, church religion!") Voltaire expressed himself plainly, if venomously, in his book *Candide,* in which the somewhat innocent hero encounters the empire-building, hypocritical Jesuit missionaries in contemporary colonized Paraguay.

Voltaire was a freethinker (i.e., an agnostic bordering on atheist). Ironically, one of this interesting man's life projects was an attempt to vin-

The society of the philosophes

dicate posthumously a Protestant man who had
been treated with extreme cruelty in 1761 and
1762 at Toulouse in France for simply being a
Protestant who would not convert to Catholicism
under France's very strict laws concerning religious conformity. When you read the story of
Voltaire's unending efforts to secure tolerance for
Protestants, not to mention concrete justice for
them, you cannot fail to be moved. When Voltaire
died, they found a picture of the Protestant man
he had championed, Jean Calas, over his bed.

Voltaire's antichurch satires were linked in
many people's minds to growing political discontent in France with the king. Anti-Christian or
antichurch sentiments became one with political
dissidence. (This was also expressed in the American colonies in fearless propagantist Tom Paine's
Rights of Man, which seemed to articulate what
many people in France were actually thinking.)
When the revolution in France broke out on July
14, 1789, the Enlightenment turned political.
The French Enlightenment became extremely
powerful politically. Many people outside France
regarded this Enlightenment with horror, especially after 1793, the year the revolution seemed
to go mad. Thousands of people were decapitated
that year in an outburst of atheistic class warfare
that now, in the light of recent history, seems
Stalinist.

If Voltaire was the key figure of the French
Enlightenment, his contemporary Swiss counter-

part was a French-speaking Protestant author, Jean-Jacques Rousseau, who was also opposed to traditional Christianity.

The impact of the French Enlightenment on world history is well known. Its impact on the Christian church was negative, as a whole. For North America, this Enlightenment came to shore in the person of Thomas Jefferson. Jefferson was a deist (i.e., he believed in God, but as a principle or cause, not as a being) and did not become a practicing Christian until the very end of his life. His approach to church and state, which has been extremely influential in America and now in the world, was rooted in Voltaire's negativity toward church expressions of Christianity.

Meanwhile, another, different Enlightenment was taking place in Germany. Because of the academic component to the Protestant Reformation in northern Europe, the Reformation movement had proved friendly to learning, specifically to university learning. Luther was himself a university professor, and his movement stressed debate and critical thinking. For Luther, there was no split in his mind (and in the minds of many of his successors) between Christianity and critical thinking. *A different Enlightenment in Germany*

Thus, when disillusionment set in throughout Europe during and after the wars of religion, Protestant intellectuals asked their questions in the context of their faith rather than in reaction to it.

The first principal Protestant Enlightenment

thinker was Gottfried Wilhelm Leibniz, who taught philosophy in Leipzig and Jena. Leibniz — like most Christians of goodwill, both Protestant and Catholic — was shocked by the sectarianism of his era. He sought to think theologically about where God was in the carnage of the world.

Lessing and
Kant

One of the two key figures of the German Protestant Enlightenment, the Voltaire of the north, was Gotthold Ephraim Lessing. Lessing was a journalist who had also had a theological education. He did not believe in Christ's miracles or in the miracles of the Old Testament, but he did consider himself to be a Christian. His short book, *The Education of the Human Race,* honors the universal truth about God and right conduct that Lessing spied in Christianity. Like Voltaire, Lessing was a liberal. Unlike Voltaire, Lessing saw a liberal version of Christianity as serving and advancing the best interests of mankind.

The intellectual pinnacle of the Protestant Enlightenment was reached in the ethical philosophy of Immanuel Kant. In Kant's famous short treatise, "What Is Enlightenment?" the philosopher defines *enlightenment* as the opportunity for adults to think for themselves. Enlightenment, he believed, is the coming of age of rational mature people. They should not be under the thumb or constraining influence of "superiors" or "superior institutions" like the church. Rather, they should be independent thinkers drawing on their God-given gifts of reason and logic.

Kant had been brought up by his pietistic (or Christian evangelical) mother. Her Bible knowledge and Christian morals were instructive. Kant rejected what he considered their dogmatic or intolerant side, but his beautiful confidence in a moral law within and a Father God above made his philosophy an act of praise. Moreover, his grasp of inward intention and also the unfailing rightness-in-principle of God's Law made him an heir of Martin Luther.

Lessing and Kant were the two key figures of the German Protestant Enlightenment. They believed themselves to be in touch with the best Christianity had to offer. They saw their work as advancing the cause of thought from a Christian basis. However, western intellectual historians have been so convinced of the central role of the French, anti-Catholic Enlightenment that they have neglected the part played by these two leading German Protestant alter egos.

Three other people need to be mentioned as representative expressions of the German Protestant Enlightenment: Georg Wilhelm Friedrich Hegel, Ferdinand Christian Baur, and Adolf von Harnack.

Hegel was a churchgoing, practicing Christian, a convinced Lutheran. In his *Philosophy of History,* which influenced Karl Marx, Hegel saw the grand design in world affairs of an ongoing progression through thesis, antithesis, and synthesis. The point for our *Primer* is that Hegel regarded

Hegel's Philosophy of History

Protestantism as the highest expression of human progress within religious terms. Although his somewhat cyclical view of history impressed many who were not Christians, Hegel viewed his picture of progress as being embodied in the progress of Christianity leading up to its most liberal and universal expression, the Reformation and its legacy. Hegel's sublime hold on Christianity breathes through every difficult sentence he wrote! I feel a kinship with him. Hegel was a student in Tübingen at the moment the French Revolution broke out. I have lived in the theological college on the roof of which Hegel is supposed to have danced a jig in celebration of the French Revolution.

Baur, the founder of biblical criticism

Ferdinand Christian Baur founded biblical criticism as we know it today. A liberal-minded Protestant who was strongly influenced by Hegel, Baur discerned a clear movement in the New Testament away from primitive or cultic Old Testament ideas to universal and nonritualized New Testament ideas. Baur saw Catholicism as essentially cultic and primitive, Protestantism as idealistic and progressive. Baur was also skeptical of all dogma as dogma. And he was a convinced Lutheran Christian.

The Protestant Enlightenment was thus liberal and also intentionally Christian. There has forever been a tension, almost a paradox, in Protestant Christianity between its libertarianism and critical independent spirit, and the element of authoritarianism or dogma in its doctrines. You might say that the spirit of dissent within Protestantism is balanced by its latent evangelicalism or religious fervor.

One final important figure of the Protestant Enlightenment is Adolf von Harnack, who taught church history in Berlin at a later period, the early twentieth century. Harnack's approach to Christianity and also to culture is a classic final phase in the movement we are tracing.

A final important figure of the Protestant Enlightenment

Harnack believed in the historical method. According to the historical method (which was accepted as true until quite recently, when it has been questioned by the postmodernists), an inquiry into the past should be an attempt to find out how a thing actually happened. In other words, with the right sources, it is possible to discover, more or less, what really happened in the past. History is objective. It is not just a matter of current opinion. We can really know what actually happened. Harnack, who was a devout Christian, wrote *History of Dogma* and, more famously, his own Christianity primer, entitled *What Is Christianity?* In these two books, he combined progressive liberal thinking with the conviction that Christ and Christianity were really true.

If you wish to read a short distillation of the Protestant Enlightenment, read Harnack's *What Is Christianity?*

✝

XVIII
PROTESTANTISM
COMES TO AMERICA

I n the modern world, it can probably be said that the Protestant version of Christianity has come to its climax in the United States of America. The country was founded primarily by two groups of Protestants: those who came to establish colonies in the southern part of American's Atlantic seaboard, and those fleeing from the English government's domination of the church who sought refuge in the seaboard's northern area. Thus, English "church Protestantism" helped shape Virginia and the Carolinas, while English Puritan or dissenting Protestantism shaped New England. American cultural life was further wedded to Protestant evangelicalism during the Great Awakening, the revival movement of the mid-eighteenth century, as I will be discussing in the next chapter. (Not until the nineteenth century did Roman Catholics come to America in large numbers, and not until the late nineteenth century did many Jews arrive.)

The three charters of American revolutionary liberty — the Declaration of Independence, the Constitution, and the Bill of Rights — all originated in Protestant notions of freedom, individual

Two groups of Protestants colonized America

responsibility, and the rights of conscience. This is an established fact, although French Enlightenment ideas also had some impact on American social thought.

What makes the United States a most impressive case of Protestant development within Christian history is the combination of explicit Christian faith (i.e., the Bible, conversion, and moral seriousness) and Christian freedom (i.e., religious tolerance and the separation of church and state), which marks the real Christian influence on America, and thus on the world, because America is now the most dominant nation in the world.

Americans are passionate for freedom

Almost all Americans are passionate for freedom, as were their Puritan ancestors who fled England to practice their religion the way they wanted. At the same time, millions and millions of Americans — the large majority — are explicitly, committedly Christian. Christian affirmations concerning the power of prayer and the idea that everything has a reason come out of the mouths of Americans with startling uniformity and regularity in services throughout the nation every Sunday. Yet Americans also wish to be free, on every front you can name. For most Americans, Christian faith and strongly held notions of autonomy and self-determination coexist. The dogmatic and evangelical part of Protestantism lives apparently and almost effortlessly with the libertarian side of the Reformation protest. This seems like a unique development in Christian history. Whether Bible conviction and radical commitment to freedom can lastingly complement each other remains to be seen. Right now, they do complement one another.

WHY SO MANY KINDS OF PROTESTANTS?

Another note on Protestantism: Unlike Roman Catholicism, which still retains a living central headquarters and a head, Protestantism is a fissiparous form of Christianity. (*Fissiparous* means "inclining to split, or to separate into parts.") Today, there exists a huge variety of Protestant churches in the United States, including Amish, Anglican, Assemblies of God, Baptist, Christian Scientist, Church of the Nazarene, Congregationalist, Episcopal, Holiness, Jehovah's Witnesses, Lutheran, Mennonite, Methodist, Moravian Brethren, Mormon, Pentecostal, Presbyterian, Quaker, Reformed, Seventh-day Adventist, Southern Baptist, Unitarian, and United Church of Christ. (A brief description of each of these major branches of American Protestantism, aimed primarily at distinguishing their prominent similarities and differences, is included in the glossary which begins on page 371.) This list, as large as it is, doesn't begin to account for the numerous branches or sects that have split off from the mother church because of one disagreement or another.

A fissiparous form of Christianity

Why are there so many kinds of Protestants? The answer has something to do with Protestant theology itself. But it probably has more to do with America, Protestantism's most influential context and environment. Yes, Protestantism encouraged Christians to read the Bible and make their own judgments concerning God and Christ. Yes, Protestantism idealized the weak person as opposed to the strong and thus gave voice to the voiceless. Yes, Protestantism challenged the church with the Gospel and thus exploded the unitary central edifice. Yes, Protestantism spoke of Grace (which results in freedom from judgment) rather than Law (which restricts and cramps and suppresses). For all these reasons, Protestantism speaks for many individuals. It moves irresistibly toward the liberation of individuals, and it also moves, inevitably, toward disagreement.

Almost from the beginning, most expressions of the Reformation in which Protestantism is rooted have multiplied at the first or second sign of disagreement. The Lutherans held together until the Reformed version challenged their rule in Germany. Each Protestant canton, or state, of Switzerland developed its own slightly different form of church. The Czech Reformation produced the Bohemian (later to be called Moravian) Brethren movement. Presbyterianism took hold in parts of Switzerland, as well as in Scotland and in Hungary, especially Transylvania. Anglicanism spawned the Puritans, who became the Pilgrim Separatists, who founded New England in 1620. The Anabaptists in Germany birthed the Mennonites and eventually the *hundreds* of Baptist denominations that are now found in America.

The Pentecostal movement, which began in its modern form in California in 1912, has followed many different paths. It has one official denomination, the Assemblies of God, but innumerable offshoots, including parties or sections within old mainline churches and even within Roman Catholicism. There are too many Protestant denominations in the United States today to even number. And the same is fantastically true of the Pentecostal house-church movement in Latin and South America.

The Pentecostal movement

But the extreme degree of fissiparousness that Protestantism now shows to the world is the creature of America. Americans wish to make their own mark. They do not like to be told what to do. Resistance to authority is locked into the DNA of this country. If I cannot do what I wish to do in England, I shall sail to Massachusetts. If the Calvinists in the Bay Colony cramp my style, then I shall snowshoe to Rhode Island. If Rhode Island bears down on me, I'll skip down to Pennsylvania and then across to Tennessee. If Tennessee won't let me be, I'll trek by covered wagon to Texas.

The reader may recall such American characters as Roger Williams, who couldn't take the direction of Massachusetts Puritans, who themselves could not abide the persecuting zeal of the high church Anglican archbishop William Laud. Then there were the Ulster Scots, for whom Pennsylvania was just not far enough away. Sam Houston, Davy Crockett, Jim Bowie, and Colonel William Travis all moved to Texas and the Alamo.

But if Texas starts to choke you, make the big move, the move to Southern California. There you can enter the New Age and dress like an Asian Buddhist. But you're a Presbyterian or a Congregationalist just the same, under the skin. So finally you move to Hawaii, where the indigenous people don't like you, or to Alaska, where there are not enough of them to put you off. I suppose the last outpost of culturally fissiparous American Protestantism is the west coast of Alaska!

The reason for the splitting up of Protestant Christianity into uncountable sects, churches, and movements is the cultural history of America. This is why the theological voice of American Protestantism often speaks more from its cultural origins than from its theological loyalties. Protestant Christianity has shaped the world in which we live more than Roman Catholic Christianity or Eastern Orthodox Christianity. Those two sisters within Christianity are still strong. But partly because of its close link to America and America's origins, the big shaping influence is Protestantism.

Protestant Christianity has shaped America

✝

XIX

THE GREAT AWAKENING
AND THE WORLDWIDE
MISSIONARY MOVEMENT

W hile the Protestant Enlightenment in Germany was seeing rich fruit in its life of the mind, and while the French, anti-Catholic Enlightenment was laying the road for the revolution of 1789 — and almost all political revolutions ever since — another form of Christianity was springing up in the British Isles. This form would have big implications for America, right through to the conversion of President George W. Bush! It would also have consequences for the "one world" of our twentieth century. Because this new expression would produce the contact of Western missionaries, and also colonialists, with all parts of the human world, Christianity was about to become a world religion in the literal sense.

The Great Awakening, which is the term used for the American expression of John Wesley's English evangelical revival, began with Wesley's conversion on May 24, 1738. Wesley was a high church Anglican priest who had experienced a nervous breakdown after a failed ministry and failed romance in the colony of Georgia. He wandered into a Bible study of pietist (or evangelical)

John Wesley's conversion

German Christians in London, known as Moravian Brethren. There, on Aldersgate Street, while listening to a passage being read aloud from Martin Luther's commentary on St. Paul's Epistle to the Romans, Wesley received the "old, old story" concerning God's Grace in the Cross of Christ. He later reported that he felt his heart "strangely warmed" and found himself, his message, and the New Testament Gospel.

Soon Wesley began to preach the Gospel to excluded sorts of people in English society, such as coal miners. The message of Grace took hold. An impressive series of outdoor meetings were held, and very shortly thousands of people began to testify to the impact in their lives of Wesley's preaching.

The Anglican church was uncomfortable with him

The Church of England became uncomfortable with Wesley's methods — he preached absolutely anywhere people would hear him, usually in the open air and thus not in church — and with his message. Wesley's emphasis on Grace sounded antinomian (i.e., as though it rejected a socially established morality). Would his message lead to moral laxity?

John Wesley, like many other inspired preachers in the history of Christianity, found himself in a Dunkirk. He was trying to reach a needy but often skeptical world, yet at the same time, the church "behind" him, the Anglican church of his birth, was uncomfortable with him.

Eventually, even though he did not wish to do

so, John Wesley was forced to leave the Church of England. The critical step occurred when he ordained bishops for his followers who were in America. His almost equally inspired brother, Charles Wesley, the writer of such hymns as "Hark! The Herald Angels Sing," never did leave.

By the time of Wesley's death in 1791, his "people," who became known as Methodists because Wesley prescribed for them certain disciplines or "methods" to sustain their faith in daily life, had become a church within a church, and not long after that, an independent Methodist church.

Wesley was humble, tireless, and visionary. Toward the end of his run, he taught a doctrine of Christian growth, called Christian perfection, which was untrue to human nature. Overall, however, John Wesley was one of the greatest men ever to surface in the Christian church. He was not a thinker with the wisdom of St. Augustine or Martin Luther, but he was the ideal churchman — notwithstanding the classic fact that his own church rejected him!

However, Wesley did retain some faithful partners and friends within that old church, the Church of England. The most famous and effective of these was George Whitefield. Whitefield preached the Gospel throughout England as successfully as Wesley, if not more so. He also crossed the Atlantic, where he preached up and down the eastern seaboard, and especially at Philadelphia,

George Whitefield

where he came quite close to converting the American skeptic Ben Franklin. He later founded what is now the University of Pennsylvania. Whitefield was buried in Newburyport, Massachusetts, where his grave became an object of Protestant pilgrimage. It can still be seen, with his bones. George Whitefield was the first "type" of the Billy Graham–style evangelist. Along with Graham, popular evangelical preachers such as Charles Finney and Dwight Moody have been frequent and important influences on American culture. Their evangelicalism is as much a part of American self-understanding as the Enlightenment-era views of Thomas Jefferson. America has lived for centuries in the tension between Protestant libertarianism, expressed in the Declaration of Independence, and Protestant evangelicalism, going back to the evangelical Anglican George Whitefield. The recently chic John Adams, second president of the United States, combined within himself both of these strands. Adams was a committed, observant, Bible Christian of Puritan sympathies who was also an independence-cherishing intellectual. Usually, however, John Adams notwithstanding, the United States has experienced an uncomfortable tension between, rather than a synthesis of, these two sides of its Protestant Christianity — its Protestant freedom and its Protestant faith.

Back in England, George Whitefield helped create a rare bird in the history of Christianity, the Anglican evangelical. As a Calvinist Reformed man, Whitefield wished to stay within the (Re-formed) Church of England as he knew it. He fought to stay within his old church, establishing within it the fire of evangelical Christianity. It was his lasting legacy. The result of his struggle was that many of his followers, especially his ordained followers, remained inside the Church of England. They became the seed of the so-called Evangelical Party. This influential group later included Charles Simeon, their great organizer; William Cowper, their hymn writer and poet; Thomas Scott, their Bible commentator; John Newton, the writer of "Amazing Grace"; and William Wilberforce, the lay politician who became the "Great Emancipator" of the slaves.

On the other side of the Atlantic, in the United States, Whitefield's legacy was preaching for conversion, for the "new birth," and the conviction that everyone needs the opportunity to respond personally to the message of God's Grace.

A big result of the Great Awakening was the worldwide missionary movement that spread first from England, Scotland, and Protestant Ireland and then from the United States. The first important overseas missionary whom Protestantism produced was the English Baptist William Carey. The Anglicans soon caught up, however, as their Church Missionary Society, founded by Charles Simeon and friends, began to send out preachers, mostly ordained, to East Africa and India.

The worldwide missionary movement

The first well-known missionary from America was Adoniram Judson, after whom Baptist churches are still named. American evangelicals went to Hawaii, south to Roman Catholic Latin America (where they had little impact until recently, but where their indigenous successors have made a giant impact), and later all over the world.

The Islamic world — the Middle East, North Africa, and also Indonesia — has been impregnable for most of these missionaries, both English and American. The theme of Muslim-Christian relations in light of Christian missionaries' hopes to reach the world of Islam has become fresh again in the light of September 11, 2001.

Establishment of Christ Church

An influential chapter in the history of Protestant evangelical missions was the establishment of Christ Church (Anglican) in 1841 at Jerusalem. This was the first Protestant church in the Middle East, and it came under the guise of a consulate church for the English at Jerusalem. But that was just cover. Christ Church's real purpose was to be a foothold in the Holy Land for evangelical Anglicans working among Jewish people. This work was undertaken in the hope that once Jews in Palestine were converted in numbers, then Christ would return. Christian Zionism, as it is known, was birthed from the Great Awakening — specifically from converted worldly men, like Anthony Ashley Cooper, 7th Earl of Shaftesbury, who understood the Bible to mean that the Jews had to be resettled in their historic land, God's gift to his people, as the precondition for the second coming of Christ.

It is not an exaggeration to say that the State of Israel could not have been founded in 1948 were it not for the support of evangelical Christian Zionists like the Christ Church founders who pressed the English government to support a Jewish homeland state. To this day, Christian Zionists are an important factor in American support for the State of Israel.

All of this derived from the revival movement dating from John Wesley's conversion on May 24, 1738.

What was happening with the other two branches of Christianity, Roman Catholicism and Eastern Orthodoxy, during this fruitful period for Protestantism? We will examine Roman Catholicism in the next chapter.

Regarding Eastern Orthodoxy, unlike Catholicism and Protestantism, it kept fully to itself. The Orthodox churches — that is, the national churches of Russia, Greece, Serbia, Armenia, Bulgaria, Romania, and the other Orthodox sectors — were mostly untouched by the evangelical revival. Nor did the secular French Enlightenment or the Protestant German/Swiss Enlightenment have any objective impact on the Orthodox churches. The reasons for this were the language barrier and the condescending opinion of most western Europeans and English intellectuals that the Orthodox

The Eastern Orthodox churches were untouched

countries were cultural backwaters. Only in Russia, because of the odd attraction French civilization held for the aristocracy and intelligentsia, did Enlightenment ideas make an impact.

The worldwide missionary movement of the nineteenth century was the child of evangelical Protestantism operating in the context of a globalizing trend brought about by the Western liberalism that had been given life and strength by the two European Enlightenments.

✝

XX

THE NINETEENTH CENTURY: MODERNISM, SCIENCE, AND THE BIBLE

T he distinguished theologian Paul Tillich called the nineteenth century "the Protestant era," and he was right. During most of the nineteenth century, Protestantism was the ascendant version of Christianity in the world because it was the dominant religion of the European technological and colonial powers — Britain, France, and Germany — as well as the United States. Whether for evangelism, commerce, or colonization, when representatives of these countries journeyed abroad, they brought with them the Protestant version of Christianity.

"The Protestant era"

At the same time, the social and cultural crises that those developed countries were experiencing were also being experienced by their Protestant churches. In fact, it was sometimes hard to tell whether a crisis spread from the church to its surrounding culture or from the culture to the church.

The Catholic church in Europe was also faced with these same social and political issues. In similar fashion to the Protestants, it sent missionaries outward throughout the world, though with a slightly lower profile. In the Catholics' case, prominent examples were the White Fathers (the French missionary order) and other religious orders of men and women, especially in Africa and India.

Also, a notable crisis for English-speaking Christianity occurred during the nineteenth century with the publication in 1859 of Charles Darwin's *Origin of Species*. Darwin's book was immediately recognized for the revolutionary idea it contained: that life had evolved from less developed to more developed forms, and that this evolution had taken place through the interplay of genetic inheritance and adaptation. Thus, although he was not an atheist, Darwin's theory of evolution challenged the idea of a God who creates something from nothing (ex nihilo, to use the medieval Schoolmen's phrase). Darwin challenged God's creation of the world at a particular point in time and definitely the creation of man and woman at a particular point in time.

Darwin's Origin of the Species

Christians, especially in England and America, reacted vigorously to Darwin's theory. The evidence seemed against them. At the same time, the Bible was increasingly coming under attack as a historical record. The natural scientists of the time could not accept miracles or actions of divine intervention outside the laws of physics. Consequently, they regarded much of the book of Genesis as myth, in the sense of fable. Jonah's being swallowed by a whale became the stone of stumbling for people who thought in rational or scientifically based terms.

In South Africa, for example, the Anglican bishop of Natal, John William Colenso, wrote a book disputing the once universally accepted idea that Moses wrote the first five books, or Pentateuch, of the Old Testament. Although his theory was repudiated by most churchmen in the English-speaking world, Colenso was never disbarred, and he continued to use his episcopal pulpit and office to advance his ideas. John William Colenso

Similarly, German university scholarship, mostly the work of liberal Lutherans in the tradition of F. C. Baur, issued numerous studies postulating that one or another of the supposed authors of the Bible did not actually write the book ascribed to him.

Because of the power and influence of its central command structure, the Catholic church was able to ward off the beast of modernism (as the movement became known) more consistently than the Protestant churches. Typically, modernism made its impact upon Catholicism in the form of socialist politics, especially in France.

However, biblical criticism did rise up within the Catholic church in the writings of Alfred Loisy. Loisy saw the development of the early church as a struggle between Paul and his Gospel of Grace and Peter and the old holdover Law. Alfred Loisy

The implications of Loisy's views, which were similar to those of F. C. Baur three-quarters of a century before, were negative for Catholic teaching. Consequently, Loisy was excommunicated in 1908.

It is hard for Christians today to realize how focused the world was on such revolutionary thinkers as Darwin, Colenso, and Loisy. But if you think how interested the Christian world has become today in the controversy surrounding homosexuality, you can appreciate the furor surrounding these three apostles of modernism and science.

There was no such furor at that time within the more stable Orthodox churches of the East, even though in Russia there were rumblings of discontent because of the reception there of Marxism and other socialist ideas.

Two reactions were triggered within Christianity by the rise of science, modernism, and biblical criticism. The first reaction was fundamentalism. The second was renewed romanticism.

Christian fundamentalism was not what people now think it is. Initially, it was a movement of retrieval and reconsideration of common orthodoxy, which was started by a series of tracts *The Funda-* called *The Fundamentals,* published between *mentals* 1910 and 1915. Even Anglican bishops were among the authors of these essays, which simply enunciated traditional positions on disputed points, such as the virgin birth and the reliability of the Old Testament for Christians. But *The Fundamentals* gave their name to a movement that, at least in the United States, became quite literalistic. American literalist fundamentalism peaked with the 1925 Scopes (or monkey) trial concerning evolution and the Bible. The fundamentalists lost, but they did not give up. The pro-life as well as the creationist schools of thought today are children of *The Fundamentals*. A great many Roman Catholics have also joined with Protestant fundamentalists in relation to pro-life or anti-abortion thought.

The second reaction to the rise of modernism, science, and biblical criticism came from intellectuals and artists in England, America, and Scandinavia who came to embrace a philosophy referred to as romanticism. In the area of religion, romanticism manifests itself in the school of thought known as liberal catholicism. Liberal catholicism is not a part of the Roman Catholic Church but is a specific version of Christianity that actually grew in liturgical Protestant churches such as the Anglican and Lutheran.

Liberal catholicism is the dominant ethos of Anglicans in England and America today. It has a strong resonance with movements in the wider culture regarding homosexuality, pluralism, and freedom of expression, *yet with taste*. We sometimes say that American Episcopalians will perform same-sex marriages, but not during Lent!

Liberal catholicism combines dignified and

beautiful worship with a sense of history and continuity *and* with modern ideas of science, the Bible, and progress. Rowan Williams, the 104th archbishop of Canterbury, is a liberal catholic, as is the current presiding bishop of the American Episcopal Church. The same is true of high church German Lutherans, a large minority of American Lutherans, and the majority of Swedish Lutherans.

Liberal catholicism has become an influential species of romanticism. It is quite opposed to traditional Anglo-Catholicism and is extremely influential among mainstream Protestant Christians today. It is deserving of more attention from historians and analysts than has thus far been given it.

†

XXI
THE TWENTIETH CENTURY: THE CHALLENGE OF THREE FORMIDABLE PROBLEMS

During the twentieth century, the Christian church was confronted with three formidable problems: the end of the ethos of cultural Protestantism, the Jewish Holocaust and the State of Israel, and the tensions created within the church by the energetic spread of Christianity into developing countries. The first problem is behind us; the other two remain.

Three formidable problems

THE END OF CULTURAL PROTESTANTISM

We now know that the tide went out on the doctrine called cultural Protestantism at midcentury. Cultural Protestantism was the consensus within the European and American Protestant nations by which civilization was assumed to be liberal but anchored in faith; tolerant but in the context of a Christian conscience; and progressive in the belief that science could manage most human problems. It manifested itself in the social and political norms of late nineteenth- and early twentieth-century Germany, England, and America, by which Protestant leaders like Otto von Bismarck, and later Woodrow Wilson and Lloyd George, were supposed and expected to solve the world's problems, especially the big one: war. Culturally Protestant were the British Empire, the German universities, and American know-how. Roman Catholicism was a foreign ethos as over against the broad assumptions of elites from Melbourne to New York, from Belfast to Johannesburg, from Bryn Mawr to New Delhi.

Cultural Protestantism ended after World War II. It ended in America as minorities of Jews and Catholics and others claimed their place in the nation. It ended in Britain with the rapid collapse of its empire after 1945. It ended for Germany in that same year on VE Day. Moreover, in Germany's case, cultural Protestantism was particularly discredited because of Nazism and the failure of the Protestant churches — though not all of them —- to protest the ideology of Hitler. All you need to do is read children's textbooks on European history that were written before the Second World War to note the collapse of cultural Protestantism.

The cultural diversity of contemporary Christianity, not to mention the secular and non-Christian world as a whole, is now the fact. I myself still hold to the cultural Protestant values of faith and freedom. But they are no longer viewed in the world as distinctively Protestant values. They are viewed now as universal cultural goods, like human rights and emancipation.

THE JEWISH HOLOCAUST AND THE STATE OF ISRAEL

The second new challenge for Christianity in the twentieth century was the rise of Holocaust awareness and the significance of the State of Israel. As a political statement of remorse and sympathy in response to the Nazi slaughter of the Jews, the United States, Britain, and the other Allies recognized the Jewish State of Israel in 1948. The Jews now had a homeland. It was now possible for Jewish people all over the world to end their diaspora from the Holy Land. The problem of the indigenous people already living there, the Palestinians, was, in the heat of the remorseful moment, brushed over. But there is no question that Israel came into existence partly from European and American *Christian* guilt over the fate of the Jews between 1933 and 1945.

With the strength and increasing strength of Israel, especially since the 1967 Six Days' War, there was a parallel movement to emphasize the importance of the Holocaust as the defining moment in twentieth-century history. For Christians, both Catholic and Protestant, their general silence during the massacre of the Jews was a talisman of shame.

A talisman of shame

The Catholic church altered its teaching

As a result of awareness of the Holocaust, the Catholic church actually altered its historic teaching concerning the Jews. Instead of saying that Jews needed to become Christians to be saved, Pope John Paul II instead declared just after the turn of the century that Jews have their own way to God and their own covenant and that these are just as valid for Jews as the New Covenant is for Christians. Roman Catholics thus now came to embrace a two-covenant theory of salvation, whereas before, the church had always taught a one-covenant theory. Such was the power of the pope that he was able with the stroke of a pen to declare null and void a position that his predecessors had taken from the earliest times. So the Holocaust had and is having a fundamental impact on Roman Catholic theology.

Protestants adopted the two-covenant theory of salvation

Among Protestants, the effects of the Holocaust, always linked to the provenance and image of Israel politically, were just as clear, if more dispersed. Many Protestant theologians adopted the two-covenant theory of salvation. This is reflected in the very Jewish Jesus of New Testament scholars today. Jesus' Judaism is now regarded as the thing! In fact, you have to look hard to find any signs of distinctive "Christianness" in the Jesus of Protestant interpreters today. For many Protestant scholars, early Christianity was a messianic variant of Judaism. Full stop.

Also, the Reformation is under a cloud today for many Protestant academics. This is because it was Lutheran in origin, and Luther is regarded as anti-Semitic; because it was German, and the Germans were the Nazis; and because it was male and robust, and male and robust people are sexists and homophobes.

The rise of Holocaust awareness has affected Christianity at its center — officially, in the case of Catholicism, and unofficially, in the case of Protestantism. The major exception among Protestants is the Southern Baptist Convention in the United States. The Southern Baptists are still attached closely enough to the Bible to be unable to reject the New Testament witness that Jews need Christ as much as Gentiles need him.

In summary, the second formidable problem for Christians that arose during the twentieth century, and still exists today, is the influence of Israel and the geometrically inflated impression of the Holocaust on American and European cultural life. Parenthetically, this second problem has apparently not yet affected Orthodox Christianity, nor has it apparently touched Spanish-speaking Christianity. Hispanic Christians do not relate to it.

The influence of Israel and the Holocaust

THE TENSIONS CREATED WITHIN THE CHURCH BY THE ENERGETIC SPREAD OF CHRISTIANITY INTO DEVELOPING COUNTRIES

The third problem that Christianity confronted in

the twentieth century is what the scholar of religion Philip Jenkins called "the next Christendom." This is the fact that Christianity has become a phenomenon of the developing world. What was once the religion of old Europe and then North America has now become *the* thriving cultural force of southern Africa, South America, and China. The growth curve is no longer with white people but with Africans, Asians, and Hispanics. Moreover, the kind of Christianity so alive in the southern hemisphere is not liturgical, or mainstream, but rather, evangelical and Pentecostal.

This new fact, that Christianity is the fastest-growing world religion, outpacing even Islam, creates problems for liberal Christianity in the West, especially liberal Protestantism. This new fact puts developing-world Christianity at ideological odds with many influential Christian churchmen in the West. It was the source of the problems that created the revolution at the 1998 Lambeth Conference, the Anglican Communion's conference of bishops, at which developing-world bishops voted overwhelmingly in favor of traditional Bible teaching concerning homosexuality. The North American bishops, and some of the British and Scottish as well, were offended by the biblical conservatism of their African and Asian colleagues. But there it was. The next Christendom is overwhelmingly poor, young, evangelical, and of color.

Whether the developing-world members of the Anglican Communion have the confidence to defend their traditional values and challenge their more liberal sisters and brothers in the West is a question.

FOUR OTHER TWENTIETH-CENTURY DEVELOPMENTS

The Failure of the Ecumenical Movement

The ecumenical movement — the bringing together of Christians of all churches into common cause and unity — came and went. Beginning as the post–World War I child of cultural Protestantism, and inspired by Archbishop Nathan Söderblom of Sweden and Bishop George Bell of England, the ecumenical movement peaked with the founding of the World Council of Churches in 1948. The Roman Catholics never joined the council, but the Orthodox churches did. Initially, there were high hopes for this movement. But those hopes are mostly gone. The continuing failure to involve the Roman Catholic Church, the decline of liberal Protestantism in numbers and money, and the rise of unecumenical evangelical Protestantism and Pentecostalism in the southern hemisphere were realities too substantial for the ecumenical movement to overcome. Ecumenical unity among the churches will have to wait for another day.

Unity among churches will have to wait for another day

The Death of Communism

Millions and millions of people, including millions of Christians, were massacred by Soviet regimes between 1917 and 1989. Consequently, the death of Communism had important implications for Christianity, especially the formally persecuted churches in Communist countries. It is also clear that the Russian Orthodox Church, whose dissidents under Stalin and his successors never fully lost heart, is experiencing some revival at present. Orthodoxy is by no means dead, and the news from Russia tells us this.

The Persecution of Christians in Muslim Areas
The Christian populations of many developing areas of the world that are predominantly Muslim, such as north central Nigeria, southern Sudan, and Pakistan, are being pressured to convert to Islam or depart. Unlike in the past, Christians are *not* persecuting Muslims these days. Just the reverse is true. And this particular persecution has implications. It is obviously difficult for Christians living on the front line in such areas to believe Muslim spokesmen from the more advanced countries who insist that Islam is a tolerant faith.

*The Demonstration of Christian Virtue by
Extraordinary Individuals*
In the twentieth century, everyday Christian saints continued to exist and have moral influence simply by virtue of leading self-sacrificing lives. Mother Teresa of Calcutta is a very well-known example of a saint. The life of this Roman

Catholic sister gave to millions of people a positive impression of Christianity's compassionate heart. Despite the many problems, challenges, and controversies with which Christianity has been confronted in the modern years of its history, it continues to be blessed by such extraordinary characters as Mother Teresa. Together with the idea of Grace and the beatitudes of Christ himself, such individuals will always be the best public face of the Christian faith.

✝

XXII
THE TWENTY-FIRST CENTURY AND BEYOND

We began the *Primer* by listing three basic elements in the identity of Christianity. They are the core of what Christianity is about. They are what the religion is saying. The first of these basic elements is the power of weakness as opposed to strength. "My power," says the revealing God to St. Paul, "is made perfect in weakness" (II Corinthians 12:9). This element has played itself out over and over again in the history of Christianity.

The second basic element is Grace as opposed to Law: the unconditional love of Christ is opposed to the distributive justice of God. The two are not in tension or in some kind of balance. They are opposed to one another. For Christians, "God has done what the law, weakened by the flesh, could not do: sending his own Son in the likeness of sinful flesh and for sin, he condemned sin in the flesh, in order that the just requirement of the law might be fulfilled in us, who walk not according to the flesh but according to the Spirit. . . . For Christ is the end of the law, that every one who has faith may be justified" (Romans 8:3–4; 10:4). Christianity declares that God relates to man and woman no longer by the Law but through his Grace. This is because of Christ's atoning death on the Cross. Like the first element, this second element shows its head again and again in its neglect and repudiation and then its triumphant reaffirmation.

The third core element in Christianity is the Gospel of God's Grace in relation to the human church. The two constantly go into collision rather than alignment. St. Augustine had to rise up and correct the teachings of the fathers of the church. Luther had to shake the apples from the Schoolmen's tree and thus plant a new tree. The Puritans were harassed by the high church Anglicans and, to quote Simon and Garfunkel, "we've all gone to look for America." John Wesley found himself rejected by the bishops, and the Methodists became a church. And so it went. And so it goes. More often than not, tension, not harmony, exists between Grace and the church.

For the *Primer,* these three basic themes in Christianity have been a kind of guide through which to narrate and interpret the history of Christianity. They are a paradigm, as historians today say, or a pattern to follow, in understanding the Christian faith in its embodiment for more than two thousand years.

A paradigm to follow for understanding

Now let us look at the status and some of the future prospects of Christianity and its three historic versions, Catholicism, Orthodoxy, and Protestantism, at the commencement of the twenty-first century. What will the future hold for what is still the largest world religion? Will the age-old three-themed paradigms stick? Will the same messes and the same sad struggles, as well as the same triumphs, continue? But first, a word about the other two "religions of the Book," Judaism and Islam. They are always with us and show no signs of disappearing or being absorbed.

JUDAISM'S ENDURING NO

Judaism's enduring no has never changed. Judaism has been strengthened immeasurably by the identity-renewing fact of the Holocaust and its political consequence, the creation of the State of Israel.

The Christian significance of Judaism's no has been worked out in changed doctrine for the Roman Catholics and sapped confidence for the Protestants. Large sectors of Christianity have lost their nerve as a result of Judaism's negation. I predict that the next thirty years will see Christians needing to work very hard to absorb the impact of Jewish perspectives without giving up their own souls. The Southern Baptists, who have not compromised in relation to "Jewish evangelism," may in fact end up carrying the soul of Bible Christianity for the rest of the Protestant churches during this era of Christian insecurity concerning the Person of Christ.

The Southern Baptists have not compromised

ISLAM'S ENDURING NO

Also on the outside of Christian faith, emphatically and committedly outside it, is Islam. Islam is a vast and universal multiplicity of ethnicities and nations united around a universal text. Like Judaism, Islam will not go away. September 11, 2001, made this plain to all.

Moreover, the pathway between Christianity and Islam is a two-way street. Christians seek to reach Muslims, for their faith is a missionary religion. But Muslims want to convert Christians, too. We hope to influence them — but have failed largely, it has to be said — and they hope to influence us. We critique their concept of power and "manifest success." We stress Grace in relation to their Shariah, or imposed law.

But we have to hear their no to Trinity, their passionate hold upon the transcendent unity of God. And we have to admire their no to church — that is, to the idea of a mediator between men and God. We have to hear what Islam is saying — at least if we expect Muslims to offer us equal consideration.

No one can predict how it will go between Christianity and Islam. Thus far, the only possible answer is "Badly!" But the image of a two-lane street is the only possible way forward for both religions. Remember, there are *fifty-three* official Islamic states, while in 2003 the European Union could not bring itself to include even

There are *fifty-three* official Islamic states

a reference to God, not to mention Christianity, in its new and very secular constitution!

CATHOLICISM

Catholicism's conservatism has been deepened and also broadened by the remarkable and versatile Pope John Paul II. The theme of conflict between Gospel and church continues to be visible, from a Protestant perspective, in Catholicism. As we previously discussed, in 2002, with "the flick of a Bic," the pope signed a recantation of classic church doctrine in relation to Judaism. (The papacy had done something similar in 1711, when Augustine's interpretation of the Bible was rejected.) This can happen in the workings of the institution. But it does not inspire trust on the part of other Christians, especially evangelical Protestants.

On the other hand, Catholicism evinces fluidity and missionary flexibility in several areas. The *visible* character of its version of Christianity remains its key point, yet also remains its characteristic weakness in relation to *invisible* Grace.

EASTERN ORTHODOXY

Eastern Orthodoxy showed great fortitude under Soviet Communism. I remember when the unbowed dissident Father Alexander Men was murdered. I was in Moscow that week. Father Men was a great man, a martyr to the Christianness of Orthodoxy. There have been many others like him. Finally, there were the first stirrings created by perestroika. Christianity is definitely coming back in Russia.

The *ethnic* character of the Orthodox Church holds it back

In general, however, the *ethnic* character of much of the Orthodox Church holds back its mission. Orthodoxy has not been able to vault over its restricted national borders and the relative obscurity of its languages. Thus it has earned a reputation for introversion. However, its great legacy of monasticism and quietness and lifelong prayer is a plus, especially in Egypt, where the Coptic Church is persecuted and unsettled. As a whole, Orthodoxy is a sleeping giant.

PROTESTANTISM

Protestantism enters the twenty-first century in possession of a heritage that contains two characteristics that are continually in conflict.

The Protestant interpretation offers freedom

On the one hand, there is the Protestant interpretation of Christianity that offers *freedom*. It has been *the* breath of fresh air in Christianity since 1517 and actually before that, in the lives of the earliest Protestants such as John Wycliffe and Jan Hus. "Liberal" Protestantism is "green," or ecologically sensitive. It is philo-Semitic, or open to Judaism. It is anti-preemptive war and pro-human rights. It loves the separation of church and state. Yet it has little to say theologically.

But Protestantism's freedom emphasis coexists with its general governing characteristic, the credo of *biblical evangelicalism,* the expression of which can sometimes be legalistic and suppressive. Evangelical Protestantism and its fast-growing offspring, Pentecostalism, is bright and affirming. It is also triumphalistic, pole-vaulting over Calvary (i.e., weakness) on the way to Pentecost (i.e., victory). The Cross is weak in its presentation, and there is a lot of demand and discipleship. There is a lot of Law, in other words. Study the writings of the giants of modern Western literature and you will find that at least half wrote in reaction to Protestant evangelicalism of one strain or another. Protestant evangelicalism's vulnerability, I think, is its unconscious conversion of Grace back into Law, especially for born-again Christians after they are converted. It remains to be seen whether the life of evangelical Protestantism can be Grace-ful enough to make a lasting impact on world culture.

PLURALISM

So we come to the big and final issue of the *Primer.* How will Christianity as a whole fare in the world of the twenty-first century — and beyond?

The big issue is pluralism. Call it diversity, the one and the many, inclusion versus exclusion. This is the future of Christianity. It is also the world's task. I believe we all know this, with our countless "wars and rumors of wars" (Matthew

24:6). It is Christianity's task, as it is also Judaism's task and Islam's task.

How can Christianity live with, and compete with, other faiths?

How can Christianity live with, and compete with, the other world faiths? How can Christianity live with Western secularism, which was, ironically, birthed by Protestantism? How can Christianity be true to its core, to its weakness, to its Grace, to Christ's "traveling light" style of life, yet live in relation to the "other"?

Christianity is exclusive. It announces its claims to truth in opposition to other views of truth. Conservative Christianity — Protestant as well as Catholic, but especially evangelical Protestant — is widely seen by non-Christians as being exclusive in its understanding of the truth. Thus, Christianity in its conservative expressions runs up against the forces of militant Islam and assertive "settler style" Judaism. In such confrontations, force will be countered by force. It seems to me that in such confrontations, Christians will always lose, because even very conservative Christians know that at the end of the day, the New Testament is not about politics. It is not about the "kingships of this world" (John 18:36).

The "inclusive" way— which is to say that all roads lead to Jerusalem, that Christianity is just one of many routes to God — also has a flawed and failing future. This is because it is patronizing. It presumes a privileged knowing. It presumes that the inclusivist understands the real facts about the "other" and is summoning it back to its essence.

Who is the inclusivist to say such a thing? How does he know? Liberal Roman Catholics used to say that Protestants are just "separated brethren." How condescending to Protestants! Liberal Protestants used to say that Pure Land Buddhists and Sufi Muslims are "anonymous Christians." The assumption — and haughty presumption — is that we are all Christians under the skin. Tell that to an Orthodox Jew or to a Muslim from Karbala! Inclusivism does justice neither to the Christian truth-claim nor to the truth-claims of others. It will probably be seen in decades to come as a subtle form of religious imperialism.

I myself wish to suggest a radically differentiated pluralism. That phrase is from John Cobb, a Christian theologian, and is an apt one. According to radically differentiated pluralism, Christianity is not Judaism and it is not western European secularism and it is not Islam. What it is, is weakness not strength, Grace not Law, Gospel not church. It is not many things, but it is also some things. Christianity can live with the "other," affirming the other's differences and its own singular character. The Muslims can make their claims; we shall make ours. We may actually debate one another, as Zwingli did with the Roman Catholics in Zurich. We shall also offer the other space, place, honor, and the dignity of their identifying difference. This is radically differentiated pluralism.

There is Christian possibility within this

Radically differentiated pluralism

species of pluralism. When you know who you are and what you think, you can, Christianly speaking, give it up. You can give it away, as Christ did, "who, though he was in the form of God, . . . emptied himself, taking the form of a servant, being born in the likeness of men. And being found in human form he humbled himself and became obedient unto death, even death on a cross" (Philippians 2:6–8).

Christ knew who he was and what he thought. Yet he gave it all away. When Christians know who they are and whom they represent, when they know this anchor-deep and without perpetual insecurity, they are able to be prepared, they become ready, to give it all up.

Lovers have been doing this, and saying it, forever and ever from the beginning of time. Sacrifice comes easily in romantic love, or at least the thought of it does. Christianity is like that. When you are differentiated in your faith and status, and only then, you are in the cruciform, or Christ-shaped, position of being able to lay it all down. The sacrifice of everything you have and are is sufficient to change the world. Christians are taught this from the Cross.

The sacrifice of everything you have and are can change the world

This, in the practice of living in the twenty-first century, is what Christians mean when they invoke the "power in the blood."

APPENDIX

St. John wrote at the end of his Gospel that "the world itself could not contain the books that would be written" about Jesus. Now add to that two thousand years of Christianity!

I have selected some very precious jewels from the literature that has been produced through the Christian tradition. Some are short, passionate bursts of theology, plain and straight; some are hymns and poems; some are manifestos that were created at points of crisis in human history. Although the texts from the New Testament are in a special category of inspiration — divinely inspired, Christians would say — all these excerpts breathe a nobility and universal reach into the human condition which makes them impressive in the extreme.

And what is more, they are only the smallest slice of the pie. Read on!

THE SERMON ON THE MOUNT
(Matthew 5:1–48)

The Sermon on the Mount is the distilled form of everything that Christ taught. The translation below is from the Revised Standard Version of the Bible.

1 Seeing the crowds, he went up on the mountain, and when he sat down his disciples came to him. ²And he opened his mouth and taught them, saying:

3 "Blessed are the poor in spirit, for theirs is the kingdom of heaven.

4 "Blessed are those who mourn, for they shall be comforted.

5 "Blessed are the meek, for they shall inherit the earth.

6 "Blessed are those who hunger and thirst for righteousness, for they shall be satisfied.

7 "Blessed are the merciful, for they shall obtain mercy.

8 "Blessed are the pure in heart, for they shall see God.

9 "Blessed are the peacemakers, for they shall be called sons of God.

10 "Blessed are those who are persecuted for righteousness' sake, for theirs is the kingdom of heaven.

11 "Blessed are you when men revile you and persecute you and utter all kinds of evil against you falsely on my account. 12 Rejoice and be glad, for your reward is great in heaven, for so men persecuted the prophets who were before you.

13 "You are the salt of the earth; but if salt has lost its taste, how shall its saltness be restored? It is no longer good for anything except to be thrown out and trodden under foot by men.

14 "You are the light of the world. A city set on a hill cannot be hid. 15 Nor do men light a lamp and put it under a bushel, but on a stand, and it gives light to all in the house. 16 Let your light so shine before men, that they may see your good

works and give glory to your Father who is in heaven.

17 "Think not that I have come to abolish the law and the prophets; I have come not to abolish them but to fulfil them. [18] For truly, I say to you, till heaven and earth pass away, not an iota, not a dot, will pass from the law until all is accomplished. [19] Whoever then relaxes one of the least of these commandments and teaches men so, shall be called least in the kingdom of heaven; but he who does them and teaches them shall be called great in the kingdom of heaven. [20] For I tell you, unless your righteousness exceeds that of the scribes and Pharisees, you will never enter the kingdom of heaven.

21 "You have heard that it was said to the men of old, 'You shall not kill; and whoever kills shall be liable to judgment.' [22] But I say to you that every one who is angry with his brother shall be liable to judgment; whoever insults his brother shall be liable to the council, and whoever says, 'You fool!' shall be liable to the hell of fire. [23] So if you are offering your gift at the altar, and there remember that your brother has something against you, [24] leave your gift there before the altar and go; first be reconciled to your brother, and then come and offer your gift. [25] Make friends quickly with your accuser, while you are going with him to court, lest your accuser hand you over to the judge, and the judge to the guard, and you be put in prison; [26] truly, I say to you, you will

never get out till you have paid the last penny.

27 "You have heard that it was said, 'You shall not commit adultery.' 28 But I say to you that every one who looks at a woman lustfully has already committed adultery with her in his heart. 29If your right eye causes you to sin, pluck it out and throw it away; it is better that you lose one of your members than that your whole body be thrown into hell. 30And if your right hand causes you to sin, cut it off and throw it away; it is better that you lose one of your members than that your whole body go into hell.

31 "It was also said, 'Whoever divorces his wife, let him give her a certificate of divorce.' 32But I say to you that every one who divorces his wife, except on the ground of unchastity, makes her an adulteress; and whoever marries a divorced woman commits adultery.

33 "Again you have heard that it was said to the men of old, 'You shall not swear falsely, but shall perform to the Lord what you have sworn.' 34But I say to you, Do not swear at all, either by heaven, for it is the throne of God, 35or by the earth, for it is his footstool, or by Jerusalem, for it is the city of the great King. 36And do not swear by your head, for you cannot make one hair white or black. 37Let what you say be simply 'Yes' or 'No'; anything more than this comes from evil.

38 "You have heard that it was said, 'An eye for an eye and a tooth for a tooth.' 39But I say to you, Do not resist one who is evil. But if any one

strikes you on the right cheek, turn to him the other also; [40] and if any one would sue you and take your coat, let him have your cloak as well; [41] and if any one forces you to go one mile, go with him two miles. [42] Give to him who begs from you, and do not refuse him who would borrow from you.

43 "You have heard that it was said, 'You shall love your neighbor and hate your enemy.' [44] But I say to you, Love your enemies and pray for those who persecute you, [45] so that you may be sons of your Father who is in heaven; for he makes his sun rise on the evil and on the good, and sends rain on the just and on the unjust. [46] For if you love those who love you, what reward have you? Do not even the tax collectors do the same? [47] And if you salute only your brethren, what more are you doing than others? Do not even the Gentiles do the same? [48] You, therefore, must be perfect, as your heavenly Father is perfect.

THE PROLOGUE TO ST. JOHN'S GOSPEL
(John 1:1–18)

This passage explains the coming of Christ. It is read traditionally at Christmas. It is often referred to as the mystery of the Incarnation.

1 In the beginning was the Word, and the Word was with God, and the Word was God. [2] He was

in the beginning with God; [3]all things were made through him, and without him was not anything made that was made. [4]In him was life, and the life was the light of men. [5]The light shines in the darkness, and the darkness has not overcome it.

6 There was a man sent from God, whose name was John. [7]He came for testimony, to bear witness to the light, that all might believe through him. [8]He was not the light, but came to bear witness to the light.

9 The true light that enlightens every man was coming into the world. [10] He was in the world, and the world was made through him, yet the world knew him not. [11] He came to his own home, and his own people received him not. [12] But to all who received him, who believed in his name, he gave power to become children of God; [13]who were born, not of blood nor of the will of the flesh nor of the will of man, but of God.

14 And the Word became flesh and dwelt among us, full of grace and truth; we have beheld his glory, glory as of the only Son from the Father. [15] (John bore witness to him, and cried, "This was he of whom I said, 'He who comes after me ranks before me, for he was before me.' ") [16] And from his fulness have we all received, grace upon grace. [17] For the law was given through Moses; grace and truth came through Jesus Christ. [18] No one has ever seen God; the only Son, who is in the bosom of the Father, he has made him known.

THE LETTER TO THE ROMANS
(Romans 3, 7, and 8)

In this letter composed by St. Paul in his full maturity as a Christian evangelist and theologian, the human condition of inherent sinfulness or fallenness is diagnosed.

All theologies of sin and redemption find their starting point in the life and teachings of Christ. They have their further and crucial explanation in chapters 3, 7, and 8 of Romans.

Romans 3:9–26

9 . . . Are we Jews any better off? No, not at all; for I have already charged that all men, both Jews and Greeks, are under the power of sin, 10 as it is written: "None is righteous, no, not one;

11 no one understands, no one seeks for God.

12 All have turned aside, together they have gone wrong; no one does good, not even one."

13 "Their throat is an open grave, they use their tongues to deceive." "The venom of asps is under their lips."

14 "Their mouth is full of curses and bitterness."

15 "Their feet are swift to shed blood,

16 in their paths are ruin and misery,

17 and the way of peace they do not know."

18 "There is no fear of God before their eyes."

19 Now we know that whatever the law says it speaks to those who are under the law, so that every mouth may be stopped, and the whole world may be held accountable to God. [20] For no human being will be justified in his sight by works of the law, since through the law comes knowledge of sin.

21 But now the righteousness of God has been manifested apart from law, although the law and the prophets bear witness to it, [22] the righteousness of God through faith in Jesus Christ for all who believe. For there is no distinction; [23] since all have sinned and fall short of the glory of God, [24] they are justified by his grace as a gift, through the redemption which is in Christ Jesus, [25] whom God put forward as an expiation by his blood, to be received by faith. This was to show God's righteousness, because in his divine forbearance he had passed over former sins; [26] it was to prove at the present time that he himself is righteous and that he justifies him who has faith in Jesus.

Romans 7:4–25

4 Likewise, my brethren, you have died to the law through the body of Christ, so that you may belong to another, to him who has been raised from the dead in order that we may bear fruit for God. [5] While we were living in the flesh, our sinful passions, aroused by the law, were at work in our members to bear fruit for death. [6] But now we are discharged from the law, dead to that which

held us captive, so that we serve not under the old written code but in the new life of the Spirit.

7 What then shall we say? That the law is sin? By no means! Yet, if it had not been for the law, I should not have known sin. I should not have known what it is to covet if the law had not said, "You shall not covet." [8] But sin, finding opportunity in the commandment, wrought in me all kinds of covetousness. Apart from the law sin lies dead. [9] I was once alive apart from the law, but when the commandment came, sin revived and I died; [10] the very commandment which promised life proved to be death to me. [11] For sin, finding opportunity in the commandment, deceived me and by it killed me. [12] So the law is holy, and the commandment is holy and just and good.

13 Did that which is good, then, bring death to me? By no means! It was sin, working death in me through what is good, in order that sin might be shown to be sin, and through the commandment might become sinful beyond measure. [14] We know that the law is spiritual; but I am carnal, sold under sin. [15] I do not understand my own actions. For I do not do what I want, but I do the very thing I hate. [16] Now if I do what I do not want, I agree that the law is good. [17] So then it is no longer I that do it, but sin which dwells within me. [18] For I know that nothing good dwells within me, that is, in my flesh. I can will what is right, but I cannot do it. [19] For I do not do the good I want, but the evil I do not want is what I do.

[20] Now if I do what I do not want, it is no longer I that do it, but sin which dwells within me.

21 So I find it to be a law that when I want to do right, evil lies close at hand. [22] For I delight in the law of God, in my inmost self, [23] but I see in my members another law at war with the law of my mind and making me captive to the law of sin which dwells in my members. [24] Wretched man that I am! Who will deliver me from this body of death? [25] Thanks be to God through Jesus Christ our Lord! So then, I of myself serve the law of God with my mind, but with my flesh I serve the law of sin.

Romans 8:1–4

1 There is therefore now no condemnation for those who are in Christ Jesus. [2] For the law of the Spirit of life in Christ Jesus has set me free from the law of sin and death. [3] For God has done what the law, weakened by the flesh, could not do: sending his own Son in the likeness of sinful flesh and for sin, he condemned sin in the flesh, [4] in order that the just requirement of the law might be fulfilled in us, who walk not according to the flesh but according to the Spirit.

A TEXT CONCERNING
ST. AUGUSTINE AND PELAGIUS

Peter Brown is a famous modern historian of late

*antiquity, the period of Rome's fall and Chris-
tianity's early ascendancy. In this passage from
Brown's biography of St. Augustine (Augustine of
Hippo: — A Biography) the conflict between
Augustine and Pelagius on the nature of the
human will and God's design is perfectly
summed up.*

The book, which Augustine himself regarded as
his most fundamental demolition of Pelagianism,
is entitled *On the Spirit and the Letter.* The clear
code of laws enforced by sanctions, which had
been welcomed by the Pelagians as a sufficient
stimulus to good action, is dismissed by Augustine
as the 'Letter that killeth,' as the Old Law. Only
God could give the 'Spirit that makes alive,' the
capacity to love goodness in itself that will ensure
that a man will grow rather than wither in the
harsh environment of God's commands. 'You
enumerate,' he says later, 'many ways in which
God helps us — the commands of the Scriptures,
blessings, healings, chastenings, excitations and
inspirations; but that He gives us love and helps
us in this way, this you do not say.'

Thus, we come to two different views of the
way in which men are able to act, and so to two
different views of freedom. For Pelagius, freedom
could be taken for granted: it was simply part of
a common-sense description of a human being.
He was assumed to be responsible (or how could
his sins be called sinful?); he was conscious of

exercising choice; therefore, Pelagius insisted, he
was free to determine his actions. *'In the beginning, God set man and left him in his own counsel. . . . He placed before you water and fire, to
have what you wish, stretch out your hand.'*

For Augustine, this description might suit an
ideal human being. What concerned him was not
'planning human nature, but how to heal it.'
Therefore, freedom for Augustine was something
that had to be achieved. He will always speak of
freedom in comparatives, of 'greater freedom,'
'fuller freedom,' 'perfect freedom.' Pelagius and
Caelestius by contrast, thought that they could
argue directly from the agreed facts of choice and
responsibility, to complete human self-determination: 'It is the easiest thing in the world,' wrote
Caelestius, 'to change our will by an act of will.'
For them, the difference between good and bad
men was quite simple: some chose the good, some
the bad. To which Augustine replied: 'I could say
with absolute truth and conviction (that men
were not sinless) because they did not want to be
sinless. But if you were to ask me *why* they did
not want to be so, then we are getting out of our
depth — *imus in longum.'*

Men choose in a way more complex than that
suggested by the hallowed stereotypes of common-sense. For an act of choice is not just a matter of knowing what to choose: it is a matter in
which loving and feeling are involved. And in
men, this capacity to know and to feel in a single,

Freedom
was some-
thing that
had to be
achieved

involved whole, has been intimately dislocated:
'The understanding flies on ahead, and there follows, oh, so slowly, and sometimes not at all, our
weakened human capacity for feeling.' Men
choose because they love; but Augustine had
been certain for some twenty years, that they
could not, of themselves, choose to love. The vital
capacity to unite feeling and knowledge comes
from an area outside man's powers of self-determination. 'From a depth that we do not see,
comes everything that you can see.' *'I know, O
Lord, that the way of a man is not in his power;
nor is it for him to walk and direct his own steps.'*

An area
outside
man's
powers of
self deter-
mination

Thus, for Augustine freedom can only be the
culmination of a process of healing. Augustine will
turn the whole of Psalm 118, ostensibly a thoroughly 'Pelagian' Psalm, containing as it does a
static code of precepts for the life of the good
man, into a treatise on the dynamic transformation of the will. The most fitting image of the
'freed' will, will be one full of motion, the baffling
resilience and activity of a great fire, that can roar
up again when beaten by the winds of adversity.

The healing process by which love and knowledge are reintegrated, is made possible by an
inseparable connection between growing self-
determination and dependence on a source of life
that always escapes self-determination. The
healed man enjoys a more acute sense of responsibility, clearer knowledge, a greater ease of
choice. He has had to achieve all that Pelagius

had thought he possessed from the start. The idea that we depend for our ability to determine ourselves, on areas that we cannot ourselves determine, is central to Augustine's 'therapeutic' attitude to the relation between 'grace' and 'free will'. It is the connection of the two, in a single healing process, that occupied all Augustine's attention: any attempt to dissect such a living relationship, to see a contrast where he saw only a vital interdependence, frankly puzzled him: 'Some men try hard to discover in our will what good is particularly due to ourselves, that owes nothing to God: how they can find this out, I just do not know.'

Freedom, therefore, for Augustine, cannot be reduced to a sense of choice: it is a freedom to act fully. Such freedom must involve the transcendence of a sense of choice. For a sense of choice is a symptom of the disintegration of the will: the final union of knowledge and feeling would involve a man in the object of his choice in such a way that any other alternative would be inconceivable.

Throughout his sermons against the Pelagians, Augustine repeats this as his fundamental assertion on the relation of grace and freedom: that the

His definition of a healthy man

healthy man is one in whom knowledge and feeling have become united; and that only such a man is capable of allowing himself to be 'drawn' to act by the sheer irresistible pleasure of the object of his love. The notorious tag of Vergil,

Trahat sua quemque voluptas, 'Each man's pleasure draws him,' occurs, surprisingly, in a sermon by the old man on the Gospel of St. John: 'And have the senses of the body their delights, while the soul is left devoid of pleasures? If the soul does not have pleasures of its own, why is it written: *"The soul of men shall hope under the shadow of Thy wings, they shall be made drunk with the fullness of Thy house, and of the torrents of Thy pleasures Thou wilt give them to drink, for in Thee is the Fountain of Life, and in Thy Light shall we see the light"?* Give me a man in love: he knows what I mean. Give me one who yearns; give me one who is hungry; give me one far away in this desert, who is thirsty and sighs for the spring of the Eternal country. Give me that sort of man: he knows what I mean. But if I speak to a cold man, he just does not know what I am talking about. . . .'

"Each man's pleasure draws him"

ST. PATRICK'S BREASTPLATE

One of the few texts that can almost certainly be attributed to the heroic Irish church planter, Patricius (Patrick), is this one, known as St. Patrick's Breastplate. It is often sung as a hymn at ordinations to the ministry.

I bind unto myself today
The strong Name of the Trinity,
By invocation of the same,
The Three in One, the One in Three.

I bind this day to me forever,
By power of Faith, Christ's Incarnation:
His baptism in the Jordan River:
His death on cross for my salvation;
His bursting from the spiced tomb;
His riding up the Heavenly way;
His coming at the day of doom:
I bind unto myself today.

I bind unto myself the power
Of the great love of cherubim;
The sweet "Well done" in judgment hour;
The service of the Seraphim;
Confessors' faith, apostles' word,
The patriarchs' prayers, the prophets' scrolls;
All good deeds done unto the Lord,
And purity of virgin souls.

I bind unto myself today
The virtues of the starlit heav'n,
The glorious sun's life-giving ray,
The whiteness of the moon at even,
The flashing of the lightning free,
The whirling wind's tempestuous shocks,
The stable earth, the deep salt sea,
Around the old eternal rocks.

I bind unto myself today
The power of God to hold and lead,
His eye to watch, his might to save,
His ear to hearken to my need;

The wisdom of my God to teach,
His hand to guide, his shield to ward;
The word of God to give me speech,
His heav'nly host to be my guard.

Christ be with me, Christ within me,
Christ behind me, Christ before me,
Christ beside me, Christ to win me,
Christ to comfort and restore me,
Christ beneath me, Christ above me,
Christ in quiet, Christ in danger,
Christ in hearts of all that love me,
Christ in mouth of friend and stranger.

I bind unto myself the Name,
The strong Name of the Trinity;
By invocation of the same,
The Three in One, and One in Three.
Of whom all nature hath creation
Eternal Father, Spirit, Word:
Praise to the Lord of my salvation,
Salvation is of Christ the Lord. Amen.

MARTIN LUTHER'S
PREFACE TO THE BOOK OF ROMANS

Written in 1522, this material has been known throughout the years as Luther's Preface to the Book of Romans. *It is one of Luther's greatest performances. In a few pages, he sums up the theology of St. Paul, his own theology as a refor-*

mer of the church, and the very heart of the Christian Gospel. Note Luther's clear, accessible definitions of theological terms.

This Epistle is really the chief part of the New Testament and the very purest Gospel, and is worthy not only that every Christian should know it word for word, by heart, but occupy himself with it every day, as the daily bread of the soul. It can never be read or pondered too much, and the more it is dealt with the more precious it becomes, and the better it tastes.

Therefore, I, too, will do my best, so far as God has given me power, to open the way into it through this preface, so that it may be better understood by everyone. For heretofore it has been evilly darkened with commentaries and all kinds of idle talk, though it is, in itself, a bright light, almost enough to illumine all the Scripture.

To begin with, we must have knowledge of its language and know what St. Paul means by the words law, sin, grace, faith, righteousness, flesh, spirit, etc., otherwise no reading of it has any value.

The little word "law" you must not take here in human fashion, as a teaching about what works are to be done or not done. That is the way it is with human laws — the law is fulfilled by works, even though there is no heart in them.

The law is fulfilled by works

But God judges according to what is at the bottom of the heart, and for this reason, His law makes its demands on the inmost heart and cannot be satisfied with works, but rather punishes works that are done otherwise than from the bottom of the heart, as hypocrisy and lies. Hence all men are called liars, in Psalm 116, for the reason that no one keeps or can keep God's law from the bottom of the heart, for everyone finds in himself displeasure in what is good and pleasure in what is bad. If, then, there is no willing pleasure in the good, then the inmost heart is not set on the law of God, then there is surely sin, and God's wrath is deserved, even though outwardly there seem to be many good works and an honorable life.

Hence St. Paul concludes, in chapter 2, that the Jews are all sinners, and says that only the doers of the law are righteous before God. He means by this that no one is, in his works, a doer of the law; on the contrary, he speaks to them thus, "Thou teachest not to commit adultery, but thou committest adultery," and "Wherein thou judgest another, thou condemnest thyself, because thou doest the same thing that thou judges;" as if to say, "You live a fine outward life in the works of the law, and judge those who do not so live, and know how to teach everyone; you see the splinter in the other's eye, but of the beam in your own eye you are not aware."

"Of the beam in your own eye you are not aware"

For even though you keep the law outwardly, with works, from fear of punishment or love of reward, nevertheless, you do all this without willingness and pleasure, and without love for the law, but rather with unwillingness, under compulsion; and you would rather do otherwise, if the law were not there. The conclusion is that at the bottom of your heart you hate the law. What matter, then, that you teach others not to steal, if you are a thief at heart, and would gladly be one outwardly, if you dared? Though, to be sure, the outward work is not far behind such hypocrites! Thus you teach others, but not yourself; and you yourself know not what you teach, and have never yet rightly understood the law. Nay, the law increases sin, as he says in chapter 5, for the reason that the more the law demands what men cannot do, the more they hate the law.

For this reason he says, in chapter 7, "The law is spiritual." What is that? If the law were for the body, it could be satisfied with works; but since it is spiritual, no one can satisfy it, unless all that you do is done from the bottom of the heart. But such a heart is given only by God's Spirit, who makes a man equal to the law, so that he acquires a desire for the law in his heart, and henceforth does nothing out of fear and compulsion, but everything out of a willing heart. That law, then, is spiritual which will be loved and fulfilled with such a spiritual heart, and requires such a spirit. Where that spirit is not in the heart, there sin remains, and displeasure with the law, and enmity toward it; though the law is good and just and holy

Accustom yourself, then, to this language, and you will find that doing the works of the law and fulfilling the law are two very different things.

The work of the law is everything that one does, or can do, toward keeping the law of his own free will or by his own powers. But since under all these works and along with them there remains in the heart dislike for the law and the compulsion to keep it, these works are all wasted and have no value. That is what St. Paul means in chapter 3, when he says, "By the works of the law no man becomes righteous before God." Hence you see that the wranglers and sophists are deceivers, when they teach men to prepare themselves for grace by means of works. How can a man prepare himself for good by means of works, if he does no good works without displeasure and unwillingness of heart? How shall a work please God, if it proceeds from a reluctant and resisting heart?

Doing the works of the law and fulfilling the law are two very different things

To fulfil the law, however, is to do its works with pleasure and love, and to live a godly and good life of one's own accord, without the compulsion of the law. This pleasure and love for the law is put into the heart by the Holy Ghost, as he says in chapter 5. But the Holy Ghost is not given except in, with, and by faith in Jesus Christ, as he says in the introduction; and faith does not come, save only through God's Word or Gospel, which preaches Christ, that He is God's Son and a man, has died and risen again for our sakes, as he says in chapters 3, 4, and 10.

To fulfil the law is to do its works with pleasure and love

Hence it comes that faith alone makes righteous and fulfils the law; for out of Christ's merit, it brings the Spirit, and the Spirit makes the heart glad and free, as the law requires that it shall be. Thus good works come out of faith. That is what he means in chapter 3, after he has rejected the works of the law, so that it sounds as though he would abolish the law by faith; "Nay," he says, "we establish the law by faith," that is, we fulfil it by faith.

Sin, in the Scripture, means not only the outward works of the body, but all the activities that move men to the outward works, namely, the inmost heart, with all its powers. Thus the little word "do" ought to mean that a man falls all the way into sin and walks in sin. This is done by no outward work of sin, unless a man goes into sin altogether, body and soul. And the Scriptures look especially into the heart and have regard to the root and source of all sin, which is unbelief in the inmost heart. As, therefore, faith alone makes righteous and brings the spirit, and produces pleasure in good, eternal works, so unbelief alone commits sin, and brings up the flesh, and produces pleasure in bad external works, as happened to Adam and Eve in Paradise.

Faith alone produces pleasure in good, eternal works

Hence Christ calls unbelief the only sin, when He says, in John 16, "The Spirit will rebuke the world for sin, because they believe not on me." For this reason, too, before good or bad works are done, which are the fruits, there must first be in the heart faith or unbelief, which is the root, the sap, the chief power of all sin. And this is called in the Scriptures, the head of the Serpent and of the old dragon, which the seed of the woman, Christ, must tread under foot, as was promised to Adam, in Genesis 3.

Between grace and gift there is this difference. Grace means properly God's favor, or the good-will God bears us, by which He is disposed to give us Christ and to pour into us the Holy Ghost, with His gifts. This is clear from chapter 5, where He speaks of "the grace and gift in Christ." The gifts and the Spirit increase in us every day, though they are not yet perfect, and there remain in us the evil lust and sin that war against the Spirit, as Paul says in Romans 7 and Galatians 5, and the quarrel between the seed of the woman and the seed of the serpent is foretold in Genesis 3. Nevertheless, grace does so much that we are accounted wholly righteous before God. For His grace is not divided or broken up, as are the gifts, but it takes us entirely into favor, for the sake of Christ our Intercessor and Mediator, and because of that the gifts are begun in us.

Between grace and gift there is a difference

In this sense, then, you understand chapter 7, in which St. Paul still calls himself a sinner, and yet says, in chapter 8, that there is nothing con-demnable in those who are in Christ on account of the incompleteness of the gifts and of the Spirit. Because the flesh is not yet slain, we still are sinners; but because we believe and have a beginning of the Spirit, God is so favorable and gracious to us that He will not count the sin against us or judge us for it, but will deal with us according to our faith in Christ, until sin is slain.

Faith is not that human notion and dream that some hold for faith. Because they see that no betterment of life and no good works follow it, and yet they can hear and say much about faith, they fall into error, and say, "Faith is not enough; one must do works in order to be righteous and be saved." This is the reason that, when they hear the Gospel, they fall-to and make for themselves, by their own powers, an idea in their hearts, which says, "I believe." This they hold for true faith. But it is a human imagination and idea that never reaches the depths of the heart, and so nothing comes of it and no betterment follows it.

Faith, however, is a divine work in us. It changes us and makes us to be born anew of God (John 1); it kills the old Adam and makes altogether different men, in heart and spirit and mind and powers, and it brings with it the Holy Ghost. Oh, it is a living, busy, active, mighty thing, this faith; and so it is impossible for it not to do good works incessantly. It does not ask whether there are good works to do, but before the question rises; it has already done them, and is always at the doing of them. He who does not these works is a faithless man. He gropes and looks about after faith and good works, and knows neither what faith is nor what good works are, though he talks and talks, with many words, about faith and good works.

Oh, it is a living, busy, active, mighty thing, this faith

Faith is a living, daring confidence in God's grace, so sure and certain that a man would stake his life on it a thousand times. This confidence in God's grace and knowledge of it makes men glad and bold and happy in dealing with God and all His creatures; and this is the work of the Holy Ghost in faith. Hence a man is ready and glad, without compulsion, to do good to everyone, to serve everyone, to suffer everything, in love and praise to God, who has shown him this grace; and thus it is impossible to separate works from faith, quite as impossible as to separate heat and light fires. Beware, therefore, of your own false notions and of the idle talkers, who would be wise enough to make decisions about faith and good works, and yet are the greatest fools. Pray God to work faith in you; else you will remain forever without faith, whatever you think or do.

Pray God to work faith in you

Righteousness, then, is such a faith and is called "God's righteousness," or "the righteousness that avails before God," because God gives it and counts it as righteousness for the sake of Christ, our Mediator, and makes a man give to every man what he owes him. For through faith a man becomes sinless and comes to take pleasure in God's commandments; thus he gives to God the honor that is His and pays Him what he owes Him; but he also serves man willingly, by whatever means he can, and thus pays his debt to everyone. Such righteousness, nature and free will and all our powers cannot bring into existence. No one can give himself faith, and no more can he take away his own unbelief; how, then, will he take away a single sin, even the very smallest? Therefore, all that is done apart from faith or in unbelief, is false; it is hypocrisy and sin, no matter how good a show it makes (Romans 14).

You must not so understand flesh and spirit as to think that flesh has to do only with unchastity and spirit only with what is inward, in the heart; but Paul, like Christ in John 3, calls "flesh" everything that is born of the flesh; viz., the whole man, with body and soul, mind and senses, because everything about him longs for the flesh. Thus you should learn to call him "fleshly" who thinks, teaches, and talks a great deal about high spiritual matters, but without grace. From the "works of the flesh" in Galatians 5, you can learn that Paul calls heresy and hatred "works of the flesh," and in Romans 8 he says that "the law was weak through the flesh," and this does not refer to unchastity, but to all sins, above all to unbelief, which is the most spiritual of all vices. On the other hand, he calls him a spiritual man who is occupied with the most external kind of works, as Christ, when He washed the disciples' feet, and Peter, when he steered his boat, and fished. Thus "the flesh" is a man who lives and works, inwardly and outwardly, in the service of the flesh's profit and of this temporal life; "the spirit" is the man who lives and works, inwardly and outwardly, in the service of the Spirit and the future life.

Paul calls heresy and hatred "works of the flesh"

Without such an understanding of these words, you will never understand this letter of St. Paul, or any other book of Holy Scripture. Therefore, beware of all teachers who use these words in a different sense, no matter who they are, even Jerome, Augustine, Ambrose, Origen, and men like them, or above them. Now we will take up the Epistle.

Beware of all teachers who use these words in a different sense

It is right for a preacher of the Gospel first, by a revelation of the law and of sin, to rebuke everything and make sin of everything that is not the living fruit of the Spirit and of faith in Christ, so that men may be led to know themselves and their own wretchedness, and become humble and ask for help. That is what St. Paul does. He begins in Chapter 1 and rebukes the gross sin and unbelief that are plainly evident, as the sins of the heathen, who live without God's grace, were and still are. He says: The wrath of God is revealed from heaven through the Gospel, upon all men because of their godless lives and their unrighteousness. For even though they know and daily recognize that there is a God, nevertheless, nature itself, without grace, is so bad that it neither thanks nor honors Him, but blinds itself, and goes continually from bad to worse, until at last, after idolatry, it commits the most shameful sins, with all the vices, and is not ashamed, and allows others to do these things unrebuked.

In chapter 2, he stretches this rebuke still farther and extends it to those who seem outwardly to be righteous, but commit sin in secret. Such were the Jews and such are all the hypocrites, who, without desire or love for the law of God, lead good lives, but hate God's law in their hearts, and yet are prone to judge other people. It is the nature of all the hypocrites to think themselves pure, and yet be full of covetousness, hatred, pride, and all uncleanness (Matthew 23). These are they who despise God's goodness and in their hardness heap wrath upon themselves. Thus St. Paul, as a true interpreter of the law, leaves no one without sin, but proclaims the wrath of God upon all who live good lives from nature or free will, and makes them appear no better than open sinners; indeed, he says that they are hardened and unrepentant.

In chapter 3, he puts them all together in a heap and says that one is like the other; they are all sinners before God, except that the Jews have had God's Word. Not many have believed on it, to be sure, but that does not mean that the faith and truth of God are exhausted; and he quotes a saying from Psalm 51, that God remains righteous in His words. Afterwards he comes back to this again and proves by Scripture that they are **By the works of the law no man is justified** all sinners and that by the works of the law no man is justified, but that the law was given only that sin might be known.

Then he begins to teach the right way by which men must be justified and saved, and says they are all sinners and without praise from God, but they must be justified, without merit, through faith in Christ, who has earned this for us by His blood, and has been made for us a mercyseat by God, Who forgives us all former sins, proving thereby that we were aided only by His righteousness, which He gives in faith, which is revealed in this time through the Gospel and "testified before by the law and the prophets." Thus the law is set up by faith, though the works of the law are put down by it, together with the reputation that they give.

After the first three chapters, in which sin is revealed and faith's way to righteousness is taught, he begins, in chapter 4, to meet certain objections. And first he takes up the one that all men commonly make when they hear of faith, that it justifies, without works. They say, "Are men, then, to do no good works?" Therefore he himself takes up the case of Abraham, and asks, "What did Abraham accomplish, then, with his good works? Were they all in vain? Were his works of no use?" He concludes that Abraham was justified by faith alone, without any works; nay, the Scriptures, in Genesis 15, declare that he was justified by faith alone, even before the work of circumcision. But if the work of circumcision contributed nothing to his righteousness, though God commanded it and it was a good work of obedience; then, surely, no other good work will contribute anything to righteousness. On the other hand, if Abraham's circumcision was an external

"Are men, then, to do no good works?"

sign by which he showed the righteousness that was already his in faith, then all good works are only external signs which follow out of faith, and show, like good fruit, that man is already inwardly righteous before God.

With this powerful illustration, out of the Scriptures, St. Paul establishes the doctrine of faith which he had taught before in chapter 3. He also brings forward another witness, viz., David, in Psalm 32, who says that a man is justified without works, although he does not remain without works when he has been justified. Then he gives the illustration a broader application, and concludes that the Jews cannot be Abraham's heirs merely because of their blood, still less because of the works of the law, but must be heirs of Abraham's faith, if they would be true heirs. For before the law — either the law of Moses or the law of circumcision — Abraham was justified by faith and called the father of believers; moreover, the law works wrath rather than grace, because no one keeps it out of love for it and pleasure in it, so that what comes by the works of the law is **Faith alone** disgrace rather than grace. Therefore, faith alone **must obtain** must obtain the grace promised to Abraham, for **the grace** **promised to** these examples were written for our sakes, that **Abraham** we, too, should believe.

In chapter 5, he comes to the fruits and works of faith, such as peace, joy, love to God and to every man, and confidence, boldness, joy, courage, and hope in tribulation and suffering. For all this follows, if faith be true, because of the over-abundant goodness that God shows us in Christ, so that He caused Him to die for us before we could ask it, nay, while we were still His enemies. Thus we have it that faith justifies without any works; and yet it does not follow that men are, therefore, to do no good works, but rather that the true works will not be absent. Of these the work-righteous saints know nothing, but feign works of their own in which there is no peace, joy, confidence, love, hope, boldness, nor any of the qualities of true Christian works and faith.

After this, he breaks out, and makes a pleasant excursion, and tells whence come both sin and righteousness, death and life, and compares Adam and Christ. He says that Christ had to come, a second Adam, to bequeath His righteousness to us through a new spiritual birth in faith, as the first Adam bequeathed sin to us, through the old, fleshly birth. Thus he declares, and confirms it, that no one, by his own works, can help himself out of sin into righteousness, any more than he can prevent the birth of his own body. This is proved by the fact that the divine law — which ought to help to righteousness, if anything can — has not only helped, but has even increased sin; for the reason that the more the law forbids, the more our evil nature hates it, and the more it wants to give rein to its own lust. Thus the law makes Christ all the more necessary, and more grace is needed to help our nature.

The law makes Christ all the more necessary

In chapter 6, he takes up the special work of faith, the conflict of the spirit with the flesh, for the complete slaying of the sin and lust that remains after we are justified. He teaches us that by faith we are not so freed from sin that we can be idle, slack, and careless, as though there were no longer any sin in us. There is sin; but it is no longer counted for condemnation, because of the faith that strives against it. Therefore we have enough to do all our life long in taming the body, slaying its lusts, and compelling its members to obey the spirit and not the lusts, thus making our lives like the death and resurrection of Christ and completing our baptism — which signifies the death of sin and the new life of grace — until we are entirely pure of sins, and even our bodies rise again with Christ and live forever

The conflict of the spirit with the flesh

And that we can do, he says, because we are in grace and not in the law. He himself explains that to mean that to be without the law is not the same thing as to have no laws and be able to do what one pleases; but we are under the law when, without grace, we occupy ourselves in the work of the law. Then sin assuredly rules by the law, for no one loves the law by nature; and that is great sin. Grace, however, makes the law dear to us, and then sin is no more there, and the law is no longer against us, but with us.

This is the true freedom from sin and the law, of which he writes, down to the end of this chapter, saying that it is liberty only, to do good with pleasure and live a good life without the compulsion of the law. Therefore this liberty is a spiritual liberty, which does not abolish the law, but presents what the law demands; namely, pleasure and love. Thus the law is quieted and no longer drives men or makes demands of them. It is just as if you owed a debt to your overlord and could not pay it. There are two ways in which you could rid yourself of the debt — either he would take nothing from you and would tear up the account; or some good man would pay it for you, and give you the means to satisfy the account. It is this latter way that Christ has made us free from the law. Our liberty is, therefore, no fleshly liberty, which is not obligated to do anything, but a liberty that does many works of all kinds, and thus is free from the demands and the debts of the law.

In chapter 7, he supports this with a parable of the married life. When a man dies, his wife is single, and thus the one is released from the other; not that the wife cannot or ought not to take another husband, but rather that she is now really free to take another, which she could not do before she was free from her husband. So our conscience is bound to the law, under the old man; when he is slain by the Spirit, then the conscience is free; the one is released from the other; not that the conscience is to do nothing, but rather that it is now really free to cleave to Christ, the second husband, and bring forth the fruit of life.

Then he sketches out more broadly the nature

A parable of the married life

of sin and the law, showing how, by means of the law sin now moves and is mighty. The old man hates the law the more because he cannot pay what the law demands, for sin is his nature and by himself he can do nothing but sin; therefore the law is death to him, and torment. Not that the law is bad, but his evil nature cannot endure the good, and the law demands good of him. So a sick man cannot endure it when he is required to run and jump and do the works of a well man.

Therefore St. Paul here concludes that the law, rightly understood and thoroughly comprehended, does nothing more than remind us of our sin and slay us by it, and make us liable to eternal wrath; and all this is taught and experienced by our conscience, when it is really smitten by the law. Therefore a man must have something else than the law, and more than the law, to make him righteous and save him. But they who do not rightly understand the law are blind; they go ahead, in their presumption, and think to satisfy the law with their works, not knowing what the law demands, viz., a willing and happy heart. Therefore they do not see Moses clearly, the veil is put between them and him, and covers him

They who do not rightly understand the law are blind

Then he shows how spirit and flesh strive with one another in a man. He uses himself as an example, in order that we may learn rightly to understand the work of slaying sin within us. He calls both spirit and flesh "laws," for just as it is the nature of the divine law to drive men and make demands of them, so the flesh drives men and makes demands and rages against the spirit, and will have its own way. The spirit, too, drives men and makes demands contrary to the flesh, and will have its own way. This contention within us lasts as long as we live, though in one man it is greater, in another less, according as spirit or flesh is stronger. Nevertheless, the whole man is both spirit and flesh and he fights with himself until he becomes wholly spiritual.

In chapter 8, he encourages these fighters, telling them not to condemn the flesh; and he shows further what the nature of flesh and spirit is, and how the spirit comes from Christ, who has given us His Holy Spirit to make us spiritual and subdue the flesh. He assures us that we are still God's children, however hard sin may rage within us, so long as we follow the Spirit and resist sin, **We are still God's children** to slay it. Since, however, nothing else is so good for the mortifying of the flesh as the cross and suffering, he comforts us in suffering with the support of the Spirit of love, and of the whole creation. For the Spirit sighs within us and the creation longs with us that we may be rid of the flesh and of sin. So we see that these three chapters (6–8) deal with the one work of faith, which is to slay the old Adam and subdue the flesh.

In chapters 9, 10, and 11, he teaches concerning God's eternal predestination, from which it originally comes that one believes or not, is rid of sin or not rid of it. Thus our becoming righteous is taken entirely out of our hands and put in the hand of God. And that is most highly necessary. We are so weak and uncertain that, if it were in our power, surely not one man would be saved, the devil would surely overpower us all; but since God is certain, and His predestination cannot fail, and no one can withstand Him, we still have hope against sin.

And here we must set a boundary for those audacious and high-climbing spirits, who first bring their own thinking to this matter and begin at the top to search the abyss of divine predestination, and worry in vain about whether they are predestinate. They must have a fall; either they will despair, or else they will take long risks.

But do you follow the order of this Epistle? Worry first about Christ and the Gospel, that you may recognize your sin and His grace; then fight your sin, as the first eight chapters here have taught; then, when you have reached the eighth chapter, and are under the cross and suffering, that will teach you the right doctrine of predestination, in the ninth, tenth, and eleventh chapters, and how comforting it is. For in the absence of suffering and the cross and the danger of death, one cannot deal with predestination without harm and without secret wrath against God. The old **Beware not** Adam must die before he can endure this subject **to drink** and drink the strong wine of it. Therefore beware **wine when** not to drink wine while you are still a suckling. **you are still** **a suckling** There is a limit, a time, an age for every doctrine.

In chapter 12, he teaches what true worship is; and he makes us all Christian priests, who are to offer not money and cattle, as under the law, but their own bodies, with a slaying of the lusts. Then he describes the outward conduct of Christians, under spiritual government, telling how they are to teach, preach, rule, serve, give, suffer, love, live, and act toward friend, foe and all men. These are the works that a Christian does; for, as has been said, faith takes no holidays.

Faith takes no holidays

In chapter 13, he teaches honor and obedience to worldly government, which accomplishes much, although it does not make its people righteous before God. It is instituted in order that the good may have outward peace and protection, and that the wicked may not be free to do evil, without fear, in peace and quietness. Therefore the righteous are to honor it, though they do not need it. In the end he comprises it all in love, and includes it in the example of Christ, who has done for us what we are also to do, following in His footsteps

In chapter 14, he teaches that weak consciences are to be led gently in faith and to be spared, so that Christians are not to use their liberty for doing harm, but for the furtherance of the weak. If that is not done, then discord follows, and contempt for the Gospel; and the Gospel is the all-important thing. Thus it is better to yield a little to the weak in faith, until they grow stronger, than to have the doctrine of the Gospel come to nought. This is a peculiar work of love, for which there is great need even now, when with meat-eating and other liberties, men are rudely and roughly shaking weak consciences, before they know the truth. In chapter 15, he sets up the example of Christ, to show that we are to suffer those who are weak in other ways — those whose weakness lies in open sins or in unpleasing habits. These men are not to be cast off, but borne with till they grow better. For so Christ has **Christ bears** done to us, and still does every day; He bears **with our** with our many faults and bad habits, and with all **many faults** **and bad** our imperfections, and helps us constantly. **habits**

Then, at the end, he prays for them, praises them and commends them to God; he speaks of his office and his preaching, and asks them gently for a contribution to the poor at Jerusalem; all that he speaks of or deals with is pure love.

The last chapter is a chapter of greetings, but he mingles with them a noble warning against doctrines of men, which are put in alongside the doctrine of the Gospel and cause offense. It is as though he had foreseen that out of Rome and through the Romans would come the seductive and offensive canons and decretals and the whole squirming mass of human law and command-ments which have now drowned the whole world and wiped out this Epistle and all the Holy Scriptures, along with the Spirit and with faith, so that nothing has remained there except the idol, Belly, whose servants St. Paul here rebukes. God release us from them. Amen.

Thus in this Epistle we find most richly the things that a Christian ought to know; namely, what is law, Gospel, sin, punishment, grace, faith, righteousness, Christ, God, good works, love, hope, the cross, and also how we are to conduct ourselves toward everyone, whether righteous or sinner, strong or weak, friend or foe. All this is ably founded on Scripture and proved by his own example and that of the prophets. Therefore it appears that St. Paul wanted to comprise briefly in this one Epistle the whole Christian and evangelical doctrine and to prepare an introduction to the entire Old Testament; for, without doubt, he who has this Epistle well in his heart, has the light and power of the Old Testament with him. Therefore let every Christian exercise himself in it habitually and continually. To this may God give His grace. Amen.

The whole Christian and evangelical doctrine

THOMAS CRANMER'S COMMUNION PRAYERS

Cranmer prepared these prayers for the first Book of Common Prayer (1549). Like the other documents in this section, the prayers are the distillation of a great mind's engagement with Bible Christianity. They survive today in some forms of the Anglican liturgy, although they have been watered down in most.

Almighty God,
Father of our Lord Jesus Christ,

Maker of all things, Judge of all men;
We acknowledge and bewail our manifold
    sins and wickedness,
Which we, from time to time, most grievous-
    ly have committed,
By thought, word, and deed,
Against thy Divine Majesty,
Provoking most justly thy wrath and indigna-
    tion against us.
We do earnestly repent,
And are heartily sorry for these our misdo-
    ings;
The remembrance of them is grievous unto
    us;
The burden of them is intolerable.
Have mercy upon us,
Have mercy upon us, most merciful Father;
For thy Son our Lord Jesus Christ's sake,
Forgive us all that is past;
And grant that we may ever hereafter
Serve and please thee in newness of life,
To the honour and glory of thy Name;
Through Jesus Christ our Lord. Amen.

We do not presume to come to this thy Table, O
merciful Lord, trusting in our own righteousness,
but in thy manifold and great mercies. We are not
worthy so much as to gather up the crumbs under
thy Table. But thou art the same Lord, whose
property is always to have mercy. Grant us therefore, gracious Lord, so to eat the flesh of thy dear

Son Jesus Christ, and to drink his blood, that our sinful bodies may be made clean by his body, and our souls washed through his most precious blood, and that we may evermore dwell in him, and he in us. Amen.

All glory be to thee, Almighty God, our heavenly Father, for that thou, of thy tender mercy, didst give thine only Son Jesus Christ to suffer death upon the Cross for our redemption; who made there (by his one oblation of himself once offered) a full, perfect, and sufficient sacrifice, oblation, and satisfaction, for the sins of the whole world; and did institute, and in his holy Gospel command us to continue, a perpetual memory of that his precious death and sacrifice, until his coming again: For in the night in which he was betrayed, he took Bread; and when he had given thanks, he brake it, and gave it to his disciples, saying, Take, eat, this is my Body, which is given for you; Do this in remembrance of me. Likewise, after supper, he took the Cup; and when he had given thanks, he gave it to them, saying, Drink ye all of this; for this is my Blood of the New Testament, which is shed for you, and for many, for the remission of sins; Do this, as oft as ye shall drink it, in remembrance of me

HYMNS OF WILLIAM COWPER AND ISAAC WATTS

William Cowper (1731–1800) was an evangeli-

cal Anglican. Isaac Watts (1674–1748) was an English nonconformist, which means a non-Anglican Protestant. Both wrote hymn texts in what is now called the "plain style" — that is, with very few words of more than two syllables. The hymns printed here have never been bettered. Unfortunately, "there is a fountain fill'd with blood" is regarded by most mainline Protestant denominations today as too vivid or heavy. Their loss!

"Praise for the Fountain Opened"

There is a fountain fill'd with blood
Drawn from Emmanuel's veins;
And sinners, plunged beneath that flood,
Lose all their guilty stains.

The dying thief rejoiced to see
That fountain in his day;
And there have I, as vile as he,
Washed all my sins away.

Dear dying Lamb, thy precious blood
Shall never lose its power;
Till all the ransomed church of God
Be saved, to sin no more.

E'er since, by faith, I saw the stream
Thy flowing wounds supply:

Redeeming love has been my theme,
And shall be till I die.

Then in a nobler sweeter song
I'll sing thy power to save;
When this poor lisping stammering tongue
Lies silent in the grave.
Lord, I believe thou hast prepared
(Unworthy tho' I be)
For me a blood-bought free reward,
A golden harp for me!

'Tis strung, and tuned, for endless years,
And formed by power divine;
To sound, in God the Father's ears,
No other name but thine.

William Cowper

"LOVE CONSTRAINING TO OBEDIENCE"

No strength of Nature can suffice
To serve the Lord aright;
And what she has she misapplies,
For want of clearer light.

How long beneath the Law I lay
In bondage and distress;
I toiled the precept to obey
But toiled without success

Then to abstain from outward sin
Was more than I could do;

Now, if I feel its power within,
I feel I hate it too.

Then all my servile works were done
A righteousness to raise;
Now, freely chosen in the Son,
I freely choose His ways.
'What shall I do,' was then the word
'That I may worthier grow?'
'What shall I render to the Lord?'
Is my inquiry now.

To see the law by Christ fulfilled,
And hear His pardoning voice,
Changes a slave into a child,
And duty into choice.

William Cowper

"CRUCIFIXION TO THE WORLD BY THE CROSS OF CHRIST"

When I survey the wondrous Cross
Where the young Prince of Glory died,
My richest gain I count but loss,
And pour contempt on all my pride.

Forbid it, Lord, that I should boast,
Save in the death of Christ, my God;
All the vain things that charm me most,
I sacrifice them to his blood.

See, from his head, his hands, his feet,
Sorrow and love flow mingled down;
Did e'er such love and sorrow meet?
Or thorns compose so rich a crown?

His dying crimson like a robe
Spreads o'er his body on the Tree,
Then am I dead to all the globe,
And all the globe is dead to me.

Were the whole realm of nature mine,
That were a present far too small
Love so amazing, so divine,
Demands my soul, my life, my all.

Isaac Watts

"MAN FRAIL, AND GOD ETERNAL"

O God, our help in ages past,
Our hope for years to come,
Our shelter from the stormy blast,
And our eternal home.

Under the shadow of thy throne
Thy saints have dwelt secure;
Sufficient is thine arm alone,
And our defence is sure.

Before the hills in order stood,
Or earth receiv'd her frame,
From everlasting thou art God,
To endless years the same.

Thy word commands our flesh to dust,
'Return, ye sons of men':
All nations rose from earth at first,
And turn to earth again.

A thousand ages in thy sight
Are like an evening gone;
Short as the watch that ends the night
Before the rising sun.

The busy tribes of flesh and blood,
With all their lives and cares,
Are carried downwards by thy flood,
And lost in following years.

Time like an ever-rolling stream
Bears all its sons away;
They fly forgotten as a dream
Dies at the opening day.

Like flowering fields the nations stand
Pleas'd with the morning light;
The flowers beneath the mower's hand
Lie withering ere 'tis night.

Our God, our help in ages past,
Our hope for years to come,
Be thou our guard while troubles last,
And our eternal home.

Isaac Watts

JOHN WESLEY'S CONVERSION

This original account of John Wesley's conversion was recorded in his journal after it happened on May 24, 1738. It is the charter document of the Methodist church.

Wednesday, 24 May — In the evening I went very unwillingly to a society in Aldersgate Street, where one was reading Luther's preface to the Epistle to the Romans. About a quarter before nine, while he was describing the change which God works in the heart through faith in Christ, I felt my heart strangely warmed. I felt I did trust in Christ, Christ alone, for salvation; and an assurance was given me that He had taken away my sins, even mine, and saved me from the law of sin and death.

I felt my heart strangely warmed

I began to pray with all my might for those who had in a more especial manner despitefully used me and persecuted me. I then testified openly to all there what I now first felt in my heart. But it was not long before the enemy suggested, "This cannot be faith; for where is thy joy?" Then was I taught that peace and victory over sin are essential to faith in the Captain of our salvation; but that, as to the transports of joy that usually attend the beginning of it, especially in those who have mourned deeply, God sometimes giveth, sometimes withholdeth, them according to the counsels of His own will.

After my return home, I was much buffeted with temptations, but I cried out, and they fled away. They returned again and again. I as often lifted up my eyes, and He "sent me help from his holy place." And herein I found the difference between this and my former state chiefly consisted. I was striving, yea, fighting with all my might under the law, as well as under grace. But then I was sometimes, if not often, conquered; now, I was always conqueror.

Now, I was always conqueror

Thursday, 25 — The moment I awakened, "Jesus, Master," was in my heart and in my mouth; and I found all my strength lay in keeping my eye fixed upon Him and my soul waiting on Him continually. Being again at St. Paul's in the afternoon, I could taste the good word of God in the anthem which began, "My song shall be always of the loving-kindness of the Lord: with my mouth will I ever be showing forth thy truth from one generation to another." Yet the enemy injected a fear, "If thou dost believe, why is there not a more sensible change?" I answered (yet not I), "That I know not. But, this I know, I have 'now peace with God.' And I sin not today, and Jesus my Master has forbidden me to take thought for the morrow."

NEGRO SPIRITUALS

Like the simple but dense hymns of William Cowper and Isaac Watts, Negro spirituals, as they are properly called, have never been im-

proved on. They emerged during the period of slavery and perfectly capture the attraction of the compassionate Christ for sufferers of all places and times.

"He Never Said a Mumblin' Word"

They led Him to Pilate's bar
Not a word, not a word, not a word, not a word
They led Him to Pilate's bar
Not a word, not a word, not a word, not a word
They led Him to Pilate's bar
But He never said a mumblin' word
Not a word, not a word, not a word, not a word

They all cried, "Crucify Him" . . .

They nailed Him to the tree . . .
They pierced Him in the side . . .

He hung His head and died . . .

Wasn't that a pity and a shame . . .

"Nobody Knows"

Nobody knows the trouble I've seen.
Nobody knows but Jesus.
Nobody knows the trouble I've seen.
Glory Hallelujah!

Sometime I'm up, sometimes I'm down,
Oh, yes, Lord,

Sometimes I'm almost to the ground,
Oh, yes, Lord.
[Refrain]

I never shall forget that day,
Oh, yes, Lord,
When Jesus washed my sins away,
Oh, yes, Lord.
[Refrain]

"STEAL AWAY"

Steal away, steal away, steal away to Jesus!
Steal away, steal away home,
I ain't got long to stay here.

My Lord, He calls me,
He calls me by the thunder;
The trumpet sounds within my soul,
I ain't got long to stay here.
[Refrain]

Green trees are bending,
Poor sinners stand a-trembling;
The trumpet sounds within my soul,
I ain't got long to stay here.
[Refrain]

My Lord, He calls me,
He calls me by the lightning;
The trumpet sounds within my soul,
I ain't got long to stay here.
[Refrain]

JOHN DAVENPORT'S CREED

The creed that follows is an early example of an American Christian statement of doctrine. It is Puritan yet also catholic, in the true sense of the word. In other words, it is purely orthodox and could be signed by almost any believer anywhere.

The prime figure in the settlement of the New Haven Colony was the Reverend John Davenport (1597–1670). The son of a Coventry alderman, he attended Oxford University but did not remain to graduate, although in 1625, owing to an exhibition of his forensic prowess at that institution, he was awarded a B.D. From November 3, 1624, until about December 3, 1633, he served as vicar at St. Stephen's Church on Coleman Street in London. After William Laud became the archbishop of Canterbury (1633), Davenport withdrew from St. Stephen's. After a stormy experience in the Netherlands, he and a group of his former London parishioners, including the able Theophilus Eaton, boarded the ship Hector *for New England. Arriving at Boston on June 26, 1637, the emigrants were welcomed cordially by the Bay Colony leaders. After a fruitless search for a suitable site in that colony, they traveled southward, reaching their final destination in April 1638. They first called their colony Quinnipiac, but in 1640 they changed its name to New Haven.*

In August 1639, the settlers "gathered" a

church in accordance with the pattern of Congregational Puritanism and called Davenport as their pastor. It is believed that when he was admitted to membership in this church, he submitted as his creed the document that is here reproduced in its entirety. This creed, which was first published in London in 1642, embraces the basic theology and ecclesiology of the first New Englanders. Evidently, John Cotton regarded the document as a representative summary of the New England Way (the approach of New England Christians to church governance) because it was republished in full in the appendix of his Covenant of God's Free Grace (1645)

I believe with all my heart, and confesse with my mouth:

1. Concerning the Scriptures.

That all Scripture is by divine inspiration, or inbreathing of God (by Scripture I mean, the Books of the old Testament, as Moses and the Prophets, and of the new Testament) and is profitable for doctrine, for reproof, for correction, for instruction in righteousness, that the man of God may be perfect, throughly furnished unto all good works, I Tim. i. 16, 17. and that in all things which concern faith and obedience, whether in Gods Worship, or in the whole conversation of men, it holdeth forth a most perfect rule, whereunto nothing may be added, nor from it may ought be diminished, Deut. A. 2. Rev. t. 18, 19.

Which also is so clear in truths necessary to salvation, that the entrance into it giveth light, yea, understanding to the simple, Psal. 19. 7.

2. Concerning the Godhead in the Unity of Essense and Trinity of Persons.

That God is a Spirit most holy, immutable, eternall, every way infinite, in greatnesse, goodnesse, power, wisdome, justice, truth, and in all divine perfections, I Tim. 6. 15, 16. Job. 4. 24. Isai. 6. 6. Exod. 34. 6, 7. And that in this Godhead, are three distinct Persons, coeternall, coequall, and co-essentiall, being every one of them one and the same God, not three Gods, and therefore not divided in essence, nature, or being, Deut. 4. 3. but distinguished one from another, by their severall and peculiar relative property; the Father is of none but of himself, the Son is begotten of the Father before all worlds, the Holy Ghost proceedeth from the Father and the Son, from all eternity, all together are to be worshipped and glorified.

3. Concerning the Decrees of God.

That God hath unchangeably decreed in himself from everlasting, touching all things, great and small, necessary, contingent, and voluntary, with all the circumstances of them, to work, and dispose them according to the counsell of his own will (yet without being Author of, or having fellowship with the sins of any) to the praise and glory of his great name. And touching the eternall estate of men, that God hath according to his most wise, free, and unchangeable purpose in himself, before the foundation of the world, chosen some in Jesus Christ to eternall life, to the praise and glory of his grace, and rejected or reprobated others to the praise of his justice.

4. Concerning Creation and Providence.

That in the beginning God made by his Word all things of nothing very good, and made man, male and female, after his own Image righteous; and as a faithfull Creator doth still uphold, dispose, and govern all things to the ends for which they were created, having care especially for man, and amongst men, chiefly for the righteous and believers; so that neither good nor evill befalls any man without Gods providence.

5. Concerning the fall of man, and originall sin.

That in as much as Adam was the root of all mankind, the Law and Covenant of works was given to him, as to a publike person, and to an head from whence all good or evill was to be derived to his posterity: Seeing therefore that by the subtilty of the Serpent, which Satan used as his Instrument, first Eve, then Adam being seduced, did wittingly and willingly fall into the disobedience of the Commandment of God; Death came upon all justly, and reigned over all, yea, over Infants also which have not sinned after the like manner of the transgression of Adam: Hence also it is, that all since the fall of Adam, are begotten in his own likenesse, after his Image, being conceived and born in iniquity, and so by nature children of wrath, dead in trespasses and sins, altogether filthy and polluted throughout in soule and body; utterly averse from any spirituall good, strongly bent to all evill, and subject to all calamities due to sin in this world, and for ever.

6. Concerning mans restitution.

That all mankind being thus fallen, yet the elect, and only they, are redeemed, reconciled to God, and saved, not of themselves, neither by their own works, but only by the mighty power of God, of his unsearchable, rich, free grace and mercy, through faith in Jesus Christ, who of God is made unto us wisdom, righteousness, sanctification, and redemption; in the relation both of a surety to satisfie God's justice for us, and of an head to restore the Image of God that was lost, and repair the nature that was corrupted in us.

7. Concerning the Person and Natures in Christ.

That the Lord Jesus, of whom Moses and the Prophets wrote, and whom the Apostles preached, is, as touching his Person, the everlasting Son of God the Father, by eternall generation, coessentiall, coequall, and co-eternall, God with him, and with the Holy Ghost; by whom he made the world, and by whom hee upholdeth and governs all the works he hath made: who also, when the fulnesse of time was come, was made of a woman, of the Tribe of Judah, of the seed of David and Abraham, viz. of Mary, that blessed Virgin, by the Holy Ghost coming upon her, and the power of the most high overshadowing her; and was in all things like unto us, sin only excepted; so that in the person of Christ, the two natures, the divine and humane, are truly, perfectly, indivisibly, and distinctly united.

8. Concerning the Offices of Christ.

That Jesus Christ is the only Mediatour of the new Testament, even of the Covenant of Grace between God and man; the Prophet, Priest, and King of the Church of God for evermore; and this office is so proper to Christ, as, neither in the whole, nor any part thereof, it can be transferred from him to any other. And to this office hee was from everlasting, and in respect of his Manhood, from the womb, called, separated, and anointed most fully with all necessary gifts, as it is written, God hath not measured out of the Spirit unto him.

9. Concerning Christs propheticall Office.

That Christ hath perfectly revealed the whole will of God, so far as it is needfull for his people, either joyntly, or severally to know, believe, or obey, and that he hath spoken, and doth speak to his church, in his own Ordinances by those instruments whom hee sendeth, and by his Spirit.

10. Concerning the Priesthood of Christ.

That Christ being consecrated, hath appeared once to put away sin, by the offering and sacrificing of himself, and hath fully performed and suffered all those things, by which God through the blood of his crosse, in a sacrifice of a sweet smelling savor, might be reconciled to his elect; and having broken down the partition wall, and finished and removed those ceremoniall rites and shadowes, is now entred into the most holy place (not made with hands), to the very heavens and presence of God, where he for ever liveth, and sitteth at the right hand of Majesty, to make intercession for such as come unto the Throne of Grace by that new and living way; and he maketh his people a spirituall house, and an holy Priesthood to offer up spirituall sacrifices acceptable to God through him.

11. Concerning Christs Kingly Office: i. In generall.

That Christ being risen from the dead, ascended up to heaven, set at the right hand of God the Father, hath all power in heaven and earth given to him, and doth exercise his power in his government of this world over all Angels and men, good and bad, to the preservation and salvation of his elect, and to the ruling and destruction of the reprobate; communicating and applying to his elect, the benefits, vertue, and fruit of his prophecie, and priesthood to their regeneration, justification, sanctification, preservation, and strengthening in all their spirituall conflicts against Satan, the world and the flesh, continually dwelling in them by his holy Spirit, begetting and nourishing in them faith, hope, love, repentance, obedience, with peace and joy unto immortality: but on the contrary, limiting, using, restraining the reprobates his enemies, by his mighty power, as seemeth good in his divine wisdome and justice, to their seduction, hardening and condemnation, till his appearing in glory with his mighty Angels to judge both quick and dead; where he will be, and separate all his elect from them for ever, punishing the wicked with everlasting perdition from his presence; and joyning together the godly with himself in endlesse glory.

12. Concerning his Kingdoms: II. In speciall.

That in the mean time, besides his absolute rule in the world, Christ hath here on earth, a spirituall Kingdome in his Church, which hee hath purchased and redeemed to himself as a peculiar inheritance, into the body whereof he doth by the power of his Word, and Spirit, gather his people, calling them through the Ministery of the Gospel out of the world, and from Idolatry, superstition, and from all works of darknesse to fellowship with Jesus Christ, and by him with the Father, and the Holy Ghost, and with his people, making them a royall Priesthood, an holy nation, a people set at liberty, to shew forth the vertues of him that hath called them out of darkness into his marvellous light, and uniteth them together as members of one body in his faith, love, and holy order unto all generall and mutuall duties: and instructs and governs them by those instruments and ordinances which he himself hath prescribed in his word for the edification of his body the Church.

13. Concerning the Application of Redemption.

That the Holy Ghost is sent by the Father and the Son to make application of Redemption only to those whom the Father hath by his eternall Decree given to Christ, and for whom Christ maketh intercession to his Father, and whom the Father accepts in Christ unto fellowship of the everlasting Covenant of his free Grace, having called them out of the world to fellowship with Jesus Christ by the Gospel, made effectually to that end, by the mighty power and operation of the Holy Ghost. Which grace of effectuall calling is thus dispensed to a poor lost sinner, awakened and humbled by the Law through the effectuall working of the spirit of bondage, judging himself worthy to be destroyed for his sins; and seeing himself utterly destitute of all help or hope of himself: The Lord, in the preaching of the Gospel by the powerfull work of the Holy Ghost, revealeth the fulnesse of all-sufficiencie of that grace, and salvation which is laid up in Jesus Christ, as the only suitable good to him; that hee also enableth him spiritually and savingly to apprehend Jesus Christ as given him of the Father. And the same Spirit, having thus enlightened him, doth leave a supernaturall vertue and impression of Gods love upon the soul, whereby the soul is drawn to close with Christ, and with that grace of God in him so entirely, that there is now nothing between Christ and the soul, but it willingly parts with all things that hinder his enjoying of Christ; and by this effectuall calling all that are brought to Christ, are, I. justified, that is, absolved from sin and death, and accounted righteous unto life, for, and through Christ apprehended, received, and relied upon by faith. II. They are adopted, that is, accepted for Christs sake to the dignity of Gods children: They are also, III. sanctified, that is, really changed by degrees from the impurity of sin, to the purity of God's Image; and lastly, they are glorified, that is, changed from the misery or punishment of sin, unto everlasting happinesse, which begins in the inward sense of Gods love to them in Christ, whence they have hope of glory, boldnesse in accesse to God, certainty of salvation, peace, joy unspeakable; and it endeth in their full perfection in soul and body.

14. Concerning a particular instituted Church, and the Priviledges thereof.

That it is a company of faithfull and holy people, or persons called out of the world to fellowship with Jesus Christ, and united in one Congregation to him as members to their head, and one with another, by a holy covenant for mutuall fellowship in all such wayes of holy worship of God, and of edification of one towards another, as God himself hath required in his Word of every Church of Christ, and the members thereof.

15. Concerning the manner of gathering a Church.

That it is the duty of all Christians, having renounced all false wayes of Idolatrous, Anti-christian, and superstitious worship, and of sin, and the world (as to instruct and govern their own families according to God, so) to joyn willingly together in Christian communion and orderly covenant, and by free confession of the faith, and profession of their subjection to the Gospel of Christ, to unite themselves unto peculiar and visible Congregations, wherein as members of one body, whereof Christ is the head, they are to worship God according to his Word: To this Church he hath given royall priviledges, as the holy Oracles, the Promises, the Seals of the Covenant, his presence, love, protection and blessing in a speciall manner, here all that acknowledge him to be their Prophet, Priest, and King, are to be inrolled amongst his household servants, and to present their bodies, and soules, and gifts, and solemn services for a spirituall sacrifice acceptable to God by Jesus Christ. Being thus united, they, to whom God hath given gifts to interpret the Scriptures, being approved by the Church, and appointed thereunto, may, and ought to teach publikely the Word of God, by prophecying according to the proportion of faith for edification, exhortation, and comfort of the Church, till such time as men may be had, fit for such office or offices, as Christ hath appointed to the publike Ministery of his Church; and then they are upon due triall, to proceed to the choyce and ordination of those officers according to God: and then the officers are to dispense the seals of the Covenant, viz. Baptisme to the seed of the faithfull in their

Infancy, and to others not yet baptised, when by profession of their faith they are added to the Church: And all of the Church that are of yeers, and are able to examine themselves, must communicate also in the Lords Supper in both kindes, viz. Bread and Wine.

16. Concerning the Sacraments

That they are in the ordinance of God, signs and seals of Gods everlasting Covenant with us, representing and offering to all receivers, but exhibiting only to true believers the Lord Jesus Christ and all his benefits unto righteousnesse, sanctification, and eternall life, through faith in his name, to the Glory and praise of God.

17. Concerning the power of every Church.

That Christ hath given the power of chusing Officers, and of receiving in, or calling of any member, to the whole body together of every Church, and not to any one member apart, or to more members sequestred from the whole, or to any other Congregation to do it for them; yet so, as every Church ought to use the best help they can hereunto, and the most meet member they have to pronounce the same in their publike Assemblies, if they want Officers. And to this censure and judgement of Christ, duly and orderly dispensed, every member of the Congregation, yea, and officer also how ecellent, or learned soever he be, is subject. Yet ought not the Church without great care and advice to proceed against such publike persons.

18. Concerning the Communion of Churches.

That although particular Churches be distinct and severall Independent bodies, every one as a city compact within it self, without subordination under, or dependence upon any other but Jesus Christ, yet are all Churches to walk by one and the same rule, and by all means convenient, to have the counsell and help one of another, when need requireth, as members of one body, in the common faith under Christ their only Head.

19. Concerning Church-officers.

That Christ, when hee ascended up on high, gave gifts unto men, and disposed of them in severall functions, and for publike ordinary ministery, he gave Pastors, Teachers, Elders, Deacons, helpers for the instruction, government, and service of his Church, to the worlds end; and that none may usurp or execute a Ministery in the Church, but such as are rightly called by the Church, whereof they stand Ministers, and being so called, they ought to give all diligence to fulfill their Ministery, and to be found faithfull, and unblamable in all things: And that this ministery is alike given to every Church of Christ, with like and equall power, and commission to have and enjoy the same as God offereth fit men, and means, and the same rules are given to all for the election and execution thereof in all places: which rules & lawes it is not lawfull for chose Ministers, or for the Church, wittingly to neglect or transgresse in any part. And those Ministers thus chosen and executing their office faithfully, every Church is bound to have them in singular love for their works sake, to reverence them according to the dignity of their office which they execute, and to provide for them, that they be not entangled with the cares of this life, according to the Law of Christ: And this to do, not as in way of courtesie or mercy, but out of duty to them in the Lord; and having hope in God, that the resurrection shall be of the just and of the unjust; of the just, to the resurrection of life, and of the unjust, to the resurrection of condemnation.

20. Concerning giving every man his due.

That unto all men is to be given whatsoever is due to them, in regard of their office, place, gifts, wages, estate, and conditions, endeavouring our selves to have always a conscience void of offence towards God, and towards men.

THE BARMEN DECLARATION

This dramatic manifesto of pure Bible Christianity was written in a time of extreme stress during the twentieth century.

After Adolf Hitler came to power in 1933, the Reich Church Administration and a faction known as the German Christians, who were sympathetic to Hitler, attempted to take over the Evangelical (Protestant) Church in Germany. The Barmen Declaration was composed by "Confessing Christian" theologians to repudiate

and refute the aims of the German Christians.
All the writers of this declaration suffered for
their words.

In view of the errors of the "German Christians"
and of the present Reich Church Administration,
which are ravaging the Church and at the same
time also shattering the unity of the German
Evangelical Church, we confess the following
evangelical truths:

We confess the following evangelical truths

1. "I am the Way and the Truth and the Life;
no one comes to the Father except through me."
John 14:6

"Very truly, I tell you, anyone who does not
enter the sheepfold through the gate but climbs in
by another way is a thief and a bandit. I am the
gate. Whoever enters by me will be saved." John
10:1,9

Jesus Christ, as he is attested to us in Holy
Scripture, is the one Word of God whom we have
to hear, and whom we have to trust and obey in
life and in death.

We reject the false doctrine that the Church
could and should recognize as a source of its
proclamation, beyond and besides this one Word
of God, yet other events, powers, historic figures
and truths as God's revelation.

We reject false doctrines

2. "Jesus Christ has been made wisdom and
righteousness and sanctification and redemption
for us by God." 1 Cor. 1:30

As Jesus Christ is God's comforting pronounce-
ment of the forgiveness of all our sins, so, with

equal seriousness, he is also God's vigorous announcement of his claim upon our whole life. Through him there comes to us joyful liberation from the godless ties of this world for free, grateful service to his creatures.

We reject the false doctrine that there could be areas of our life in which we would not belong to Jesus Christ but to other lords, areas in which we would not need justification and sanctification through him.

3. "Let us, however, speak the truth in love, and in every respect grow into him who is the head, into Christ, from whom the whole body is joined together." Eph. 4:15–16

The Christian Church is the community of brethren in which, in Word and Sacrament, through the Holy Spirit, Jesus Christ acts in the present as Lord. With both its faith and its obedience, with both its message and its order, it has to testify in the midst of the sinful world, as the Church of pardoned sinners, that it belongs to him alone and lives and may live by his comfort and under his direction alone, in expectation of his appearing.

We reject the false doctrine that the Church could have permission to hand over the form of its message and of its order to whatever it itself might wish or to the vicissitudes of the prevailing ideological and political convictions of the day

4. "You know that the rulers of the Gentiles lord it over them, and their great ones are tyrants over them. It will not be so among you; but who-

ever wishes to have authority over you must be your servant." Matt. 20:25–26

The various offices in the Church do not provide a basis for some to exercise authority over others but for the ministry [lit., "service"] with which the whole community has been entrusted and charged to be carried out.

We reject the false doctrine that, apart from this ministry, the Church could, and could have permission to, give itself or allow itself to be given special leaders [Führer] vested with ruling authority.

5. "Fear God. Honor the Emperor." 1 Pet. 2:17

Scripture tells us that by divine appointment the State, in this still unredeemed world in which also the Church is situated, has the task of maintaining justice and peace, so far as human discernment and human ability make this possible, by means of the threat and use of force. The Church acknowledges with gratitude and reverence toward God the benefit of this, his appointment. It draws attention to God's Dominion [Reich], God's commandment and justice, and with these the responsibility of those who rule and those who are ruled. It trusts and obeys the power of the Word, by which God upholds all things.

We reject the false doctrine that beyond its special commission the State should and could become the sole and total order of human life and so fulfil the vocation of the Church as well.

We reject the false doctrine that beyond its

special commission the Church should and could take on the nature, tasks and dignity which belong to the State and thus become itself an organ of the State.

6. "See, I am with you always, to the end of the age." Matt. 28:20

"God's Word is not fettered." 2 Tim. 2:9

The Church's commission, which is the foundation of its freedom, consists in this: in Christ's stead, and so in the service of his own Word and work, to deliver all people, through preaching and sacrament, the message of the free grace of God.

We reject the false doctrine that with human vainglory the Church could place the Word and work of the Lord in the service of self-chosen desires, purposes and plans.

The Confessing Synod of the German Evangelical Church declares that it sees in the acknowledgment of these truths and in the rejection of these errors the indispensable theological basis of the German Evangelical Church as a confederation of Confessing Churches. It calls upon all who can stand in solidarity with its Declaration to be mindful of these theological findings in all their decisions concerning Church and State. It appeals to all concerned to return to unity in faith, hope and love.

An appeal for a return to unity in faith, hope, and love

Verbum Dei manet in aeternum.

The Word of God will last for ever.

INDEX AND GLOSSARY OF IMPORTANT SUBJECTS, EVENTS, AND WRITINGS MENTIONED IN THE TEXT

Against Julian
Six anti-Pelagian tracts written by St. Augustine in 419 **167**

Age of Faith
The Middle Ages in Europe, viewed by some as a time of serenity and grace for the Christian church **199, 202**

"Ah, Holy Jesus"
Poem written in 1630 by German Protestant poet Johann Herrmann **39**

Alexandria
City in Egypt, founded in 332 B.C. **141, 197**

Allah
The Supreme Being of the religion of Islam **184**

Amish
A Protestant group, part of a larger group called the Pennsylvania Dutch, that originated in Switzerland (where its followers were called Mennonites). The Amish are now concentrated in the states of Ohio, Pennsylvania, Indiana, and Iowa, as well as Canada. They teach separation from

the world, and members of the sect are forbidden from going to war, swearing oaths, or holding public office. Their doctrine requires farming and calls for personal simplicity in all aspects of life. **265**

Anabaptists
The Reformation name for Baptists, deriving from the Greek word meaning "to baptize again" **267**

Anathematize
To declare an idea blasphemous and wrong, and hence officially heretical **242**

Anatolia
Turkey **65, 113**

Anchorites
Monks who live alone, as hermits **149, 150**

Anglican Communion
See Anglicans

Anglican orders
Monastic orders of men and women during the late nineteenth century in Europe, particularly in England, whose members held liberal and romantic viewpoints of Christian faith **159**

Anglicans
Members of the Christian church originating in England. *Anglicanism* is generally used in reference to the world-

wide family of churches that are in communion with the Church of England. Sometimes *Anglicanism* is also used to refer to a moderate species of Christian believing that does not go to extremes. That use of the word, a misnomer in this case, has existed only since the Oxford or high church movement of the nineteenth century. **160, 235, 238–239, 265, 266, 273, 288, 294**

Ante-Nicene Fathers
Fathers or teachers of the church who wrote and thought before the First Council of Nicaea in 325. Most of the Ante-Nicene Fathers had an inflated and nonbiblical view of human nature. **144**

Antinomianism
The idea that the Grace of God renders null and void the Law of God in the lives of believers — an idea much voiced in the United States in the expression "God loves you as you are." Antinomianism loses sight of the Cross and also the cost to God of his acceptance and forgiveness of human beings. **118–119, 270**

Antioch
City in northern Turkey founded about 300 B.C. Until about A.D. 900 it was the capital of Syria. **65, 101, 118, 141**

Anti-Semitism
Hostility or prejudice against jews **45, 98, 251-252**

Apocalyptic
Describing vividly and visually the end of the world **88, 89**

Apollinarianism
According to Apollinarianism, taught by Apollinarius, Christ had no human spirit. This heresy overemphasized the divine character of Christ against his human character. It was condemned by the Council of Constantinople. **144**

Aramaic
The language Jesus spoke at home, derivative but also different from ancient Hebrew **58**

Arian heresy
The idea that the Son of God is inferior to God the Father. It is considered a Christian heresy and is similar to Socinianism, which is the original name for Unitarianism. **132, 141–142, 186**

Arianism
See Arian heresy

Aristotelian method
The philosophical study of the principles of reality and knowledge, including questions of epistemology (i.e., how do we know what we know?) and system (i.e., what data belongs in this category and not in that category?) **212–217**

Ascension
The return of Christ to heaven and his Father forty days after his resurrection. The story of the ascension is told in Acts 1:6–11. **74**

Assemblies of God
The largest Pentecostal denomination in the world, developed from a revival movement during the early twentieth century. It teaches that the Bible is infallible, and it recognizes speaking in tongues and other "gifts of the Holy Spirit" as visible signs of a person's successful relationship with God. **266, 267**

Atonement
The sacrifice of substitution that Christ made on the Cross for the sins of the world. The atonement is the leverage in theology by which God reconciles his necessary demand for justice with his charter of forgiving love. There are several theories in Christian thought of how atonement works, the most powerful in application being Christ's substitution for us, hence our freedom now from past guilt. **79–81, 117, 183**

Augsburg Confession
The first Protestant confession of faith, offered by Luther's disciple, Melanchthon, to the Holy Roman emperor in 1530 **228, 232**

Augustinianism
The theological school of thought derived from the later writings of St. Augustine. The Augustinian approach stresses mankind's paralyzed fallenness; his radical need for saving, which has to come from outside himself; and the awesome finality of Christ's work on the Cross. Augustinianism influenced all the Protestant reformers greatly and therefore became tainted in the minds of many Roman

Catholics. It was removed by the pope from privilege within Catholicism in the year 1711. **163–174, 313–317**

Babylonians

Residents of the ancient empire of Babylonia, located in the Euphrates Valley of southwestern Asia, prominent from about 2000 to 1000 B.C. **19**

Baptism

The sacrament of Christian initiation by water. It symbolizes purification, the washing away, of indwelling or original sin. Most churches believe in baptizing infants; some baptize adults only. In most Catholic and Protestant churches, baptism is performed by pouring or sprinkling water upon an individual's body; in the Eastern Orthodox Church and many evangelical Protestant churches, baptism is practiced by submerging or immersing a person's entire body in water. **85–86**

Baptists

A large Protestant religious group (initially called Anabaptists) that developed as an offshoot of English Congregationalism in the early seventeenth century. Baptists oppose the baptism of infants, believing instead that baptism should be restricted to persons old enough to make their own declaration of faith. The first Baptist church in America was founded by Roger Williams in Rhode Island in 1639. Since then, Baptists have made up the largest Protestant denomination in America, and about half of this group belong to the Southern Baptist Convention. **265, 267, 274**

Barmen Declaration
A statement of religious beliefs by a group of Protestant theologians repudiating and refuting the pro-Nazi position of the German Evangelical Church **366-370**

Basilica
See St. Peter's Basilica

Battle of Lepanto
A battle in 1571 in which Christian forces defeated the Turks lead by the Barbary corsair Barbarossa **249**

Battle of the Boyne
Battle in England in 1690 between the forces of the Protestant King William III and those of the Catholic King James II, supported by Louis XIV of France. The Protestants won, a crucial victory for the forces of religious freedom and Reformed faith. **130, 135, 165, 240**

Battle of the Milvian Bridge
Famous battle at a bridge on the Flaminian Way near Rome on October 28, 312, between the forces of Roman emperors Constantine the Great and Maxentius. Constantine emerged victorious, resulting in the unification of the eastern and western branches of the Catholic church and the legalization of Christianity within the Roman Empire. **131**

Beauvais Cathedral
See Saint-Pierre Cathedral

Benedictines
A monastic order established by Saint Benedict about A.D. 529 **152, 158**

Bethlehem
A town near Jerusalem where David lived and Jesus was born **18**

Bohemian Brethren
See Moravian Brethren

Bondage of the Will
A book by Martin Luther, published in 1525, that presented his theories on why human beings cannot do anything to contribute to their salvation **232**

Book of Common Prayer of the Church of England
See English Prayer Book

Books of Sentences
Books written in 1150-52 by Peter Lombard, a theologian and member of the philosophical group known as Schoolmen, containing quotations or summaries of dogma compiled from the Bible and church tradition **213**

Boyne
See Battle of the Boyne

Buddhism
One of the major religions of the world, founded about 500 B.C. in India by a wandering monk from Nepal called

Buddha. The principal teaching of Buddha, called the *dharma*, is the concept that life is a continuing cycle of death and rebirth, and that each person's status in his present life is determined by his behavior in previous lives. Today Buddhism has about 330 million followers, most of whom are in Southeast Asia. **1, 30, 268, 301**

Bull
An official letter and proclamation from the pope that defines correct doctrine and incorrect heresy **241**

Caesaropapism
The idea that the pope is the successor to the Roman emperor, unifying church and state in the bishop of Rome **137**

Calvary
The elevated rock outcropping on which Christ was crucified. It can still be seen and touched in the Church of the Holy Sepulchre at Jerusalem. **299**

Calvinism
The theology of Protestant pastor John Calvin, developed in Switzerland in the mid-sixteenth century. Calvin's French followers were called Huguenots; his English followers, Puritans. Calvinism is now expressed in the teaching of the Reformed or Presbyterian churches. It is sometimes a code word for the ideas of total human fallenness and absolute divine predestination. **163, 233–236, 238, 249, 273**

Candide
The best-known work of Voltaire (the pen name of François Marie Arouet, a French author and philosopher), published in 1759. It is recognized as a brilliant philosophical inquiry into the nature of good and evil. **255**

Canossa
Site of a castle in central Italy where Henry IV, emperor of the Holy Roman Empire, is said to have stood three days in the snow as penance to obtain from Pope Gregory VII a withdrawal of the excommunication that Gregory had levied against him. Henry was absolved, but the peace between him and the pope was short-lived. **136, 201**

Canterbury
Famous English cathedral **200**

Catharism
A heresy advocated by members of a religious sect of the Middle Ages that believed in dualism (i.e., the belief in a principle of good and evil — the former creating the invisible and spiritual universe, the latter creating the author of the material world) **153**

Catholicism
The faith, doctrine, system, and practice of a Catholic church, especially the Roman Catholic Church **128–130, 199–210, 241–252**

Celtic Christianity
The form of Christianity practiced by the Christians of

Ireland, Scotland, and western England in the Dark Ages. It really existed, but there is little surviving literary evidence. It has become a fad among English-speaking Christians. **129, 194–197**

Cenobitic monasticism
A form of religious life in which monks live in community (that is, together) rather than alone (as anchorites) **150**

Chartres
Famous French cathedral **200**

Christ Church (Anglican)
First protestant church in the Middle East, established in Jerusalem in 1841 **274–275**

Christian Science (Church of Christ, Scientist)
A Protestant denomination founded upon the principles of divine healing and upon laws expressed in the acts and sayings of Jesus, as set forth by its founder, Mary Baker Eddy, in 1866. Adherents rely on spiritual rather than medical or material means for the healing of sickness. The denomination is located primarily in the United States, although members can be found in seventy countries throughout the world. **36, 265**

Christian Zionism
The idea deriving from Anglican evangelicals in the early nineteenth century that the geographic land of Israel has an indispensable place in God's plan for the history of the world. According to Christian Zionism, if the Jews are

resettled in their covenanted land in high enough numbers, Christ will return as messiah and king. Lord Shaftesbury was the first leading Christian Zionist, although Christian Zionism is also found in the thinking of Oliver Cromwell. **274–275**

Christocentric
The belief that Christ is the center of human existence, the center of history, and the center between God and nature **196**

Church of England
The national church of England and the mother church of the worldwide Anglican Communion. The church came into existence in the mid-sixteenth century, when Henry VIII declared the king to be head of the church in the place of the Catholic pope. It recognizes the Old and New Testaments as its authority for doctrine. Its principles and teachings are set forth in the Thirty-nine Articles of the Church of England. The church is divided into two provinces, Canterbury and York, each of which is governed by an archbishop. The archbishop of Canterbury is considered by all Anglicans as their spiritual leader. Numerous references throughout the text. Principal discussion **160, 236–240, 270–273**

Church of the Holy Sepulchre
A church in Jerusalem that is the holiest Christian site, the place of Jesus Christ's burial and resurrection **206**

Church of the Nazarene
A Protestant denomination, established in Texas in 1908,

that is an offshoot of the Methodist church. It has approximately 9,000 congregations throughout the world. **265**

Cistercian Church of Saint Anne
An ancient church constructed in Jerusalem by the Crusaders in the twelfth century. It is regarded as one of the finest examples of Crusader architecture. **207**

Cistercian movement
A reforming French monastic order founded by Robert of Molesmes in 1098 that stressed simplicity, poverty, and solitude. It was a form of the puritan impulse in Christianity, the surviving church buildings of which epitomize "low church" ideas concerning worship. **152–153, 158, 209**

City of God
A book written by St. Augustine of Hippo in the late fourth century that presents the history of humanity **166**

Communism
A social system characterized by the absence of classes and by common ownership of the means of production and subsistence **181, 289-290, 297**

Confessions
One of the first great autobiographies, written by St. Augustine of Hippo in the late fourth century **164–166**

Congregationalists
Members of a Protestant religious group, originally a

branch of Puritanism, who were initially known as Separatists. They broke away from the Church of England and settled Plymouth Colony in Massachusetts, where they became known as Pilgrims, and later as Congregationalists. Congregationalism was the dominant religious tradition in New England from 1620 to about 1800. During that time, the Congregational church advocated liberal social goals, education, and local control of religious matters. As a result, Congregationalist doctrine had a strong influence on the development of civil government in America. Congregationalists believe that each congregation should control its own affairs, including the selection of ministers, and that there should be no intermediaries, such as councils or bishops, between themselves and Jesus. Today, most Congregational churches are members of the United Church of Christ. During the early nineteenth century, many Congregational churches voted to become Unitarian. **265–268**

Constantinople
City in Turkey, first named Byzantium, which was renamed by Constantine the Great in 330 and replaced Rome as the capital of the empire. **107, 144, 175-178, 197, 207, 247**

Consubstantiation
Martin Luther's attempt to reconcile his biblical theology with the worship of the church of Rome. He taught that the bread and wine of the Lord's Supper became the body and blood of Christ but remained also and at the same time bread and wine. Consubstantiation is a surprising version,

from an otherwise thoroughly consistent mental giant, of trying to have your cake and eat it, too. **229**

Coptic Christianity
A form of Christianity that exists to this day in Egypt and Ethiopia. It is rooted in monasticism and from a Western perspective is slightly heretical, in part. **298**

Council of Chalcedon
The fourth Nicene Council, held in 451, to which was presented a famous letter from Pope Leo I, called the *Tome*, setting forth his belief that in Christ, human nature and the divine are distinct, yet also united, in opposition to the doctrine of Monophysitism **145**

Council of Constantinople
Council convened in 381 to affirm the full deity of the Holy Spirit and to confirm the Nicene Creed **144**

Council of Ephesus
The third general council of the Catholic church, held in Ephesus in 431, to condemn the heresy of Nestorianism **144**

Council of Nicaea
Popular name for the First Council of Nicaea, which was convened in Nicaea (now northwest Turkey) in 325 by Emperor Constantine to settle the dispute that had arisen in the Roman Catholic Church over the Arian heresy. Its most famous product was the Nicene Creed, which reaffirmed the church's adherence to the doctrine of the Holy Trinity. A second Nicene council was held in 787. **135, 143**

Council of Nicaea II
The seventh general council of the Catholic church, held in Nicaea in 787, to rebut the doctrine of iconoclasm **143**

Council of Orange
A gathering of Catholic bishops and scholars in 529 **172**

Council of Trent
The nineteenth ecumenical council of the Roman Catholic Church, which convened at Trent, Italy, at various times during the years 1545–1563 to meet the crisis of the Protestant Reformation **242–243**

Counter-Reformation
The Roman Catholic movement of reaction against Protestantism that culminated in the Council of Trent. It ended some abuses in the church but reaffirmed medieval doctrine. It also succeeded in bringing back into the Catholic fold several countries and regions that had turned Protestant. **Numerous references throughout text. Principal discussion 241–252**

Covenant of God's Free Grace
Book written in 1645 by Puritan minister John Cotton **354**

Crucifixion
The putting to death of Christ on a cross at Calvary **46–47, 188**

"Crucifixion to the World by the Cross of Christ"
Famous hymn by Isaac Watts **346–347**

Cowley Fathers
A liberal religious community, or order, founded in England during the late nineteenth century within the Church of England. Also known as the Society of St. John the Evangelist. **160**

Creationism
A doctrine that ascribes the origin of all matter and living forms as they now exist to distinct acts of creation by God **281**

Crusades
Eight wars fought between 1096 and 1270 with the idea of safeguarding and guaranteeing Christians' access to the Christian holy sites of Palestine. European kings, nobles, and knights fought Muslim armies for possession of the Holy Land. The Christians finally gave up and never tried again. **181, 199, 203, 204, 205–208**

Cuius regio, cuius religio
The principle of a geographic region's religion being the same religion as that of its ruling monarch. It was put into European law by the Peace of Westphalia. Parts of Europe were declared lastingly Protestant, and larger parts remained Catholic. **139, 253**

Cultural Protestantism
A term for late nineteenth and early twentieth-century northern European and North American culture, which was typified by a loose consensus of Protestant values and Protestant religion. Cultural Protestantism ended in

Europe after the First World War and in America by the late 1960s. **283–285**

Czech Reformation
A movement to reform the Roman Catholic Church in Bohemia, led principally by Jan Hus, who was burned at the stake on July 6, 1415, more than one hundred years before Martin Luther nailed his Ninety-five Treatises to the church door in Wittenberg to inaugurate the far more influential Protestant Reformation. **266**

Damascus
Capital of Syria and one of the world's oldest cities, founded about 5,000 years ago **57, 61, 62, 63, 72, 76, 81, 86, 92**

Dark Ages
The period between the fall of Rome (410–476) and the building of the European cathedrals (the mid-eleventh century and following) **191–198, 211**

Davenport, John (Creed of)
Celebrated statement of the theology of the first New Englanders by Puritan pastor John Davenport, published in 1642 **354–366**

Deist
One who believes that although God did create the universe, he assumes no control over life, exerts no influence on natural phenomena, and gives no supernatural revelations **257**

Diaspora
The exile or dispersion of an ethnic or religious group from its original geographic point of origin. We speak of the Jewish Diaspora after the fall of Jerusalem and the French Protestant diaspora after the revocation of the Edict of Nantes in 1685. **103**

Didache, The
Didache is the Greek word for "teaching." Today the word has come to be recognized as the short title of an ancient document believed to have been written around A.D. 150 that contains some very early Christian doctrines. **120**

Dispensationalism
The idea held by some Christians that Christ's miracles were confined to his thirty-three years on earth. This view asserts that God works differently in different dispensations or time periods — that was then, this is now, so forget about miracles today. **36**

Docetic
A member of a heretical sect in the early Christian church that believed that Christ had no human body and only appeared to have died on the cross **113**

Dominicans
A monastic order established by Saint Dominic in 1215 **153, 158, 161, 204**

Donatists
Followers of a belief that flourished in North Africa during

the fourth and fifth centuries and that was considered a heresy by the Roman Catholic Church **165**

Double predestination
The idea that God predestines some people to salvation and others to damnation. Single predestination affirms the first point only; the second point is much more controversial. **232**

Easter (day and season)
A festival in the Christian church commemorating the Resurrection of Christ, celebrated on the first Sunday following the full moon that occurs on or next after March 21 **37, 50-55**

Eastern Orthodox Church
The ancient Catholic churches of the European and Middle East that split from Rome in 1054. They have a distinct ethos of transcendent worship, icons, and popular devotion to the figure of Christ. They are governed by geographic patriarchs rather than by a single spiritual leader or pope. **Numerous references throughout text. Principal discussion 176–181, 247–250, 275–276, 297–298**

Ecumenical movement
A modern initiative instituted by a number of Protestant leaders in the early twentieth century to foster unity among Christian churches throughout the world. It culminated in the formation of the World Council of Churches in 1948. This organization, which was endorsed by the Roman Catholic Church at the Second Vatican Council,

works to reduce differences on doctrine and promote Christian unity. **289**

Education of the Human Race
A book by German journalist and philosopher Gotthold Ephraim Lessing, published in 1780, extolling the virtues of Christianity **258**

Emancipation Proclamation
A proclamation issued by President Lincoln, effective January 1, 1863, declaring the freedom of all slaves in territories still at war with the Union **130**

Encyclopédie
The most renowned of all encyclopedias, compiled by the French philosopher Denis Diderot and others in France in 1772 **255**

English Prayer Book
The Book of Common Prayer of the Church of England, first published in 1549. The first edition — it has undergone many revisions since — was largely the work of Thomas Cranmer, a notable archbishop of Canterbury during the sixteenth century. **85, 116, 238, 341–342**

Enlightenment
A philosophical movement of the eighteenth century concerned with the critical examination of previously accepted doctrines and institutions **252, 256–261, 269, 275, 276**

Ephesus
An ancient Greek city **67, 113, 114, 115**

Episcopal
A Protestant religion closely related to the Anglican Church, with a government of bishops **265, 281**

Episcopal Church, USA (ECUSA)
An eccentric sect of liberal catholics who combine high church liturgy with whatever ideas are strongest in the surrounding culture. ECUSA was once a full part of the worldwide Anglican Communion. **119, 265**

Epistemology
See Aristotelian method

Epistles
Letters written by apostles, consisting of 21 books in the New Testament **108, 234**

Epistle to the Romans
The sixth book of the New Testament, a letter from St. Paul to the Christians in Rome, probably written about A.D. 56 **27, 108, 168, 170, 270, 309–312, 349**

Eschatology
Theology concerning the end of the world, from the Greek word meaning "last things" **88**

Essays
A famous philosophical work by Michel de Montaigne, published in 1575 **254**

Essence
A philosophical term describing the intrinsic nature of a thing **176–177**

Essenes
Jewish separatist monks who lived in the area of the Dead Sea at the time of Christ **19**

Eucharist
See Holy Communion

Evangelical
A Christian who emphasizes the Gospel of Grace, the centrality of the Bible, the atonement of Christ on the Cross, and the importance of personal conversion **13, 259, 263, 269, 272–276, 288, 299, 300**

Evangelist
A person who seeks to share the Gospel with others in hopes of their embracing it for themselves **43, 63, 107, 114, 160, 180, 196, 272**

Exodus
The departure of the Jews from Egypt, as related in the book of Exodus of the Bible — the second of the five books of the Law (the Torah) — that relates primarily to the bondage of the Jews in Egypt and their exodus under the leadership of Moses, and the handing down of the Ten Commandments at Mount Sinai **130**

Exorcism
The expelling of evil spirits with earnest and solemn argument **33–34, 40**

Filioque
Latin for "and the Son," added after the declaration that

the Holy Spirit proceeds from the Father, in the version of the Nicene Creed used by the Western church **179**

First Apostolic Council
Meeting between Paul, Peter, James, and the other apostles, as described in the Bible's book of Acts, chapter 15 **66**

First Nicene Council
See Council of Nicaea

First Temple
First Jewish temple built by King Solomon between 960 and 925 B.C., and destroyed by Nebuchadnezzar in 587 B.C. **19**

Forum (Roman)
A section of ancient Rome that served as the legal, administrative, and legislative center of the Roman Republic and Roman Empire from approximately 150 B.C. to A.D. 400 **72**

Franciscans
Members of a monastic Roman Catholic religious order founded by St. Francis of Assisi in 1209. Early Franciscans devoted themselves to preaching and caring for the basic needs of people. The order later involved itself in social work and missionary tasks. **11, 153–155, 161, 204**

Freedom of a Christian Man, The
A tract written by Martin Luther, published in 1520 **140**

French Revolution
A political movement, lasting from 1789 to 1799, which

succeeded in overthrowing the monarchy but ultimately failed to accomplish its original democratic goals **260**

Fundamentalism

A large movement within Protestant denominations in the United States, first enunciated in the early twentieth century by the tracts called *The Fundamentals*. Fundamentalists try to preserve the basic ideas of Christianity, in opposition to criticism by liberal theologians. The basic tenets of the movement are the beliefs that the Bible is infallible, including its stories of the creation and its accounts of miracles, the virgin birth and the deity of Jesus, Christ's atonement (through his crucifixion) for mankind's sins, and Christ's physical resurrection and return at the Second Coming. Its largest following is among the Baptist, Presbyterian, Church of God, Assemblies of God, and Pentecostal churches. **280–281**

Fundamentals, The

A series of twelve small volumes published from 1910 to 1915, written by anonymous authors, that set forth what the authors regarded as basic Christian doctrines that should be accepted without question by all Christians **280–281**

Galilean ministry

In Christian theology, the period in the life of Christ when he performed miracles **35**

Galilee

Region that was the northernmost part of Palestine in Roman times, now a part of Israel **17, 21, 43, 125**

Gentile
A non-Jew **65–66, 69–70, 106, 108, 287**

Germanic tribes
Primarily four groups of primitive, warlike people — the Vandals, Angles, Saxons, and Jutes — from the area of what is now Denmark and northern Germany. Early in the fourth century, the Vandals invaded Rome, Spain, and northern Africa. In the fourth and fifth centuries, the Angles, Saxons, and Jutes invaded England. **192**

Gethsemane
Garden outside Jerusalem that was the scene of Jesus' agony and arrest **44, 105**

Glorious Revolution
The bloodless coup by which the Dutch Protestant William of Orange became king of England in 1688, supplanting James II **136, 239**

Good Friday
The Friday before Easter **38, 39, 45**

Gospel
The word has two meanings. The first is the Good News of salvation through Christ's Grace alone received by faith alone on account of Christ's sacrificial death alone. The second meaning is each of the first four books of the New Testament. The Gospels of the New Testament are biographies of Jesus. **Numerous references throughout text. Principal discussion 105–108, 113–114**

Gothic style
Medieval or medieval-inspired architecture that is based upon the pointed arch **200**

Grace
Unmerited favor for the sinner, which in Christian theology comes from the character of God as expressed in Jesus **Numerous references throughout text. Principal discussion 8–14, 117–122, 225–226**

Great Awakening
The evangelical movement of the mid-eighteenth century that had tremendous impact in the United States **11, 263, 269, 273**

Great Schism
The separation in 1054 of the Eastern Orthodox churches from the Roman Catholic Church. The gap has never been bridged. **2, 176, 179**

Hagia Sophia
Eastern Roman Catholic cathedral in Constantinople (now Istanbul), particularly famous as the site where in 1054, the papal ambassador to Constantinople placed upon the cathedral's high altar a letter excommunicating its patriarch, which, in turn, precipitated the Great Schism **176**

Hellenistic
Coming from the period after the death of Alexander the Great (336 B.C.), the period after Greece's Golden Age, in which Greek ideas were spread throughout the Mediter-

ranean world. Christ was born and the Roman Empire flourished in late Hellenistic times. **21, 107**

"He Never Said a Mumblin' Word"
Famous Negro spiritual **48, 351**

Heresy
An incorrect teaching about God and about man in relation to God that wounds and corrupts the outward and inward lives of everyday Christians **141–147, 244**

Heretics
Persons opposed to the church's teachings **125**

Hermeneutics
The science of interpretation, especially biblical interpretation: what rules are we to use in attempting to understand in the now a text that was written back then? **83–84, 215**

Herrnhut
Protestant community near the German border with the Czech Republic **159**

History of Dogma
A seven-volume work of German church historian Alfred von Harnack. An English edition was published between 1894 and 1899. **261**

Holiness denominations
Theologically conservative Protestant denominations that arose in the United States toward the end of the nineteenth century and that later became the foundation for a number

of organizations — including the Holiness Church, the Church of the Nazarene, and the Salvation Army — as well as Pentecostal Christianity **265**

Holocaust
The systematic state-sponsored murder of millions of Jews and others during World War II (1939–1945) **38, 39, 244, 283, 285–287**

Holy Communion
The Christian sacrament (holy ceremony) of the Lord's Supper. Most protestants call the sacrament the *Lord's Supper*. Anglicans, Roman Catholics, and members of the Eastern Orthodox churches call it the *Eucharist* or *Holy Communion*. **44, 75, 86–88, 113, 226, 229–230, 235**

Holy Roman Empire
The European concept of a Catholic-Christian successor-kingdom to the Christian church that existed during the time of the ancient Roman Empire **136–137, 193–195**

Holy Trinity
Doctrine that God is three Persons (Father, Son, and Holy Spirit) in one God **Numerous references throughout text. Principal discussion 90–91, 187, 190**

House churches
Extended families, or small communities, of Christians in the religion's earliest days **126–128**

Huguenots
Slang name, which stuck, for the French Protestants. They were expelled from France by King Louis XIV in 1685. **246**

Huns
A warrior tribe of northern Europe that invaded the Roman Empire in the fourth century. They achieved their greatest success with the invasion of Gaul (now mainly France) under their great leader Attila, but they were ultimately defeated in 451. **192**

Hussites
Followers of the early fifteenth-century Bohemian religious reformer Jan Hus **11**

Icon
A holy painted image of Jesus, Mary, or one of the saints. Icons are believed by Eastern Orthodox Christians to have divine properties. **177**

Iconoclasm
The doctrine of destroying sacred images **143**

Iconoclast
A person who believes that icons break the second commandment, which bans images **196**

Incarnation
The "coming into flesh," which is the literal translation of this word, of God. It refers to Christ Jesus being God's presence on earth in a human body. **187, 307**

Indulgences
Formal certificates of promise sold by the Roman Catholic Church guaranteeing to the buyer that his beloved deceased would spend less time in puratory **224, 227**

In Praise of Folly
A satirical work by the Dutch priest and reformer Desiderius Erasmus, published in 1511, that criticized the Roman Catholic clergy for abandoning the principles of piety, morality, and dedication to truth **221**

Inquisition
A special court created by Pope Gregory IX in 1231 to investigate and punish those whom the church deemed to be heretics (persons opposed to the church's teachings) **204–205**

Islam
The religion founded by the prophet Muhammad in the seventh century. Islam means "submission (to the will of God.)" **1, 11, 138, 165, 183–190, 248, 274, 288, 295–296, 300**

Israel
The Biblical Holy Land, located between the Mediterranean Sea and the Jordan River, occupied by the Hebrew people during the second millennium B.C. and the scene of most of the events described in the Bible. Now a modern democratic state. **20, 23, 24, 29, 43, 275, 283, 285–287**

Jansenism
The school of thought within seventeenth-century French Catholicism that rediscovered St. Augustine's theology as the hoped-for fountain of Catholic Christian truth. The Jansenists started out with impressive patrons and influence but were eventually almost completely silenced and nullified by the Jesuit order. **158–159, 161, 173–174**

Jamnia
Biblical city located on the coast of Israel, south of Jaffa **104**

Jehovah's Witnesses
An evangelical religious group that evolved from the Seventh-Day Adventists. Jehovah's Witnesses believe there is one God, Jehovah. Although they consider Jesus to be divine, they do not consider him, as God's Son, as being equal to God. The movement was organized in Pennsylvania in the late nineteenth century by Charles Taze Russell and his associates. Jehovah's Witnesses are particularly well known today for their magazine *The Watchtower,* which is printed in one hundred languages. Membership is about four million worldwide. **265**

Jerusalem
Capital and largest city of Israel, one of the world's holiest cities **18, 19, 36, 47, 66, 68, 69, 93, 205, 206, 207, 300**

Jesuit order (Society of Jesus)
The order founded by Ignatius Loyola in the mid-sixteenth

century. The Jesuits were Catholic priests who dedicated themselves one hundred percent to doing what they considered the pope wanted done. They later had to be reined in by the Vatican. **157–158, 161, 174, 244–245, 247, 255**

Jewish Sabbath
The seventh day of the week, Saturday, named in the Ten Commandments as the day of rest and worship for Jews **28, 40**

Jordan (River)
Principal river of Israel, flowing from northern Israel through the Sea of Galilee to the Dead Sea **27**

Judaism
The monotheistic religion of the Jewish people, tracing its origins to Abraham **1, 20, 64, 75, 79, 84, 98, 124–125, 176, 183, 250–252, 286, 295, 297, 300**

Judean (or Jerusalem) ministry
In Christian theology, the time of the suffering and death of Christ **35**

Jude the Obscure
Novel by English author Thomas Hardy, published in 1895 **118**

Justification by faith
The idea that God declares sinful human beings righteous even though they are not in themselves righteous. God justifies them by regarding them — through the lens, so to

speak, of Christ's perfection — as righteous. **Numerous references throughout text. Principal discussion 76–79, 225–226**

Lambeth Conference
Conference of Anglican bishops, held at Lambeth palace, London, at which they voted overwhelmingly in favor of traditional Bible teaching concerning homosexuality **288**

Lambeth Palace
The archbishop of Canterbury's residence in London **248**

Last Supper
Christ's supper with his disciples the night before his Crucifixion **43, 86–88**

Law of Moses
The code of moral principles, also known as the *Mosaic Code*, assembled by the Jewish people during the period from about 1000 to 400 B.C. It included the Ten Commandments and key parts of the first books of the Hebrew Bible and later, the Christian Bible **20, 47**

Les Miserables
Novel by French author Victor Hugo, published in 1862 **95**

Letter of Clement
A famous letter believed to have been written around A.D. 96 from Pope Clement I to the church in Corinth. The letter strongly condemmed pride and arrogance within the

church and clarified the order of succession within the church hierocracy. It is the oldest surviving Christian text except for the Scriptures. **120**

Liberal catholicism
A post-Reformation movement, most prominently peopled by upper-class and well-educated members of the Church of England, who looked backward with an unrealistic and romantic view at the Middle Ages and the monastic communities of that era **160, 281–282**

Liturgical churches
Churches that worship from a previously agreed-upon script or book. Roman Catholic, Eastern Orthodox, Anglican, and most Lutheran churches are liturgical. **59, 143**

Lord's Supper
See Holy Communion

"Love Constraining to Obedience"
Famous hymn by William Cowper **345–346**

Lutherans
Members of the largest Protestant denomination; there are more than sixty million Lutherans worldwide. Lutheranism is based primarily upon the doctrines and beliefs of its founder, Martin Luther. Lutherans emphasize congregational participation in a liturgy that generally follows the style of the Roman Catholic Mass. They place special emphasis upon Luther's concept of justification by faith

(i.e., that God's forgiveness is solely the gift of God's grace and cannot be earned by good deeds or piety). **139, 233, 238, 265, 266, 279, 282, 287**

Macedonianism
In Macedonianism, the Holy Spirit was subordinated to God the Father; just as in Arianism, Jesus Christ was lowered in relation to God the Father. Macedonianism was taught by Macedonius and refuted by the great Gregory of Nazianzus. It was condemned by the Council of Constantinople. **144**

Magyars
Ethnic Hungarians who became Protestant in the sixteenth century and whose Protestantism helped them retain their group identity and finally win their independence from the Austrian Hapsburg dynasty **249**

"Man Frail, and God Eternal"
Famous hymn by Isaac Watts **347–348**

Manichaeanism
An ancient Middle Eastern religious conception that understood the world and universe to be locked in a battle between two forces: the force of cosmic good and the force of cosmic evil **164–165**

Martyr
A word from the Greek word for "witness," meaning someone who dies for his or her faith, usually during a time of persecution **60, 165**

Mecca

The sacred city of Muslims, located in western Saudi Arabia. It is the birthplace of Muhammad, the prophet of Islam. In the heart of the city stands the Great Mosque, the center of worship for all Muslims. Islam requires that every Muslim make the hajj (a pilgrimage to Mecca) at least once during his lifetime if he is physically able to do so. **183–184**

Medievalists

A group of eighteenth-century English critics and philosophers, among them John Ruskin and John Henry Newman, who considered the Middle Ages to be a glorious epoch in human history **202**

Medina

A sacred city of Muslims, located in western Saudi Arabia. Medina is the site of the Prophet's Mosque, which contains the tomb of the Islamic prophet Muhammad. **184**

Mennonites

Early Baptists, now sometimes known as Amish, who stressed community and also separation from the world. The first Mennonites belonged to a church organized in Switzerland, where its members called themselves Swiss Brethren. Later they were nicknamed Anabaptists. Beginning in the early sixteenth century, they came to call themselves Mennonites, a word derived from the name of their leader, Menno Simons, a former Roman Catholic priest. To escape persecution in Europe, many Mennonites traveled to Pennsylvania and joined the Pennsylvania Dutch residing there. **267**

Messiah
The promised divine savior of Israel, who would rescue the Jews from their enemies and establish a permanent kingdom of harmony and abundance **19, 24–25, 31, 33, 41, 67, 94, 106, 250**

Methodists
Followers of the English cleric John Wesley, who laid down a method, or rule of life, for Bible-reading everyday Christians. The Methodist church began as a movement at England's Oxford University in the early eighteenth century. Students helped each other to be disciplined and methodical in their religious study, which earned them the nickname "methodists." Today, the Methodist church is divided into a number of churches, including the United Methodist Church, the Methodist Episcopal Church, the African Methodist Church, and the Church of the Nazarene. **265, 271, 294, 349**

Middle Ages
The period between ancient and modern times in western Europe **17, 63, 137, 150, 160, 172, 192–212**

Milvian Bridge
See Battle of the Milvian Bridge

Modernism
A specific movement within twentieth-century Catholicism that tried to reconcile contemporary science with traditional Christianity. It failed, and its founder, Alfred Loisy, was excommunicated. **279–281**

Mohacs
Site in Hungary of a famous battle in 1526, in which Hungarian Catholics were defeated by invading Ottoman Muslims **249**

Monasticism
A form of religious life in which one flees the world and lives apart from it, alone or in a group, focusing on prayer, simple self-sufficiency, and routine **149–161**

Mongols
A group of nomadic tribes, originally from Mongolia, Manchuria, and Siberia, who, under the leadership of Genghis Khan and later his grandson Kublai Khan, created the largest land empire in history, extending from eastern Asia to eastern Europe during the twelfth to fourteenth centuries **180**

Monophysitism
A heresy that stresses Christ's divinity at the expense of his humanity. In Christ, according to Monophysitism, the divine and human natures are mixed to form one nature. **145, 186**

Montanist Pentecostals
A group in Asia Minor around the year 170 who subscribed to the teachings of their founder Montanus, teachings that were in opposition to the Roman Catholic Church. Montanists spoke in tongues, endorsed an apocalyptic outlook on life, and regarded themselves as martyrs completely alienated from the world. **130**

Monte Cassino
A magnificent monastery located about halfway between Rome and Naples, founded by St. Benedict in the sixth century. It was completely destroyed during World War II. **152**

Moral Law
In Christian theology, Moral Law refers to the Ten Commandments of the Old Testament, whereas Ceremonial Law refers to the principles of ritual, sacrifice, and purity that governed the liturgical or cultic life of the Jewish people. The Jewish Ceremonial Law is not binding on Christians. **66**

Moravian Brethren
A group of Protestants initially known as the Bohemian Brethren. The Moravian Church was founded in Bohemia (now part of the Czech Republic) in 1457. Persecution from without and dissension from within brought about the decline and near extinction of the Brethren during the sixteenth and seventeenth centuries. The movement was renewed and gained new life and vigor in 1722 under the leadership of German count Nikolaus Ludwig von Zinzendorf. Today, this Bible-believing and personally pious, or pietistic, community of German Protestant Christian Moravians is still going strong, with more than 160 congregations in Germany, Great Britain, and the United States. **265, 266, 269–270**

Mormons
The name commonly given to members of the Church of Jesus Christ of Latter-day Saints, so called because of their belief in The Book of Mormon. The Mormon Church was

founded in Palmyra, New York, in 1830. Today, the Mormon Church consists of more than seven million members, located predominantly in the western United States, with headquarters in Salt Lake City, Utah. Mormons believe that the Christian church as established by Christ and his apostles did not survive in its original form but was altered and restored by divine means through the works of the Mormon Church's founder and prophet, Joseph Smith. **265**

Moslem
See Muslim

Mount of Olives
A hill east of Jerusalem **44**

Mount Sinai
Mountain in Egypt where Moses received the Ten Commandments **130**

Muslim
A member of the nation of Islam **65, 81, 165, 205, 207, 260, 290, 296, 301**

Nazarenes
An early name for Christians **125**

Nazareth
A town in the region of Galilee **5, 17**

Nazism
The National Socialist German Workers' Party, founded in Germany in 1919 and brought to power under Adolf Hitler in 1933 **251, 284-285, 287**

Nestorianism
A heresy that is quite complicated but generally emphasizes Christ's human nature at the expense of his divine nature. According to this doctrine, the creation of Theodore of Mopsuestia, Christ is two Persons (God the Son and the human Jesus), each acting through his own nature. This idea put emphasis on the humanity of Christ. It was refuted by Cyril of Alexandria, who taught that Christ is one Person (God the Son), acting through two natures, divine and human. **144**

New Covenant
See the New Testament

New Testament
The proper term for the Christian Scriptures of the Bible **Numerous references throughout text. Principal discussion 103–122**

Nicaea
City in northwestern Turkey and site of the First Council of Nicaea in 325 **142-143**

Nicene Creed
The declaration of Christian faith adopted by the First Nicene Council in 325. It reaffirmed the Catholic church's adherence to the doctrine of the Holy Trinity and is recited today in Catholic and Protestant liturgical churches several times each year. **143, 179**

Nicomachean Ethics
A book written by Aristotle in 350 B.C. **214**

Ninety-five Theses, The
Document announcing Martin Luther's insight of justification by faith and denouncing the Catholic church's practice of selling indulgences **227, 241**

Norman style
Early medieval form of architecture that is based on the rounded arch. It is part of the Romanesque style. **200**

Novum
A Latin word meaning "new thing," or breakthrough **27–29, 33, 76**

"Nobody Knows"
Famous Negro spiritual **351-352**

Odium theologicum
Odium theologicum literally means "theological hatred," referring to the fact that when religious convictions are seriously held, they can result in crippling divisions between people and between groups of people. **254**

Old Testament
The Jewish Scriptures of the Bible **124–125**

On the Spirit and the Letter
Letter written by St. Augustine in A.D. 412 refuting the doctrine of Pelagianism **313**

Original sin
The brokenness, sickness, and aggression in human beings that is a part of who we are, not just what we do. In

Christianity, original sin goes with the territory of being human. **168**

Origin of Species, The
A book by Charles Darwin, published in 1859 and bearing the full title *On the Origin of Species by Means of Natural Selection; or, The Preservation of Favoured Races in the Struggle for Life*. The work announced Darwin's revolutionary theory of evolution. **278**

Orthodox Church
See Eastern Orthodox Church

Ottoman Empire
Muslims from Turkey who expanded the rule of Islam westward during the sixteenth century, threatening Christian Europe **248, 249, 251**

Palm Sunday
The Sunday before Easter, commemorating Christ's entry into Jerusalem, when palm fronds were strewn before him **41**

Parable
A simple story from everyday life that illustrates a point about God and God's relation to man. Jesus made many of his points using parables. **32**

Participationism
The idea that the essence of being a Christian is being one with or part of the cosmic Christ. Some scholars think that St. Paul taught this. He did, but not in a big way. **74**

Passion of Jesus
Jesus' suffering during the last days of his life **46, 47, 106**

Passover
The annual Jewish feast and holiday that celebrates the hasty departure of the Israelites under Moses from their slavery in Egypt **41, 42**

Patmos
Remote island off the coast of Greece where St. John wrote the book of Revelation **114–115**

Pastoral Epistles
St. Paul's letters to Timothy and Titus **110-111**

Pauline Letters
The letters of St. Paul, principally to Christian congregations he had founded **108-112**

Pelagianism
The idea, taught by the British monk Pelagius, that men and women have the capacity to do what God commands in the Law, hence the capacity to save themselves. Augustine argued against it, but it lives in unquiet earth. It is always stirring in the heart. **167–169, 313–316**

Pella
Capital of the Macedonian kingdom about 400 B.C. **104**

Pentateuch
The first five books of the Bible **279**

Pentecost
Both a Jewish festival and a Christian festival. For Chris-

tians, Pentecost is the day when the Holy Spirit came upon the disciples after Christ's ascension, enabling them to speak in tongues and thus communicate with foreigners. **57–58, 299**

Pentecostal Christianity
The belief of a group of Protestant churches that trace their origins to a religious revival that began in Topeka, Kansas, in 1901. Today, some of the world's largest and fastest-growing Protestant denominations are Pentecostal. Their members view evangelism as a solemn obligation to prepare the world for Jesus' return, and they believe that they can receive gifts from the Holy Spirit, including the power of physical healing, the ability to prophesy, and the power to speak and understand unknown tongues. In the United States, there are more than thirty varieties of Pentecostal churches, chief among them the Holiness Church, the Church of God, and the Assemblies of God. **13, 36, 58, 91, 108, 245, 267, 288–289, 299**

Perestroika
A series of economic and cultural reforms in the former Soviet Union that were initiated by Premier Mikhail Gorbachev in the late 1980s **298**

Pharisees
Jews of Christ's time who subscribed to a conservative school of thought that emphasized observance of the Law. They also believed in the resurrection of the dead. **19, 30, 61**

Philo-Semitic
Love of the Jews **250, 298**

Philosophes
The leading philosophical, political, and social writers of the French Enlightenment in the eighteenth century **255**

Philosophy of History
A book by Georg Wilhelm Friedrich Hegel, published in 1805 **259**

Pilgrims
Separatist Puritan Christians from England who emigrated to Massachusetts in the early seventeenth century. It is also a general term for people on their way to a heavenly and divine destination. **206**

Poor Clares (Sisters of St. Clare)
Female monastic order founded by St. Francis of Assisi in 1212 through his friend and disciple, St. Clare of Assisi **154**

Post-modernism
Modern school of thought that the Protestant Reformation was not a watershed event, but only one of a number of equally important societal changes that took place in sixteenth-century Europe **219**

Post-Nicene Fathers
Theologians and teachers in the period after the First Council of Nicaea (325). They mostly had a more realistic view of human nature and sin than the Ante-Nicene Fathers, and thus a view of the Cross more in keeping with the Bible and St. Paul. **144**

"Praise for the Fountain Opened"
Famous hymn by William Cowper **344-345**

Predestination
The idea that God elects the righteous to salvation and is the author of all cause and effect. This idea can be relatively weak, as in single predestination, which affirms only heaven; or strong, as in double predestination, which affirms both heaven and hell. **Numerous references throughout text. Principal discussion 93–97, 170–171, 230–233**

Preface to the Book of Romans
A famous 1522 writing of Martin Luther **319–341**

Presbyterianism
Another word for Reformed or Calvinist theology and church life. It is from the Greek word for "elder," and refers to the government of local churches by presbyteries of elders. **228, 236, 249, 265, 266, 268**

Protestantism
The faith, doctrine, system, and practice of all sects of Christianity that have descended from those that seceded from the Roman Catholic Church at the time of the Reformation **Numerous references throughout text. Principal discussion 219–240, 263–276**

Protestant Reformation
A religious movement that began in 1517 when Martin Luther, a German Catholic priest, publicly protested

against certain practices of the Roman Catholic Church. Luther's ideas rapidly spread throughout Europe during the next forty years, exerting a tremendous impact on social, political, and economic life. **Numerous references throughout text. Principal discussion 219–240**

Protest of the Lutheran Nobles
A document presented by a group of Lutheran nobles to the German Reichstag meeting at Speyer, Germany, on April 19, 1529. The nobles were protesting that legislative body's restoration of Roman Catholic doctrine and authority in the Holy Roman Empire. **228**

Purgatory
In Roman Catholic theology, the state in which the souls of those who have died in Grace must expiate their sins **163, 224**

Puritans
Members of the Church of England who wished to "purify" that church of all Roman Catholic–seeming, non-biblical ceremonies and practices. The Puritans failed to accomplish their objectives. Many of them emigrated to America. **233, 263, 264, 265, 272,**

Quakers
A popular name for the Religious Society of Friends, a Protestant Christian sect that developed in England in the seventeenth century. Today, there are sizable populations of Quakers in Great Britain and Kenya, but the majority of the sect's members are located in the United States. **265**

Qur'an (Koran)
Muslim book and Holy Scripture dictated to the prophet
Muhammad by an angel from God **184–188**

Radically differentiated pluralism
A philosophical definition of Christianity, first enunciated
by Christian theologian John Cobb, according to which
Christianity is not Judaism, western European secularism,
or Islam. Rather, Christianity is weakness not strength,
Grace not Law, Gospel not church. Christianity honors its
own identity, and that of all other religions, and thus is able
comfortably to coexist with them **301–302**

Reformation
See Protestant Reformation

Reformation, The
A new historical study, published in 2004, by distinguished
British historian Patrick Collinson **219**

Reformed churches
See Presbyterianism

Renaissance
A period of revival of interest in classical art, literature,
and learning that originated in Italy during the fourteenth
century and later spread throughout Europe **137, 221**

Resurrection
With a small "r," the restoration of a dead person to life
through God's power. The resurrection of Jesus as
described in all four Gospels is referred to as the
Resurrection (with a capital "R"). **Numerous references
throughout text. Principal discussion 50–55, 59**

Rights of Man
Thomas Paine's celebrated book on the principles of republican government, published in two parts in 1791 and 1792 **256**

Roman Catholic Church
The largest Christian denomination in the world, numbering more than one billion members. It had its beginnings early in the first century A.D., and by the end of that period, it was centered primarily in Vatican City in Rome, which remains its headquarters today. The church is organized in a hierarchical structure, headed by a pope in Rome, who is regarded as being a successor to the first pope, St. Peter, and Christ's representative on earth. Roman Catholics believe in the teachings of the Bible and Jesus, the Holy Trinity, sin, the Incarnation, and salvation. The Roman Catholic Church has a long, glorious, turbulent history, the highlights of which are discussed in this Primer. **Numerous references throughout text. Principal discussion 237–239**

Roman Empire
The Roman Empire was the dominant political power of the Western world for hundreds of years before and after the birth of Christ. At its height, it covered a vast territory, including about half of Europe, much of the Middle East, and northern Africa. The empire was the successor first to the city of Rome and later to the Roman Republic. According to legend, the city of Rome was founded in 753 B.C., and within several hundred years, it controlled most of the Italian peninsula. In 509 B.C., the Roman Republic was established. It lasted almost five hundred years, until the

Roman Empire was established in 27 B.C., after the republic had been destroyed by a series of civil wars. Over the next two hundred years, the empire reached the zenith of its power and influence. Thereafter, in the face of onslaughts from Visigoths, Vandals, and other Germanic tribes, its power began to decline, and it finally fell into disarray in A.D. 476. **Numerous references throughout text. Principal discussion 126–135, 175–181, 191–210**

Romanesque style
An architectural style that was prevalent in Europe from the ninth to the twelfth centuries **200**

Romanticism
The act of seeing something through idealistic and rose-colored glasses because it seems to fulfill an idea you have of it that pleases you. Thus, nineteenth-century church people had a romantic but not a realistic idea of the Middle Ages. **280–281**

Sacraments
Rites of the Christian church considered to have been instituted by Jesus **88, 243**

Sadducees
Members of a party of Jewish teachers at the time of Christ who were ethical but not supernaturally religious. They believed in observance of the Law but had no confidence in an afterlife with God. **19**

St. John's Gospel (Prologue to)
A celebrated passage from the New Testament which explains the coming of Christ **307–308**

St. Peter's Basilica
Originally called St. Peter's Church when it was built about 330, it became the famous site of what is now known as St. Peter's Basilica in Rome's Vatican City, the headquarters of the Roman Catholic Church. *Basilica* is the Latin word for a large Roman hall design that Christian architects borrowed for their church architecture **245, 330**

St. Peter's Breastplate
Text and hymn believed to have been written by St. Patrick **317–319**

Saint-Pierre Cathedral
The cathedral in Beauvais, near Paris. Begun in 1227 it collapsed in 1284. It is symbolic of the grandeur and pathos of the Christian Middle Ages in Europe. **203, 245**

St. Sophia Cathedral
See Hagia Sophia

Sanhedrin
The governing body of the Jewish temple. Its members condemned Christ to death for blaspheming but they did not have the legal authority to carry out the sentence. **45, 48**

Saracens
The tribe of Muslims who fought and beat the Crusaders **205, 207**

Saxons
Members of a Germanic tribe who invaded England during the fifth and sixth centuries **195**

Saxony
Formerly a region of northwestern Germany **139, 220, 251**

Sea of Galilee
A lake in northern Israel, fed by the River Jordan, cele-brated as the site where Christ appeared to Peter after the Resurrection 100 (John 21:1-7) **100**

Second-Temple Judaism
This is the commonly used term for Jewish life and thought at the time of Christ. The Second Temple was constructed in the 400s B.C. under the leadership of Nehemiah and Ezra, and later adorned by King Herod the Great, to replace the First Temple, which had been constructed by King Solomon but destroyed by the Babylonians **19, 20, 21, 22, 23, 24, 26, 28, 41, 62, 80, 103**

Semi-Pelagianism
The heretical but still very common idea that God cooper-ates with human efforts to create righteous deeds and thus righteous lives. Subscribers to this notion believe: "I alone cannot save myself, but with God's added help, I can." ("I get by with a little help from my friends" [the Beatles]). **223–224**

Sepphoris
The capital city of Galilee **21**

Sermon on the Mount
A famous speech of Christ, recorded in Matthew 5:1-48, containing a number of famous beatitudes, or sayings,

including "Blessed are the poor in spirit, for theirs is the kingdom of heaven" and "Blessed are the meek, for they shall inherit the earth". It is reproduced in the appendix on page 303. **35, 303–307**

Sermon on the Plain
A famous speech of Christ, recorded in Luke 6:20–49, that (according to Luke) was delivered on a plain at the foot of the mountain from which Christ delivered the Sermon on the Mount. Although it contains some subject matter that is similar to that of the better-known Sermon on the Mount, it is only one-third as long. **35, 106**

Seventh-day Adventists
Members of an evangelical Protestant denomination that was organized in 1863 by the followers of Baptist minister William Miller and that focuses on the second coming of Christ. Seventh-day Adventists observe the Sabbath on Saturday, the seventh day of the week. The denomination has about six million members throughout the world. Its international headquarters is in Silver Spring, Maryland. A later outgrowth of the Seventh-day Adventist Church in the late nineteenth century was the Jehovah's Witnesses movement. **265**

Scholasticism
The broad name for medieval theology as it was centered at the University (or school) of Paris in the twelfth century. Scholasticism was academic in the bloodless sense of the word. The proponents of scholasticism were called Schoolmen. **211–217, 278, 294**

Schoolmen
See Scholasticism

Simplicissimus
A German novel first published in 1668, with the full title of *The Adventures of Simplicissimus Teutsch, attributed to Hans Jakob Christoffel von Grimmelshausen.* The book tells the story of the quixotic adventures of a simpleton during the Thirty Years' War. **254**

Sisters of St. Margaret
A woman's liberal religious community, or order, founded in England during the late nineteenth century within the Church of England **160**

Six Days' War
The 1967 war fought and won by Israel against Egypt, Syria, and Jordan **285**

Slavic churches
The Orthodox churches of the Slavic peoples, such as the Russians **180**

Slavonic churches
See Slavic churches

Society of Jesus
See Jesuit order

Socinianism
See Socinians

Socinians
Followers of Arianism, an unorthodox movement of the late sixteenth century that rejected the deity of Christ and broke decisively with classical Reformed Christianity. In the early nineteenth century, the Socinians (who were named for their teacher, Fausto Sozzini) organized the Unitarian Church. **143**

Southern Baptist Convention
The largest Baptist organization in the world. It was created in 1845 as a result of division among the Baptists over the issue of whether slaveholders should be appointed as missionaries. Today, the Southern Baptist Convention consists of more than 37,000 churches in the United States and its possessions, as well as 3,600 missionaries in other countries, and it numbers more than fifteen million members. **265, 287, 295**

Spanish Armada
The Spanish fleet of 130 warships that attempted an invasion of England in 1588. It was defeated by the English navy, with a loss of 63 ships. **239, 246**

Spanish Inquisition
The official interrogation and execution of heretics and undesirable nonbelievers that was undertaken by the Catholic church in Spain during the sixteenth century **204–205, 208**

"Steal Away"
Famous Negro spiritual **352**

Stigmata
The spontaneous manifestation of bloody wounds on a person's hands, feet, and side — similar to the wounds of the crucified Jesus **154**

Stoic
A Greek school of philosophy that held that men should be free of passions and calmly accept all occurrences as the unavoidable result of divine will **254**

Sufism
A mystical school of thought within Islam that has several parallels with the Christian theology of Grace. Sufis claim to have a special and intimate relationship with God. **301**

Suras
Chapters of the Qur'an **184**

Synod of Whitby
A meeting of leaders of the Roman Catholic Church in 664 at Whitby, a monastery on the northeastern coast of England, at which the leaders chose to follow Roman Catholicism rather than the Irish-Celtic style of Christianity of St. Patrick and his followers **197**

Synoptic Gospels
The New Testament books of St. Matthew, St. Mark, and St. Luke, which are generally so similar in content that they are called synoptic ("look-alike") **105–108**

System
See Aristotelian method

Tarsus
A city in Cilicia (now part of Turkey), the birthplace of St. Paul **70**

Third Crusade
The Crusade in which Christians fought against Muslims in the Holy Land from 1189 to 1193 **207**

Thirty-nine Articles of the Church of England
The doctrinal or confessional statement of the Church of England composed during the Reformation and ratified by Queen Elizabeth I in 1562. It is basically Lutheran and also moderately Calvinist in its expression of the faith. **238, 247**

Thirty Years' War
The extremely destructive European war between Catholics and Protestants in the first half of the seventeenth century. It caused widespread disillusion within the Christian church generally, as well as disillusion with its chief theological concerns and divisions. **136, 241–247, 253, 254**

Tome
A 451 writing of Pope Leo I, fully entitled *Tome to Flavian* **145**

Torah
The proper Hebrew word for the Jewish Law. It is intended to be memorized and observed in its full detail. **61, 184**

Tours
Site in France of a famous battle between the Franks and Islam in 733 that saved Europe for Christianity **197**

Transubstantiation
The Roman Catholic doctrine, rejected by all Protestants, that the bread and wine of the Mass are transformed into the body and blood of Christ one hundred percent and corporeally. It was made an official doctrine of the church in 1215. **229–230**

Transylvania
A region which was formerly central Rumania **24**

Trinity
See Holy Trinity

Trintarian
Describing or relating to the Holy Trinity **196**

Tritheism
The belief that mankind has three gods **187**

Ulster Scots
Scots who migrated to the northern province in Ireland (Ulster) beginning about 1605 **268**

Unitarianism
The Christian school of thought that rejects the Trinity and the divinity of Jesus. According to Unitarianism, Christ is a great teacher and an outstanding example of the moral life, but he is not divine. Unitarianism originated in Poland at the time of the Reformation and took hold in Puritan New England during the early nineteenth century. **143, 205, 265**

United Church of Christ
A Protestant religious group, an offshoot of the Congregational church, that was formed in 1957. It has about 1,600,000 members in the United States. **265**

Vandals
A member of the Germanic tribes of northern Europe who invaded Spain, Rome, and northern Africa in the early fourth century **193**

Vatican
The church and building where the pope sits; his headquarters and the seat of authority of the Roman Catholic Church. The word refers not just to the building but also to the whole governing authority of the church of Rome. **72, 129, 226**

Vikings
Scandinavian invaders of England who pushed Christianity to the west, especially to Ireland. They wore horned helmets, drank a kind of ale called mead, and had a colorful idea of the afterlife. **193**

Wesley, John (conversion of)
An excerpt from Wesley's journal, the charter document of the Methodist church **349–350**

What Is Christianity?
A book on the Protestant Enlightenment, published in 1901 by German historian Adolf von Harnack. The work is a classic yet orthodox statement of liberal theology. **261**

"What is Enlightenment?"
Famous 1784 essay by philosopher Immanuel Kant **258**

White Fathers
French Catholic missionary order **278**

Wittenberg
University in Saxony (now east central Germany) where Martin Luther was a Catholic priest and professor of biblical theology **241**

World Conference on Faith and Charity
(1965) **112**

Worms
A German city which was the site of the Diet of Worms (1521) at which Martin Luther was declared to be a heretic **241**

Zealots
Jewish political radicals who sought to overthrow the Romans by force. They were well known when Jesus was alive — one of his disciples, Simon the Canaanite, was a zealot — and became ascendant in Palestine. They are best remembered for their defense of the Masada fortress, where 960 men, women, and children held out for three years, committing suicide at the end rather than surrendering to the Romans. The zealots were completely obliterated in 135 after the Bar Kokhba revolt. **19, 70**

INDEX AND BIOGRAPHICAL SKETCHES OF PRINCIPAL PERSONS MENTIONED IN THE TEXT

Abelard, Peter (1079-1142)
Scholastic theologian and philosopher who came to be associated with the University of Paris. He was an early "Schoolman" and "liberal" in theology because he stressed Christ's *example* rather than Christ's *sacrifice*. He had a famous and disastrous love affair with Héloise which destroyed his career. **212**

Adams, John (1735-1826)
Second president of the United States **272**

Aidan (Saint) (?–651)
Influential Celtic Christian monk and missionary **196**

Ambrose (Saint) (ca. 339–397)
Bishop of Milan. He challenged the authority of the Roman emperor Theodosius and won, preparing the way for the triumph of the church over the state. **164**

Andrew (Saint) (first century A.D.)
An apostle of Jesus **42**

Anselm of Canterbury (ca. 1033–1109)
English theologian who stressed the atonement of Christ as a judicial transaction between the Father and the Son **212**

Anthony the Hermit (ca. 250–355)
Early anchorite, or solitary monk, who was a classic model of a hermit tempted by sexual fantasies and demonic visions. He was given the grace to resist them. **149**

Apollinarius (?–ca. 390)
Bishop of Laodicea in Syria, a friend of Athanasius, and formulator of the heresy that the humanity of Christ was incomplete **144**

Apuleius, Lucius (125?–170?)
Roman writer of the only preserved novel in Latin, *Metamorphoses,* or *The Golden Ass* **126**

Aquinas, Thomas (Saint) (1225–1274)
Catholic theologian and philosopher and a leader of the school of scholastic theology. After Aristotle, he is the most influential theology professor in history. He is the most admired and quoted academic in the history of Roman Catholicism. **172, 213, 214**

Archibishop of Mainz
See Boniface (Saint)

Aristotle (384–322 B.C.)
With Plato, the most important of all Greek philosophers. His views on justice and ethics crucially influenced the medieval church. The Protestant reformers saw Aristotle as the cause of the church's bad theology. **211, 213, 214, 215, 216, 217**

Arius (ca. 256–336)
Libyan theologian who formulated the Arian heresy **141, 142**

Athanasius (328–373)
Egyptian theologian and pope of Alexandria who opposed the teachings of Arius and defended the doctrines of the Nicene Creed **142, 147**

Augustine of Hippo (Saint) (354–430)
The second greatest Christian theologian. He changed his mind in late career and lowered his estimation of human nature while lifting his estimation of the Cross and God's relation to human destiny. He wrestled with guilt concerning early sexual sin but came to peace and extraordinary wisdom in his maturity. **Numerous references throughout text. Principal discussion 163–174, 313–317**

Augustus (63 B.C.–A.D. 14)
Arguably the most important figure in Roman history, Augustus (meaning "the exalted") presided over the Roman Empire during an era of peace, prosperity, and cultural achievement that became known as the Augustan Age. **17**

Aurelius, Marcus
See Marcus Aurelius

Avicenna (980–1037)
Islamic philosopher and physician **213**

Barabbas
A Jew who was a prisoner of the Romans at the same time as Jesus. He is briefly mentioned in all four Gospels. **168, 231**

Barnes, Robert (1495–1540)
The first English Lutheran and a theologian of courage and grit. He was burned at the stake under King Henry VIII. **236**

Bartholomew (Saint) (first century A.D.)
An apostle of Jesus **42**

Baur, Ferdinand Christian (1792–1860)
Grandfather of liberal biblical criticism. He tried to understand earliest Christianity as a dynamic struggle between spokesmen for Grace (i.e., St. Paul's group) and spokesmen for Law (i.e., St. Peter's group). He is often seen as more skeptical about the Bible than he really was. **259–260, 280**

Becket, Thomas à (Saint) (ca. 1118–1170)
Archbishop of Canterbury who was murdered in his own cathedral by order of King Henry II. Unlike Ambrose of Milan and Leo the Great, Becket lost in the struggle of church versus state. **201**

Bell, George K. A. (1883–1958)
Bishop of Chichester. Prophetic wartime leader in the Church of England, friend of the German martyr Dietrich Bonhoeffer, and patron of the arts. One of the great Christians of the twentieth century. **289**

Benedict of Nursia (Saint) (ca. 480–ca. 550)
Founder of the most successful form of group monastic life. His "rule of life" is overvalued today. It is authoritarian and ultimately superficial. **152, 161**

Bernini, Gian Lorenzo (1598–1680)
Italian sculptor and architect of St. Peter's Basilica. Bernini was a dominant force in the development of the Italian baroque style of architecture. **245**

Beza, Theodore (1519–1605)
Systematician of Reformed theology and successor to John Calvin. He moved Calvin's concept of God further in the direction of predestination. **232**

Bismarck, Otto von (1815–1898)
Prussian military leader and statesman who became chancellor of Germany in 1871 **284**

Boleyn, Anne (1507?–1536)
Second wife of King Henry VIII. Their marriage initially precipitated the English Reformation. She was an ardent Protestant. **237**

Bonhoeffer, Dietrich (1906–1945)
Theologian and Protestant martyr under Adolf Hitler. He spoke strongly against the persecution of the Jews and was executed by the Nazis. **63**

Boniface (Saint) (675–754)
English-born Christian missionary who became known as the Apostle of Germany. He was instrumental in organizing Christian churches and monasteries in Germany and later became archbishop of Mainz. **224**

Bunyan, John (1625–1688)
English Puritan writer and preacher. His allegory of

Islam at the battle of Tours in 732 and thus saved Europe for Christianity. He is reported to have said of Christ's crucifixion: "If I and my Franks had been there, it never would have happened." **197**

Chrysostom, John (Saint) (ca. 347–407)
Mellifluous and persuasive preacher of early catholic Christianity. His name means "golden tongue." He became the patriarch of Constantinople in 398 and is considered one of the greatest preachers in the history of the church. His statue is found on many pulpits. When you read the texts of his sermons, however, they don't catch fire. But as always in good preaching, it was an event. You had to be there! **144**

Clare (Saint) (ca. 1193–1253)
Colleague of St. Francis who organized women into a parallel religious order with the Franciscan brotherhood. The women were called the Poor Clares. **154**

Clement I (Clement of Rome) (Saint) (second century A.D.)
First official pope and author of a famous letter that almost made it into the New Testament **129, 144**

Clement of Alexandria (ca. 155–220)
The first known Christian scholar. He stressed Jesus' embodiment as the Word or *logos* of God. **144**

Cobb, John B., Jr. (1925–)
Prominent American Christian theologian, ordained Methodist minister, and professor at Claremont School of

Theology in California. He is the author of numerous books on contemporary Christian thought, including *Christ in a Pluralistic Age* (1975), and is the formulator of the doctrine of radically differentiated pluralism. **301**

Colenso, John William (1814–1883)
Heretical South African bishop who attacked the historical truth of the Bible, especially the Old Testament, and split the Anglican church in South Africa **279, 280**

Collinson, Patrick
Distinguished British historian, emeritus professor of history at Cambridge University, and author of *The Reformation* **219**

Columba (Saint) (521–597)
Most illustrious Irish church leader of the sixth century. He created a mission to the Picts, jumping off from the tiny Scottish island of Iona. **196**

Constantine I (Constantine the Great) (ca. 275–337)
First Christian emperor of Rome. Converted through a vision before a battle in 312, he gave official recognition to Christianity. He also led the church through the first phase of the Arian heresy. He called together the Council of Nicaea. **132–133, 135–142**

Cooper, Anthony Ashley
See Shaftesbury, 7th Earl of

Cotton, John (1584-1652)
An influential Puritan minister and author, Cotton became

New England's spokesman against the extreme baptist views of Roger Williams, founder of the Rhode Island colony **354**

Cowper, William (1731–1800)
Evangelical poet of the "plain style" who wrote many hymns that are still sung today. One of his most famous compositions is the hymn "Praise for the Fountain Opened," with its vivid first line, "There is a fountain filled with blood" which is reproduced in the appendix on page 344. **273, 344–346**

Cranmer, Thomas (1489–1556)
Architect of the English Reformation and the Book of Common Prayer. He was burned at the stake under Mary Tudor, Queen Mary I, as a Protestant heretic. **116, 171, 230, 237, 341–343**

Cyril (Saint) (827–869)
Courageous and brilliant evangelist, together with his companion Methodius, to the Slavic peoples. He is the charter saint for the Orthodox churches of the European East. **180, 248**

Darwin, Charles (1809-1882)
British naturalist, author of *On the Origin of the Species by Means of Natural Selection, or the Preservation of Favoured Races in the Struggle for Life* (1859) **278, 280**

Davenport, John (1597-1670)
An English Puritan and clergyman, Davenport migrated to

America in 1637, and became a leading figure in the founding of the colony of Quinnipac (a name later changed to New Haven). He was the author of a number of influential theological writings. One of most celebrated is" John Davenport's Creed" which is reproduced in the appendix on page 353. **353–366**

Diderot, Denis (1713–1784)
French philosopher and principal writer and editor of the *Encyclopédie* **255**

Dominic (Saint) (1170–1221)
Celebrated preacher and founder of the preaching order, the Dominicans. He is overrated, but in his day he was a fierce hammer of heretics. **63, 153, 161**

Domitian (51–96)
Emperor of Rome late in the first century A.D., he was an avid supporter of Roman religion, identifying himself with the gods Minerva and Jupiter **114, 115, 131, 135**

Duns Scotus, John (1266–1308)
Scholastic theologian whose thought was very intricate but whose writings were later derided, resulting in the creation of the word *dunce,* from *Duns,* meaning one whose ideas are obscure or hard to understand **213**

Eck, Johann (1486–1543)
German Roman Catholic theologian who condemned the new theses of Martin Luther and was a leading opponent of the Reformation in Germany **241**

Edward III (1312-1377)
King of England during the Hundred Years' War **201**

Edward VI (1537–1553)
King of England who championed the Reformation. His early death crippled the movement. **238**

Elizabeth I (Elizabeth Tudor) (1533–1603)
Queen of England. Under her reign, a moderate state-Protestantism became the established religion of England. **238**

Erasmus, Desiderius (ca. 1466–1536)
Critic of abuses by the Catholic church, but a "liberal" in theology, who disagreed with Luther fundamentally about human nature **221–222**

Eutyches (ca. 380–ca. 456)
A priest and archimandrite (head of a monastery) in Constantinople and a supporter of Cyril of Alexandria, who vehemently opposed Nestorianism **145**

Finney, Charles Grandison (1792–1875)
A Presbyterian and Congregational revival preacher who also served as president of Ohio's Oberlin College from 1851 to 1866 **272**

Francis of Assisi (Saint) (ca. 1182–1226)
A sanctified and wholly committed medieval holy man who influenced thousands to join his monastic order and way of life. He loved animals, nature, and the poor with whom he lived. **69, 130, 153–155, 161**

Freud, Sigmund (1856–1939)
Austrian psychiatrist and founder of the psychoanalytic method **64**

Galileo (1564–1642)
Great Italian astronomer, mathematician, and physicist **215**

George, Lloyd (1863–1945)
British Liberal Party leader and prime minister from 1914 to 1918 **284**

Gibbon, Edward (1737–1794)
Ironic English humanist who hated Christianity and blamed it for the fall of the Roman Empire **192**

Graham, Billy (1918–)
American evangelist of worldwide impact **272**

Gregory VII (Hildebrand) (Saint) (ca. 1023–1085)
As pope, he faced down Henry IV, the emperor, and won, thus strengthening further and inflexibly the church of Rome **136**

Gregory IX (ca. 1155–1241)
Roman Catholic pope who created the Inquisition **204**

Grosseteste, Robert (ca. 1175–1253)
Bishop of Lincoln, the most populous diocese in England at that time. He taught at Oxford University. One of the most learned men of the Middle Ages, Grosseteste was particu-

larly noted for his study of Aristotle and early Christian history, as well as his opposition to the papal administration of the Roman Catholic Church. **213**

Gutenberg, Johannes (ca. 1400–1468)
Inventor of movable type. Because of his invention, the Protestant Reformation was able to spread rapidly. **222**

Hardy, Thomas (1848–1928)
English novelist and poet who wrote a number of famous novels, including *Jude the Obscure* (1895) **118**

Harnack, Adolf von (1851–1930)
The greatest and best of the nineteenth-century "liberal" German theologians. Not liberal by our contemporary standards, he understood the Christian Gospel in its essence, and the insight of Martin Luther best of all. **259, 261**

Heermann, Johann (1585–1647)
Polish Lutheran pastor and hymn writer **39**

Hegel, Georg Wilhelm Friedrich (1770–1831)
Lutheran philosopher who understood Protestant Christianity as the highest point of God's dynamic in history **259–260**

Helena (Saint) (ca. 248–ca. 327)
The mother of Constantine the Great. Helena excavated and established the locations of the most important holy sites in Jerusalem and Bethlehem. Were it not for Helena,

we would not know where Jesus was crucified and where he was born. **132**

Henry II (1133–1189)
King of England. In Christian history, he is chiefly remembered for his quarrel with Thomas à Becket, whom he had made archbishop of Canterbury, with jurisdiction of the church courts. Their quarrel ended with the assassination of Becket in 1170, for which Henry was at least indirectly responsible. **201**

Henry IV (1050–1106)
Emperor who opposed Pope Gregory VII and lost, in a memorable, humiliating display of public penitence **136**

Henry VIII (1491–1547)
English king who approved the Church of England's separation from Rome. He was unscrupulous and persecuted Catholics and Protestants equally. He ended up becoming a Protestant. **138, 201, 237**

Herod I (Herod the Great) (ca. 73–4 B.C.)
Herod, who came from the ruling family in Palestine, ruled as king of Judea until his death. He was a ruthless leader, as amply demonstrated by his order to slaughter the "innocents," or infant boys, in and around Palestine in an attempt to kill the infant Jesus. **19, 20**

Hippolytus (Saint) (ca. 170–ca. 236)
Early Christian codifier and observer of liturgy who is highly regarded today. He was probably a heretic, and we know a lot less about him than many think we do. Hippolytus is a modern-day sacred cow. **144**

Hitler, Adolf (1889-1945)
Dictator of Germany from 1933 to 1945 **284, 366**

Holbein, Hans (ca. 1497–1543)
Swiss painter who understood and put into visual grammar the underlying theological issues of the Reformation **211, 217**

Hooper, John (?–1555)
The first Puritan bishop, burned at the stake for his Protestant convictions **230**

Hugo, Victor (1892–1885)
French novelist; author of *Les Misérables* (1862) **95**

Hus, Jan (ca. 1369–1415)
A very early religious reformer from Czechoslovakia who was burned at the stake at the Council of Constance **130, 221, 298**

Irenaeus (Saint) (ca. 130–ca. 200)
Early apologist for Christianity against Christian heretics. He was an impressive example of an orthodox bishop. **144**

Isabella I (1451–1504)
Queen of Spain whose fame today rests chiefly upon her financing of the voyages of Christopher Columbus **205**

Iscariot, Judas (first century A.D.)
The apostle who betrayed Jesus **42, 44, 57, 188**

James (Saint) (first century A.D.)
An apostle of Jesus and brother of St. John **42, 64, 117–119**

James II (1633–1701)

The king of England who tried to convert his country back to Catholicism. He almost succeeded but was defeated decisively by William of Orange at the Battle of the Boyne in 1690. He fled to France and lived there under the patronage of Louis XIV. **239–240**

Jansen, Cornelius (1585–1638)

Roman Catholic bishop and theologian. The scales fell from his eyes after he read St. Augustine. He became the founder of the Jansenist school of thought in France, which was exterminated by Louis XIV. **173**

Jefferson, Thomas (1743–1826)

Third president of the United States. He was a student of the French Enlightenment and detested Christianity. He made his personal peace with it, however, during his last term as president. **257**

Jenkins, Philip (1952–)

Distinguished professor of history and religious studies at Pennsylvania State University and author of numerous works on Christianity, including *The Next Christendom: The Coming of Global Christianity* (2002) **288**

Jerome (Saint) (ca. 342–420)

Monk who translated the Bible into a Latin edition that became known as the Vulgate. The Vulgate served the Catholic church until Erasmus' translation of the New Testament in 1516. Jerome lived much of his life in a cave in Bethlehem. **69, 144**

Joan of Arc (1412?-1431)

A peasant girl who led the French army to a great victory over the English at the siege of Orleans. She was later convicted of witchcraft and heresy and burned at the stake **140**

John (Saint) (first century A.D.)

An apostle who was sometimes called the Beloved Disciple, because he was especially trusted by Jesus. He is the author of the Gospel according to St. John, and probably the book of Revelation. **Numerous references throughout text. Principal discussion 112–115, 307–308**

John the Baptist (Saint) (ca. 6 B.C.–A.D. 28)

A Jewish prophet who was regarded as the forerunner of his cousin, Jesus. John lived in the wilderness of Judea, where he proclaimed the coming of God. He baptized people, including Jesus, in preparation for the coming of one who would baptize them in the Holy Spirit. Feared by the Romans and Jews of Palestine, he was arrested by Herod Antipas (governor of Galilee and son of Herod the Great), imprisoned, and eventually executed. **23, 24–27, 32**

John Paul II (1920–2005)

Polish pope of the Roman Catholic Church, elected in 1978 and noted for his conservative theology **278, 286**

Joseph (Saint) (first century A.D.)

Husband of Mary and foster father of Jesus Christ. Joseph, a carpenter by trade, was likely born in Bethlehem but later moved to Nazareth (where he married Mary) and, still later, to Galilee. There are apocryphal stories that Joseph had previously been married for a long time and became Mary's husband when he was a very old man. **18**

Josephus, Flavius (ca. 37–100)
Jewish historian who wrote *The Jewish War,* a history of the war between the Jews and the Romans, and *Jewish Antiquities,* a history of the Jews **20**

Judson, Adoniram (1788–1850)
American Baptist missionary **274**

Julian of Eclanum (380–ca. 455)
Heretical bishop who followed the teachings of Pelagius concerning human nature and free will. Augustine refuted his position **166–167**

Julian the Apostate (ca. 331–363)
Roman emperor who persecuted the Christians and loved every minute of it **131, 135**

Kant, Immanuel (1724–1804)
Influential German Enlightenment philosopher who worked from an unspoken but definite Lutheran-Protestant understanding of the moral life **258–259**

Käsemann, Ernst (1906–1998)
Protestant theologian of the New Testament who started the second quest for the historical Jesus **63, 76, 112**

Kepler, Johannes (1571–1630)
German astronomer and mathematician who developed the three laws of planetary motion **215**

Kierkegaard, Søren (1813–1855)
Danish philosopher and theologian who pioneered modern existentialism, which stresses personal decision and personal risk. He was depressed and introverted. **117, 220**

Latimer, Hugh (1485–1555)
English reformer who was regarded as the best preacher of his generation. He was burned at the stake under Mary Tudor. **230**

Laud, William (1573–1645)
Extremely "high church" archbishop of Canterbury. Laud persecuted the Puritans. He received his reward when he was beheaded during the English Civil War. **268**

Leary, Timothy (1920–1996)
Controversial psychologist and author who used psychedelic drugs to enhance his observations of the mind **149**

Leibniz, Gottfried Wilhelm (1646–1716)
Protestant Enlightenment philosopher who wrote in the disillusioned aftermath of the Thirty Years' War. He did not lose his Christian faith, however, and taught something like "God's in his heaven — all's right with the world." **258**

Leo I (Leo the Great) (ca. 400–461)
Famous and powerful pope who broke a theological dead-

lock concerning Christ's divinity and humanity by writing his *Tome to Flavian* in 451 **145**

Leo X (1475-1521)
Renaissance pope in power at the time of the Reformation **224**

Lessing, Gotthold Ephraim (1729–1781)
German Enlightenment playwright and journalist who was a Christian, but an antichurch one. He stressed the freedom tradition in Protestantism more than the faith tradition. **258–259**

Loisy, Alfred (1857–1940)
Radical French New Testament scholar. A hard, unyielding man, he founded Catholic modernism. He was excommunicated by the church in 1908. **279, 280**

Lombard, Peter
See Peter Lombard

Louis IX (1214-1270)
King of France who led two crusades **201**

Louis XIV (1638–1715)
Fiercely anti-Protestant and megalomaniacal king of France. He fell under the influence of one mistress after another and, finally, the Jesuit order. **174, 253**

Loyola, Ignatius (1491–1556)
Founder of the Jesuit order. He would do absolutely anything to advance the interest, as he saw it, of the popes of Rome. **157**

Lucaris, Cyril (1572–1638)
"Protestant" patriarch of Constantinople. He tried to bring Orthodox Christianity into line with the Reformation, was murdered by soldiers of the sultan, and was later declared a heretic by the church he had led. **247, 248**

Luke (Saint) (first century A.D.)
A Gentile apostle of Jesus and the author of the Gospel according to St. Luke **106, 107**

Luther, Martin (1483–1546)
Protestant reformer and the greatest theologian of all time. He perfectly integrated his psychological search for unity with the core theological concerns of the New Testament. **Numerous references throughout text. Principal discussion 219–236, 250–252, 319–341**

Maccabaeus, Judas (200–160 B.C.)
A leader of the Jews in their struggle for independence in the second century B.C. **24**

Macedonius (?–ca. 517)
Patriarch of Constantinople who was exiled by the emperor Anastasius for his support of the Council of Chalcedon and his rejection of the heresies that admitted two Sons or two Christs or that divided the two natures, divine and human, of Christ **144**

Maimonides, Moses (1135–1205)
Jewish student of Aristotle. He was more like a Christian scholastic theologian than a rabbinic scholar of the Book. **213**

Marcion of Sinope (?–ca. 160)
Bishop from Turkey's Black Sea coast who was the first to gather into one volume the main books of the New Testament. He perceived legalistic heresy in several of the biblical books and is considered a heretic by most Christians. He did understand St. Paul. **106–107, 120–122**

Marcus Aurelius (121–180)
Roman emperor, philosopher, and a follower of Stoic philosophy, which believes, among other things, that the world is ruled by a benevolent spirit, and that there is a divine spirit in all things **131, 135**

Mark (Saint) (first century A.D.)
Not one of the original twelve apostles, but an early follower of Jesus who wrote the Gospel according to St. Mark **105–106**

Martel, Charles
See Charles Martel

Martyr, Justin (ca. 100–165)
Early apologist for Christianity against Greek philosophy and Judaism. He was executed for his faith. **144**

Marx, Karl (1818–1883)
German social philosopher and chief theorist of the doctrines of modern socialism and communism **259**

Mary (Saint) (?–ca. 63)
The mother of Jesus Christ. She is also known as the Virgin

Mary, the Blessed Virgin Mary, and the Blessed Virgin. According to the Gospels of Matthew and Luke, she gave birth to Jesus in Bethlehem, where, according to Luke, she had gone with her husband Joseph to have their names recorded as members of the house of David. **17, 113**

Mary I (Mary Tudor) (1516–1558)
Queen of England known as Bloody Mary because she persecuted the Protestants. She was a reactionary Roman Catholic who was totally sincere. She married King Philip II of Spain and died of a cancer that she mistakenly thought was his child inside her. **238**

Mary Magdalene (Saint) (first century A.D.)
A follower of Jesus, she is best remembered as the first person to see Jesus after he arose from the tomb. She reputedly came from the village of Magdala (hence her name). **51**

Matthew (Saint) (first century A.D.)
An apostle who was a tax collector. He later wrote the Gospel according to St. Matthew. **106**

Maxentius (278-312 A.D.)
Roman emperor whose army was defeated by Constantine at the Battle of the Milvian Bridge in 312 A.D. Maxentius died in the battle. **131**

Matthias (Saint) (first century, A.D.)
An apostle of Jesus. He was chosen by the other apostles to replace Judas Iscariot after his suicide **57**

Melanchthon, Philipp (1497–1560)
Luther's principal student and best colleague. He com-

posed most of the Augsburg Confession (1530), Protestantism's first confession of faith. **232**

Men, Alexander (1935–1990)

Russian Orthodox priest. Born a Jew, Men was baptized by his mother, who had become a member of the underground church in Russia during the Soviet suppression. After formal theological training, he served as a priest for thirty years, the last twenty in a small wooden church outside Moscow, where he preached to a congregation of thousands. He was a spiritual counselor to such notables as Andrey Sakharov and Aleksandr Solzhenitsyn. He was a prolific writer and public speaker, stressing a fearless faith in Christ open to dialogue with the world. This commitment provoked anti-Semites, atheists, and the KGB into despising him. He was murdered by an ax blow to the back of the skull, a crime that has never been solved. He is regarded today as the architect of Christian renewal in Russia and a modern martyr. He believed that Grace and truth could be found in all Christian traditions. Regarding the divisions to be found within Christianity, he once said, "The walls that we erect between ourselves are not high enough to reach up to God." **297**

Merton, Thomas (1915–1968)

The most read and thus most popular monk of the twentieth century. He was particularly interested in Indian mysticism. **159**

Methodius (Saint) (826–885)

Roman Catholic priest from Constantinople who was active in missionary work in Moravia, Bohemia, and

Poland. Known as the Apostle of the Slavs, Methodius translated the Bible into the Slavonic languages. **180**

Milton, John (1608–1674)
English poet and political writer **140**

Montaigne, Michel de (1533–1592)
French writer whose most celebrated work is his *Essays,* published in 1575 **254–255**

Montesquieu, Charles de Secondat, baron de La Brède et de (1689–1755)
French jurist and political philosopher. His greatest work is *The Spirit of Laws* (1748), a study of government. **255**

Moody, Dwight (1837–1899)
American evangelist who founded two secondary schools in Northfield, Massachusetts, and the Moody Church and Moody Bible Institute in Chicago **272**

Moses (thirteenth century B.C.)
A prophet and the principal leader and teacher of the Israelites. Moses is one of the most important figures in the Bible. He led his people out of slavery in Egypt to their homeland in Canaan, later called Palestine; declared the Ten Commandments as their Law; and established a nation under his leadership. **27, 28, 34, 40**

Muhammad (ca. 570–632)
Founder of Islam. An inspired prophet, he composed the Qur'an and later founded a militant worldwide missionary and political movement. **183–188**

Nero, Claudius (37–68)
Roman emperor who persecuted Christians as well as others whom he regarded as threats to Rome. He was responsible for the deaths of St. Peter and St. Paul. **71, 101, 131, 135**

Newman, John Henry (1801–1890)
An Anglican evangelical clergyman who developed into a "high churchman" and founded the Oxford movement, which influenced the Church of England in a high church direction. He later became a Roman Catholic and ended up a cardinal. Newman was also part of a group of intellectuals knows as medievalists, who regarded the Middle Ages as a beautiful epoch in human history. **202**

Newton, Sir Isaac (1642–1727)
Scientific genius who was also a convinced Puritan — a classic product of Protestantism at its best **157**

Newton, John (1725–1807)
Leading Anglican evangelical clergyman who started out as a sailor on a slave ship. He wrote many hymns, including the Christian anthem "Amazing Grace." **273**

Nicholas I (Saint) (?–867)
One of the great popes of the Middle Ages **177**

Ockham, William of (ca. 1280–ca. 1349)
Scholastic philosopher and logician who fell out with the pope in favor of Emperor Louis of Bavaria. He was a simplifier in philosophy, believing that less is more, and he regretted the overemphasis on the philosophy of Aristotle. **213**

Origen (ca. 185–ca. 254)
Wonderful early Christian thinker and interpreter of the Bible. His writings today seem obscure, to say the least. He was a passionate and fanatical man who castrated himself at age fourteen and later became an early Arian. **144**

Pachomius (Saint) (ca. 290–346)
Egyptian monk who first gathered solitary or anchorite monks into communities for support and for purposes of physical and mental health **150, 151**

Pagels, Elaine (1943–)
Professor of early Christian history at Princeton University. For her views on St. Augustine and his times, see her book *Adam, Eve, and the Serpent* (1988). **163**

Paine, Thomas (1737–1809)
Radical American author of *Common Sense* (1776) and *The Rights of Man* (1791–1792). He was a deist, arguing for a passive God who is uninvolved in history and exists from a distance. **256**

Palestrina, Giovanni Pierluigi da (ca. 1525–1594)
One of the great composers of the Italian Renaissance. He is particularly acclaimed for the choral works and masses that he composed for the Roman Catholic Church. **245**

Parr, Catherine (1514–1548)
English Protestant noblewoman who became the sixth wife of King Henry VIII. She narrowly escaped martyrdom when she came under suspicion for influencing Henry's

choice concerning Protestant or Catholic regents for his son Edward. **237**

Pascal, Blaise (1623–1662)

Mathematician and genius in many disciplines who was converted to Jansenism and thus to the theology of St. Augustine. The French Jesuits regarded him as a crypto (i.e., hidden)-Protestant and refused to let him receive Holy Communion on his deathbed. **174**

Patrick (Saint) (ca. 390–ca. 461)

Apostle to the Irish. He was born in present-day Scotland, was imprisoned in Ireland by pirates as a teenager, escaped, but returned to bring the Gospel to his captors. Although a lot of fog and legend covers his life, Patrick was a genuinely impressive man and saint. **195–196, 317–319**

Paul (Saint) (first century A.D.)

One of the most important figures in Christianity, Paul is sometimes referred to as an apostle, although he was not one of the twelve apostles of Jesus. He became famous as a missionary and founder of Christian congregations throughout Asia Minor and southeastern Europe. His letters, called Epistles, form a significant part of the New Testament. **Numerous references throughout text. Principal discussion 57–102, 108–112, 309–312**

Pelagius (ca. 354–ca. 418)

British heretical theologian who taught that human beings have it in them to save themselves and can do so if they just put their wills into it. St. Augustine refuted his ideas, but the notions of Pelagius are built into the edifice of human self-deception and denial. **166–169, 172, 313–317**

Peter (Saint) (?–ca. 64)
A leading apostle of Jesus Christ and a prominent figure in the New Testament. His original name was Simon. Jesus gave him the name Peter, which means "rock" in Greek. Some years after leaving Jerusalem, Peter became the first bishop of Rome, where, it is believed, he died as a martyr at the hands of Emperor Nero. According to tradition, he is buried under what is now St. Peter's Basilica in Vatican City. **Numerous references throughout text. Principal discussion 71–72, 98–101**

Peter Lombard (ca. 1095-1169)
Key figure in scholastic theology who composed the textbooks known as the *Books of Sentences*. Late in his career, he veered into heresy concerning the humanity of Christ. **213**

Philip (Saint) (first century A.D.)
An apostle of Jesus **42**

Philip II (1527–1598)
King of Spain. During his reign, Spain underwent severe economic decline and bankruptcy, and its armada suffered defeat at the hands of the English navy. **246**

Photius (ca. 820–ca. 892)
Greek churchman and theologian, and patriarch of Constantinople **177–178**

Pilate, Pontius (first century A.D.)
Roman governor of Judea who ordered the crucifixion of Jesus **21, 39, 45–46**

Polycarp (Saint) (ca. 69–ca. 155) Early Christian martyr and bishop. He was very much a father figure, and his death as a result of persecution had an effect on the Roman world. **128**

Richard I (1157-1199)
King of England, popularly known as Richard the Lionhearted **207**

Ridley, Nicholas (ca. 1500–1555)
Reforming bishop and theologian who was burned at the stake back-to-back with Hugh Latimer. Latimer said to Ridley, "Play the man, Master Ridley; we shall this day light such a candle, by God's grace, in England, as I trust shall never be put out." **230**

Robert of Molesmes (Saint) (1029–1111)
Founder of an anchorite monastery at in the valley of Langres, France, in 1075 **152**

Rousseau, Jean–Jacques (1712–1778)
French Enlightenment thinker who disliked Christianity but, unlike his colleagues such as Voltaire, came from a Protestant background. His view of human nature was inflated. His thought has always been popular in the United States. **257**

Rubens, Peter Paul (1577–1640)
Great Flemish painter who received many commissions from the Roman Catholic Church **245**

Rublev, Andrei (1370–1430)
Celebrated Russian icon painter. His most famous work is *The Holy Trinity* icon. **69**

Ruskin, John (1819–1900)
English writer who wrote influential criticism on the art, literature, and social issues of the Victorian Age. He was also a member of a group known as medievalists, who regarded the Middle Ages as a beautiful epoch in human history. **202**

Sabellius (fl. ca. 220)
A heretic and radical monotheist who taught in Rome from 198 to 217. He questioned the Trinity, saying that God is One and that the three Persons (Father, Son, and Holy Spirit) are roles or parts played by the One. The church corrected Sabellius by saying that God is One but that he also contains three (divine) Persons; and that there is only one divine will and mind, one set of divine attributes, but these attributes are all used by the three divine Persons. **144**

Savonarola, Girolamo (1452–1498)
Florentine reformer of the Roman Catholic Church who has never received his due from Christian historians. He was executed by being slowly roasted over a fire. **221**

Schweitzer, Albert (1875–1965)
Skeptical scholar of the origins of Christianity who lost his

faith in the historical Jesus and thus in Christianity as a whole. He became a humanitarian agnostic and gave decades of service as a medical missionary in Africa. **82, 85**

Scott, Thomas (1747–1821)

English theologian and Bible commentator. He was a follower of George Whitefield and a member of the Evangelical Party. Scott's most famous publication is a commentary on the Bible. **273**

Shaftesbury, 7th Earl of (Anthony Ashley Cooper) (1801–1885)

English earl whose evangelical views resulted in important social legislation and political action. He was also a Christian Zionist, and his founding of an Anglican ministry to Jews at Jerusalem set the early stage for the founding of the State of Israel. **274–275**

Simeon, Charles (1759–1836)

Anglican clergyman who organized the Evangelical Party in the Church of England. He was vicar of Holy Trinity Church in Cambridge for fifty years, where his many influential converts included Patrick Brontë, father of the famous authors. **273**

Simon the Canaanite (Saint) (first century A.D.)

An apostle of Jesus **42**

Smart, Christopher (1722–1771)

Author of one great poem, *Song to David* (1763) **18**

Socrates (469–399 B.C.)
Greek philosopher and mentor of Plato. Socrates was known for his consideration of philosophy as a proper and necessary pursuit by man. **216**

Söderblom, Nathan (1866–1931)
Archbishop of Sweden and recipient of the Nobel Peace Prize in 1930 **289**

Solomon (tenth century B.C.)
Third king of ancient Israel, and builder of the First Temple and his palace in the capital (Jerusalem). A fine administrator and international leader, he reorganized and developed the large kingdom that his father, King David, had conquered. **19**

Stephen (Saint) (first century A.D.)
The first Christian martyr. He was stoned to death outside Jerusalem sometime after the Resurrection. **59–62**

Teresa, Mother (1910–1997)
Twentieth-century model of Christian activist compassion. She worked in Calcutta with the poorest of the poor. In 1979, she won the Nobel Peace Prize. **154, 291**

Tertullian (Quintus Septimius Florens Tertullianus) (ca. 160–ca. 220)
Christian apologist and hammer of heretics. He used his fine legal mind to create metaphors and exact vocabulary for ideas such as atonement and vicarious sacrifice. He was also a puritan and a Pentecostal. **121, 144**

Tetzel, Johann (1465–1519)
A hawker of indulgences, he was the first public antagonist of Martin Luther **224**

Thaddeus (Saint) (first century A.D.)
An apostle of Jesus **43**

Thomas (Saint) (first century A.D.)
An apostle of Jesus. He is known as Doubting Thomas because at first he did not believe that Jesus had risen from the dead. **42, 53**

Tillich, Paul (1886–1965)
American philosopher and theologian. An ordained Lutheran minister, he taught theology at several universities in Germany. He was dismissed from his last German professorship, at the University of Frankfurt, for his opposition to the Nazi regime. He then came to America and taught at Harvard and the University of Chicago. **277**

Timothy (Saint) (first century A.D.)
Friend of Paul and recipient of two of Paul's pastoral Epistles **111, 128**

Titus (Saint) (first century A.D.)
Friend of Paul and recipient of one of Paul's pastoral Epistles **111, 128**

Torquemada, Tomás de (1420–1498)
Inquisitor general of the Spanish Inquisition. He persecut-

ed all whom he regarded as deviants from the Catholic norm. **205**

Tyndale, William (ca. 1494–1536)
First translator of the whole Bible into English, and a Protestant martyr. Before he was strangled and burned at the stake, he said, "God, open the king of England's eyes." **236**

Urban II (Saint) (ca. 1042–1099)
French pope who was an eloquent spokesman for the necessity of the Crusades **206**

Vladimir (Saint) (956–1015)
Grand prince of Kiev in Russia who accepted Christianity, like his grandmother Olga. Vladimir is responsible for the Christianization of Mother Russia. **180**

Voltaire (1694–1778)
The pen name of François-Marie Arouet, a French Establishment novelist and thinker. He hated the Christian church. But he also defended persecuted French Protestants and regarded his defense of them as one of his greatest contributions to mankind. **255–256, 257, 258**

Watts, Isaac (1674-1748)
An English nonconformist, which means non-Anglican Protestant. He wrote more than 700 hymns and psalms, including "Crucifixion to the World by the Cross of Christ," with its famous opening line, "When I survey the wondrous Cross," which is reproduced in the appendix on page 346. **346–348**

Wesley, Charles (1707–1788)
The "sweet singer" of Methodism and brother of John, he wrote thousands of hymns, including "Hark! The Herald Angels Sing." **271**

Wesley, John (1703–1791)
Founder of Methodism and one of the most influential Christians of the eighteenth century. Wesley developed a doctrine of "Christian perfection" toward the end of his ministry; this doctrine inadvertently contributed to the legalism and gaps in reality of American evangelicalism. **18, 83, 269–271, 275, 349–350**

Whitefield, George (1714–1770)
George Whitefield and John Wesley were the leading English evangelists of the English-speaking world in the eighteenth century. Unlike Wesley, Whitefield was a moderate Calvinist who stayed within the Church of England. Together with Charles Simeon, Whitefield founded the Evangelical Party in Anglicanism. **63, 271–273**

Wilberforce, William (1759–1833)
English evangelical nobleman who became known as the Great Emancipator because he led the finally successful campaign to emancipate the slaves in the British Empire. He was one of a group of aristocratic evangelicals known as the Clapham sect. **273**

William I (William the Conqueror) (ca. 1027–1087)
First Norman king of England. He assumed the throne in 1066 after his army's victory over the Anglo-Saxons at the Battle of Hastings. **199**

William III (William of Orange) (1650–1702)
The Dutch Protestant leader of the Netherlands who was invited to England by Protestant politicians to assist them in overthrowing the Catholic King James II. Their revolution — known as the Glorious Revolution — succeeded, and William became king. He is a hero to all who cherish the Protestant tradition of faith and freedom. **239, 253**

William of Ockham
See Ockham, William of

Williams, Roger (ca. 1603–1683)
Puritan clergyman and founder of Rhode Island **267**

Williams, Rowan (1950–)
The 104th archbishop of Canterbury. Born in Wales, Williams was ordained a priest in 1978 and thereafter served as a teacher, dean, and chaplain at Cambridge and then as a professor of theology at Oxford. An outspoken liberal (some would say radical), Williams acknowledged knowingly ordaining a gay priest and described the United States' bombing of Afghanistan after September 11, 2001, as "morally tainted." **282**

Wilson, Woodrow (1856-1924)
President of the United States during World War I **284**

Wycliffe, John (ca. 1329–1384)
A very early religious reformer and philosopher. His followers translated the New Testament into English. Wycliffe's body was dug up after his death and burned, because his teachings, especially against transubstantia-

tion, were regarded as heretical. They were not. **221, 236, 298**

Xavier, Francis (Saint) (1506–1552)
Basque Jesuit missionary and one of the founders of the Society of Jesus. He was one of the greatest Christian missionaries, traveling for many years in the Far East, where he died. **158**

Zinzendorf, Count Nikolaus Ludwig von (1700–1760)
Founder of the Moravian church and Christian Pietist who wrote many hymns and poems. He was a mystic who befriended John Wesley. The church he founded is still strong and was the force behind the founding of Winston-Salem, North Carolina. **159**

Zwingli, Huldrych (1484–1531)
Reformer of Zurich. A great and courageous man, he was rejected by Martin Luther because of a difference over the theology of Holy Communion. Zwingli was killed in action at the Battle of Kappel, after and because of which the Reformation in Switzerland was completely halted by the Roman Catholic cantons (Swiss states). **229, 233, 301**

ABOUT THE AUTHOR

Paul F. M. Zahl is a Christian theologian. His academic credentials include an A.B., magna cum laude, from Harvard College; an M.Phil. from England's University of Nottingham; a diploma in pastoral studies, with distinction, from St. John's Theological College; and a Dr.theol., magna cum laude, from Eberhard-Karls-Universität, Tübingen, Germany.

In 2004, Dr. Zahl was appointed dean and president of Trinity Episcopal School for Ministry in Ambridge, Pennsylvania. Earlier in his career, he served as pastor in several Episcopal parishes in the United States; as visiting scholar at Wycliffe Hall, Oxford, England; and, for almost a decade, as dean of the Cathedral Church of the Advent (Episcopal) in Birmingham, Alabama.

He is a regular columnist for *The Anglican Digest* and the author of numerous theological articles and reviews, as well as seven books: *The First Christian: Universal Truth in the Teachings of Jesus Christ* (2003); *Five Women of the English Reformation* (2001); *A Short Systematic Theology* (2000); *The Collects of Thomas Cranmer* (with C. Frederick Barbee) (1999); *The Protestant Face of Anglicanism* (1998); *Die Rechtfertigungslehre Ernst Käsemanns* (1996); and *Who Will Deliver Us?* (1983).